CASEBOOK SERIES

JANE AUSTEN: *Emma* David Lodge
JANE AUSTEN: *'Northanger Abbey' & 'Persuasion'* B. C. Southam
JANE AUSTEN: *'Sense and Sensibility', 'Pride and Prejudice' & 'Mansfield Park'* B. C. Southam
BECKETT: *Waiting for Godot* Ruby Cohn
WILLIAM BLAKE: *Songs of Innocence and Experience* Margaret Bottrall

SHAKESPEARE: *Coriolanus* B. A. Brockman

SHAKESPEARE: *Early Tragedies* Neil Taylor & Bryan Loughrey
SHAKESPEARE: *Hamlet* John Jump
SHAKESPEARE: *Henry IV Parts I and II* G.K. Hunter
SHAKESPEARE: *Henry V* Michael Quinn
SHAKESPEARE: *Julius Caesar* Peter Ure
SHAKESPEARE: *King Lear* Frank Kermode
SHAKESPEARE: *Macbeth* John Wain
SHAKESPEARE: *Measure for Measure* C. K. Stead
SHAKESPEARE: *The Merchant of Venice* John Wilders
SHAKESPEARE: *'Much Ado About Nothing' & 'As You Like It'* John Russell Brown
SHAKESPEARE: *Othello* John Wain
SHAKESPEARE: *Richard II* Nicholas Brooke
SHAKESPEARE: *The Sonnets* Peter Jones
SHAKESPEARE: *The Tempest* D. J. Palmer
SHAKESPEARE: *Troilus and Cressida* Priscilla Martin
SHAKESPEARE: *Twelfth Night* D. J. Palmer
SHAKESPEARE: *The Winter's Tale* Kenneth Muir
SPENSER: *The Faerie Queene* Peter Bayley
SHERIDAN: *Comedies* Peter Davison
STOPPARD: *'Rosencrantz and Guildenstern are Dead', 'Jumpers' & 'Travesties'* T. Bareham
SWIFT: *Gulliver's Travels* Richard Gravil
SYNGE: *Four Plays* Ronald Ayling
TENNYSON: *In Memoriam* John Dixon Hunt
THACKERAY: *Vanity Fair* Arthur Pollard
TROLLOPE: *The Barsetshire Novels* T. Bareham
WEBSTER: *'The White Devil' & 'The Duchess of Malfi'* R. V. Holdsworth
WILDE: *Comedies* William Tydeman
VIRGINIA WOOLF: *To the Lighthouse* Morris Beja
WORDSWORTH: *Lyrical Ballads* Alun R. Jones & William Tydeman
WORDSWORTH: *The 1807 Poems* Alun R. Jones
WORDSWORTH: *The Prelude* W. J. Harvey & Richard Gravil
YEATS: *Poems 1919–35* Elizabeth Cullingford
YEATS: *Last Poems* Jon Stallworthy

Issues in Contemporary Critical Theory Peter Barry
Thirties Poets: 'The Auden Group' Ronald Carter
Tragedy: Developments in Criticism R.P. Draper
Epic Ronald Draper
Poetry Criticism and Practice: Developments since the Symbolists A.E. Dyson
Three Contemporary Poets: Gunn, Hughes, Thomas A.E. Dyson
Elizabethan Poetry: Lyrical & Narrative Gerald Hammond
The Metaphysical Poets Gerald Hammond
Medieval English Drama Peter Happé
The English Novel: Developments in Criticism since Henry James Stephen Hazell
Poetry of the First World War Dominic Hibberd
The Romantic Imagination John Spencer Hill
Drama Criticism: Developments since Ibsen Arnold P. Hinchliffe
Three Jacobean Revenge Tragedies R.V. Holdsworth
The Pastoral Mode Bryan Loughrey
The Language of Literature Norman Page
Comedy: Developments in Criticism D.J. Palmer
Studying Shakespeare John Russell Brown
The Gothic Novel Victor Sage
Pre-Romantic Poetry J.R. Watson

Shakespeare
Antony and Cleopatra

A CASEBOOK

EDITED BY

JOHN RUSSELL BROWN

Revised Edition

MACMILLAN

First published 1968 by
THE MACMILLAN PRESS LTD
Houndmills, Basingstoke, Hampshire RG21 2XS
and London
Companies and representatives
throughout the world

ISBN 0–333–53359–3 hardcover
ISBN 0–333–53360–7 paperback

A catalogue record for this book is available
from the British Library.

Printed in Hong Kong

Twelfth reprint 1988
Revised edition 1988
Reprinted 1992, 1993

CONTENTS

ACKNOWLEDGEMENTS

Georg Brandes, *William Shakespeare: A Critical Study* (William Heinemann Ltd); review by Ivor Brown in the *Observer*, 13 May 1951; review by Harold Hobson in the *Sunday Times*, 13 May 1951; review by Jeremy Treglown in *Plays & Players*, xxvi, 3, December 1978; review by Michael Billington in the *Guardian*, 11 April 1987; A. C. Bradley, *Oxford Lectures on Poetry* (the executors of the late A. C. Bradley); Harley Granville-Barker, *Prefaces to Shakespeare* (B. T. Batsford Ltd and Princeton University Press); John Middleton Murry, *Shakespeare* (Jonathan Cape Ltd and The Society of Authors); Professor Franklin Dickey, *Not Wisely But Too Well* (The Huntington Library); Maurice Charney, *Shakespeare's Roman Plays: The Function of Imagery in the Drama* (Harvard University Press; © the President and Fellows of Harvard College 1961); *Some Shakespearean Themes* (Chatto & Windus Ltd and Stanford University Press; © L C. Knights 1959); H. A. Mason, '*Antony and Cleopatra*: Telling *versus* Shewing', in the *Cambridge Quarterly*, 1 (1966); Michael Long, *The Unnatural Scene: A Study in Shakespearean Tragedy* (Methuen, 1976); Leonard Tannenhouse, *Power on Display: The Politics of Shakespeare's Genres* (Methuen, 1976); Kay Stockholder, *Dream Works: Lovers and Families in Shakespeare's Plays* (University of Toronto Press, 1987).

GENERAL EDITOR'S PREFACE

Each of this series of Casebooks concerns either one well-known and influential work of literature or two or three closely linked works. The main section consists of critical readings, mostly modern, brought together from journals and books. A selection of reviews and comments by the author's contemporaries is also included, and sometimes comments from the author himself. The Editor's Introduction charts the reputation of the work from its first appearance until the present time.

What is the purpose of such a collection? Chiefly, to assist reading. Our first response to literature may be, or seem to be, 'personal'. Certain qualities of vigour, profundity, beauty or 'truth to experience' strike us, and the work gains a foothold in our mind. Later, an isolated phrase or passage may return to haunt or illuminate. Where did we hear that? we wonder – it could scarcely be better put.

In these and similar ways appreciation begins, but major literature prompts to very much more. There are certain facts we need to know if we are to understand properly. Who were the author's original readers, and what assumptions did he share with them? What was his theory of literature? Was he committed to a particular historical situation, or to a set of beliefs? We need historians as well as critics to help us with this. But there are also more purely literary factors to take account of: the work's structure and rhetoric; its symbols and archetypes; its tone, genre and texture; its use of language; the words on the page. In all these matters critics can inform and enrich our individual responses by offering imaginative recreations of their own.

For the life of a book is not, after all, merely 'personal'; it is more like a tripartite dialogue, between a writer living 'then', a reader living 'now', and whatever forces of survival and honour link the two. Criticism is the public manifestation of this dialogue, a witness to the continuing power of literature to arouse and excite. It illuminates the possibilities and rewards of the dialogue, pushing 'interpretation' as far forward as it can go.

And here, indeed, is the rub: how far can it go? Where does 'interpretation' end and nonsense begin? Why is one interpretation superior to another, and why does each age need to interpret for itself? The critic knows that his insights have value only in so far as they serve the text, and that he must take account of views differing sharply from his own. He knows that his own writing will be judged as well as the work he writes about, so that he cannot simply assert inner illumination or a differing taste.

The critical forum is a place of vigorous conflict and disagreement, but there is nothing in this to cause dismay. What is attested is the complexity of human experience and the richness of literature, not any chaos or relativity of taste. A critic is better seen, no doubt, as an explorer than as an 'authority', but explorers ought to be, and usually are, well equipped. The effect of good criticism is to convince us of what C. S. Lewis called 'the enormous extension of our being which we owe to authors'. A Casebook will be justified only if it helps to promote the same end.

A single volume can represent no more than a small selection of critical opinions. Some critics have been excluded for reasons of space, and it is hoped that readers will follow up the further suggestions in the Select Bibliography. Other contributions have been severed from their original context, to which some readers may wish to return. Indeed, if they take a hint from the critics represented here, they certainly will.

A. E. Dyson

INTRODUCTION

I

Shakespeare probably wrote *Antony and Cleopatra* late in 1606 or very early the following year. In Barnaby Barnes's *Devil's Charter*, performed at Court on 2 February 1607 and 'augmented' for publication by October, there is probably an allusion to Cleopatra's death as it was shown in Shakespeare's play, and in the same year Samuel Daniel issued a new edition of his tragedy *Cleopatra*, which reflects Shakespeare's in phrases, names and stage-business, as the earlier edition of 1594 did not. On 20 May 1608 a manuscript in possession of the publisher Edward Blount was registered for printing as 'A book Called Anthony and Cleopatra', together with 'The booke of Pericles prynce of Tyre'.

For the story of this tragedy Shakespeare had returned to Plutarch's *Lives of the Noble Grecians and Romans* in Sir Thomas North's translation of a French version, published in 1579. He had used this earlier for *Julius Caesar*, but now he was more deeply interested in Plutarch's account of character and history; and he went to the same source for his very next play, the tragedy *Coriolanus*. For *Timon of Athens*, written at about the same time as the two Roman tragedies, he used details from two of Plutarch's *Lives*. No single writer had exercised such a hold over Shakespeare since Holinshed and Hall had yielded material for the history plays; in *Antony and Cleopatra* the source is often followed closely and yet with independent judgement.

So, after four major tragedies – *Hamlet* (1600–1), *Othello* (1604–5), *King Lear* (1605–6) and *Macbeth* (1605–6) – each set in an exotic or mysterious kingdom, each centred on a single hero and often sustained at important crises by soliloquies that progressively reveal his inner hopes and fears, Shakespeare now chose a broader theme – Rome, the Roman Empire and Egypt; Antony *and* Cleopatra – and a style of presentation that involved a far larger cast of named characters, numerous short scenes, rapid changes of location and very few and brief soliloquies. In many ways *Antony and Cleopatra* was a new departure for Shakespeare in tragedy. And after *Coriolanus* he wrote only comedy and history: *Pericles, Cymbeline, Winter's Tale, The Tempest* and *Henry VIII* (1608–12), and possibly some parts of *The Two Noble Kinsmen* and the lost *Cardenio*.

For Shakespeare personally, 1606–7 may well have been a time of prosperity and added security; he seems to have given up acting after 1603, and in 1605 he purchased for £440 an interest in a parcel of tithes from property in his local Stratford on Avon; in 1607 his elder daughter, Susanna, married John Hall of Stratford, a physician of more than local fame. But for England these were the years of increasing dissatisfaction with James I, and a heightening of political and religious tensions. In 1605 Ben Jonson and Chapman were imprisoned for writing against the Scots in a comedy called *Eastward Ho!* In 1606 *The Revenger's Tragedy* gave a merciless picture of a 'new age', composed of lust, ambition, cunning and folly; its virtue is rare and on the defensive. The same year saw Dekker's weighty pamphlet on *The Seven Deadly Sins of London* and Barnaby Rich's somewhat more sprightly *Faults, Faults, and nothing but Faults.* While Shakespeare complimented King James in some episodes of *Macbeth*, in the same play he also portrayed political dissimulation and suspicion with new intensity. In *Timon of Athens* he created two fierce and unrelenting misogynists and showed the one faithful character, Flavius, as useless in helping his master and unrelated to the corrupt political bosses. Written in this context, *Antony and Cleopatra* shows both technical mastery and experimentation: a work written at the height of its author's powers, but without relaxed assurance, deeply conceived and deeply questioning, energetic and yet ambiguous, rich yet severe.

Early performances have left no record beyond those echoes in Daniel and Barnes, and certainly the play was never a favourite in its own time, as were *Richard III* or *Hamlet* or a dozen or so of Shakespeare's works revived during the first decades of the seventeenth century. Despite its early registration, the text was not published until (after a further registration as if the publisher had forgotten his ownership) it was included in the posthumous folio edition of Shakespeare's *Comedies, Histories and Tragedies* of 1623. From this good text all modern editions are directly and solely derived. Its stage-directions are often elaborate, and these, together with variations in the spelling of proper names, omission of some entrances and the presence of characteristic spellings and misprints, all suggest that the manuscript used by the original printer was

Shakespeare's own careful draft, possibly the autograph manuscript from which the theatre's promptbook had been transcribed and edited. (In IV xv some editors believe that Shakespeare has left his first version side by side with his improved version; perhaps he meant to erase everything from the second half of line 11 to the first of line 29.)

II

The Lord Chamberlain's records for 1669 tell us that *Antony and Cleopatra* was 'formerly acted at the Blackfriars', a small, indoor theatre belonging to the King's Men from 1609 to 1642. But we have no details of these performances, nor any evidence of further revivals from after the Restoration until a shortened and modified version ran for six nights only in 1759 during Garrick's management of Drury Lane. The few passing references to the play in performance during the seventeenth century take special note of the 'crimes' or 'defects' of the principal characters, as the reprints in this volume will show; and then, from 1677 onwards, Dryden's rehandling of the theme in his *All For Love*, using shreds and patches of Shakespeare's text, usurped most attention by reason of its frequent performance. Dryden's tragedy was more regular and less demanding in its stagecraft and, as its sub-title, *The World Well Lost*, suggests, more simple to grasp than Shakespeare's.

Samuel Johnson's short note in his edition of 1765, shortly after Garrick's attempted revival, gives the first sustained account of Shakespeare's play. Praise and blame are here curiously mixed, but in noting the 'low' arts of Cleopatra, the energy of the action and Shakespeare's presentation of history, Dr Johnson adumbrated the main critical reactions until the end of the nineteenth century. As exemplified in Coleridge's admiration for the art that allowed our 'sense of criminality' in Cleopatra's passion to be 'lessened by our insight into its depth and energy', a fascination with 'character' dominated English criticism. Although intent on describing the 'moral characteristics' of women, Mrs Jameson in 1833 wrote of Cleopatra as a 'glorious riddle, whose dazzling complexity continually mocks and eludes us'; she found a 'consistent inconsistency', mingling 'all that we most hate with what we most admire'. In the appreciation of character, moral judgement was dominant, usually of blame, but sometimes of acceptance, depending on the creed of the critic.

Shakespeare's presentation of historical events at the cost of regular tragic form, led the German critic, A. W. Schlegel (1809–11), to consider *Antony and Cleopatra* as a historical drama that placed two characters against a wide, specifically Roman background, with one major contrast in the figure of Octavius Caesar. With Hazlitt (1817) and, more thoroughly, with the Danish theatre critic and philosopher, Georg Brandes (1896), this approach led to a fuller vindication of the structure of the play; Brandes so emphasised Shakespeare's concern with the 'course of history and the fate of empires' that he rated most highly 'that sense of universal annihilation' which he believed this play to share with *King Lear*.

Edward Dowden's criticism (1875) benefited from its place in a general account of the development of Shakespeare's 'Mind and Art'. Like Coleridge and Hazlitt before him and Swinburne after him, Dowden acclaimed the sensuous and imaginative poetry and the vigour of conception and execution, but, from a comparison with *Julius Caesar* and *Macbeth* and with Milton's *Samson Agonistes*, he also argued that 'at every moment . . . we assist at a catastrophe – the decline of a lordly nature'; because of its plot, structure and dramatic contrasts, 'The spirit of the play, though superficially it appear voluptuous, is essentially severe.' Its conclusion showed the 'remorseless Nemesis of eternal law'.

III

In 1849 at the Sadler's Wells theatre, Samuel Phelps mounted the first production that was essentially faithful to Shakespeare's text, with himself as Antony and Eleanor Glyn as Cleopatra. Miss Glyn's performance, emphasising the dignity and splendour of an Egyptian Queen, became one of her most triumphant roles and was repeated several times, notably at the Princess's Theatre in 1867. But Phelps did not succeed in gaining general acceptance for *Antony and Cleopatra* in Shakespearian repertoires. Only at the very end of the century did productions of this play become common: that of Louis Calvert and Janet Achurch in 1897 (which Bernard Shaw said achieved its one 'really tragic effect' in a burst of laughter when

Antony, dying, learns that Cleopatra is in fact not dead), that of the Bensons in 1900, and that of Beerbohm Tree in 1906. From Robert Atkins's production of 1922 onwards, the play was often produced at the Old Vic, the Royal Shakespeare Theatre, the Canadian Stratford Festival and many other long-run and repertory theatres. Its new theatrical popularity was much indebted to the enhanced technical resources of stage-production, the lights, sound and machinery which enabled the many and various scenes to follow each other smoothly and swiftly so that the text's suggestions of magnificence and sensuality were realised on stage in ways unimagined by Shakespeare. The increased control exercised by theatre directors over stage-business, minor roles and supernumeraries, which followed the visit of the Duke of Saxe-Meiningen's company to London in 1881, also proved vitalising for this play. In the Meiningen production of *Julius Caesar* the crowd had had a dominant role for the first time, and the public meetings and battles were alike fully realised; this success showed actor-managers, and then directors, how to stage the later Roman tragedy. Some credit for the new interest in *Antony and Cleopatra* must also go to the taste for exotic dramas, poems, novels and paintings which thrived at the turn of the century.

A considerable time was to pass before spectacular staging and star performances were displaced as the main attractions in performance. But their success was seldom secure; some critics would dislike or disbelieve the artifice that captured the imaginations of other critics; and outright defeat for the actors was always possible. However, the death of Cleopatra, helped by textual cuts and evocative staging, has seldom failed to hold attention with its more sustained and more concentrated focus. Reviews of productions starring Vivien Leigh and Laurence Olivier, and Peggy Ashcroft and Michael Redgrave, exemplify this period of the play's stage-history in this Casebook.

But with the 1970s a new critical interest stirred. Now directors became more important than actors, as they probed the sources of action and speech, tried to establish distinct modes of thought for Egypt and Rome, used more of Shakespeare's text, and took the political issues more seriously and more subtlely. Reviews of productions by Peter Brook and Peter Hall exemplify this work. The former was stripped of scenic grandeur, the latter set the whole action against a dark red portico, effecting frequent changes of mood by means of light and music. Both critics, reprinted here, register their surprise at what they witnessed, and their conviction.

IV

In the present century the printed text of *Antony and Cleopatra* has been constantly under critical scrutiny. Andrew Bradley did a perhaps unsuspecting service to the play by omitting it from consideration in his book on *Shakespearean Tragedy* (1904) and then, in *Oxford Lectures on Poetry* (1909), publishing an eloquent, clear-headed and balanced account of its unique qualities. Once he had acknowledged the play's lack of compelling and concentrated narrative, and of a passionate quest by its protagonists for morally right and psychologically true action, and the fact that it did not excite pity and terror with a force commensurate with other Shakespearian tragedies, Bradley proceeded to describe the play's political irony, its supernatural elements, magnitude of setting, impressions of swift thought and feeling, and sense of disenchantment: and he did so with a precision that necessarily added to a reader's appreciation and so turned description into praise. After Bradley came many less gifted pleaders for the play, and more and more explanations of its hold over a reader and perhaps an audience. Not only was Bradley's a liberating tactic, but his discrimination, mature sensitivity and close knowledge of Shakespeare made this lecture one of his own finest achievements as a critic; no one before had said, for example, that Cleopatra's 'ecstasy' at the end of the play appears 'not factitious, but an effort strained and prodigious as well as glorious, not, like Othello's last speech, the final expression of character, of thoughts and emotions which have dominated a whole life'.

Since Bradley, there have been three main streams of critical attention: first a gathering of information about Elizabethan thought and life, to provide a glass through which to view the play and so correct misreadings caused by the changes the passage of time has brought to language, thought and feeling. M. W. MacCallum's *Shakespeare's Roman Plays and their Background* (1910) made a notable advance in this direction and his perspective has now been assimilated into most editions and works of criticism. Willard Farnham, having written a general study of *The Medieval Heritage of Elizabethan Tragedy* (1936), brought the same interests to a further study of *Shakespeare's Tragic Frontier: the World of his Final Tragedies* (1950). Now, for example, the importance of the 'time of universal peace' announced by Caesar (IV vi 5) and of Antony's and, later, Cleopatra's growing concern with 'nobleness' are more fully understood, and the play can be judged in a tradition of history plays and narrative tragedies, as opposed to the classical tradition of tragedies of crisis. In 1957 Franklin Dickey's *Not Wisely, But Too Well* traced the medieval and renaissance origins of the love-theme, and other scholars, in specialised articles, have shown how Shakespeare presented Cleopatra as mother, nurse and goddess, or echoed – even as he criticised – the extreme renaissance misogynists. We have also been taught to recognise the consistent and significant references to Fortune and gaming thoughout the play, and how the traditional association of food and sex reflects, in vocabulary and stage imagery, the traditional moral judgements against Antony's indulgences.

The new surge in historical criticism that occurred in the 1970s and 80s and sought to understand the place of the plays in the social consciousness of their times, considered both the sexual and political ideas inherent in *Antony and Cleopatra*. In 1986, for example, Leonard Tennenhouse argued that this tragedy was 'Shakespeare's elegy for the signs and symbols' which had been used to legitimise political power in the earlier Elizabethan age (*Power on Display*, p. 146). Robert Grudin's *Mighty Opposites: Shakespeare and Renaissance Contrariety* (1979) considered notions about wisdom and education which were new in England at the beginning of the seventeenth century and, quoting extensively from Montaigne's *Essays* (first published in translation in 1603), argued that Cleopatra is not a compromise between two views of greatness. For Grudin, Cleopatra 'represents a new and positive sense of the indivisibility of spirit and body, form and matter, and being and change' (p. 173).

The second, and more prolific, line of critical attention has been directed to the language and imagery of the play. Wilson Knight, in *The Imperial Theme* (1931), noted recurring words speaking of power, magnificence, nature, ascent and spiritual life, the general verbal acuity and the glow and strangeness of imagery throughout the play. For him the allusive life of the poetry, the play's 'visionary imaginations', far outweighed the purely human and narrative element, such as the 'minor stressing of Antony's shame or disgrace' (p. 255) noted by more traditional and historically minded critics.

Read in this way the play neither condemns nor vindicates two merely human lovers, but celebrates a triumph of 'transcendental humanism', the politicians become negligible and the lovers die into spiritual life:

> Now we feel the pressure of our 'mating' references throughout, the constant stress on 'melting', 'dissolving', 'mingling', till 'strength' of eternity and 'force' of time are inextricably 'entangled' (IV xiv 48), and 'death' . . . but the simplification, the freeing and unloosing of Life's 'intrinsicate' (V ii 307) knot. . . . In death man is triumphant, a 'conqueror' (IV xiv 62). (p. 262)

Knight's account is too long for inclusion in this volume, and too sustained and intricate to quote fairly in part. His approach is represented here by the chapter on the play in Middleton Murry's *Shakespeare* (1936). This notices particularly the words describing royalty and loyalty, and directs attention to the unifying concepts in the play as a whole. For Murry, too, the power of poetry, as appreciated through close verbal analysis 'overrode' drama and psychology: 'We cannot judge a play such as this as a record of action merely; if we do, its essence escapes our judgement. And by essence here, I do not mean something vague, such as we might call the "soul of the play"; but its vital inward unity.' He, like Wilson Knight, believed that the conclusion of the play presents and vindicates spiritual, not material, values.

From Wilson Knight many critics who do not insist on a wholly mystical conclusion seem to have taken their cue. These include John Dover Wilson in the Introduction of the New Cambridge edition (1950) and Harold Goddard in his *Meaning of Shakespeare* (1951), both of whom joined an appreciation of poetic values to a renewed interest in the psychology of the drama – Goddard in particular reconciling a triumphant conclusion with Cleopatra's continued deceit and prevarication by arguing that after the death of Antony she decided to deceive everyone as to her innermost determination to die with her 'husband', and that she deceived most readers as well as the Romans of the drama.

While the study of 'poetic texture' has often led to a reading of the tragedy as a vindication or even transformation of human love, it has also led to a closer appreciation of ambiguities within the play, as in L. C. Knights's *Some Shakespearean Themes* (1959), or in John Danby's account of the oppositions of imagery in the chapter on the play in his *Poets on Fortune's Hill* (1952). B. T. Spencer's article in

Shakespeare Quarterly, IX (1958), on 'Antony and Cleopatra and the Paradoxical Metaphor', drew attention to the prevalence of verbal paradox and suggested that the play itself is a paradox, affirming both Roman and Egyptian values. Ernest Schanzer's *Problem Plays of Shakespeare* (1963) noted the frequency with which Antony and Cleopatra use the same words and the insistent parallels with Hercules, Dido, Mars and Venus; he argued that the audience was left to choose its own reaction, of approval or disapproval.

Ambiguities were also noticed by those critics who examined the theatrical techniques of the play. At first this critical approach was concerned chiefly with dramatic structure and the creation of an impression of living characters. L. L. Schücking's *Character Problems in Shakespeare's Plays*, published in Leipzig in 1919, is instructive and challenging: here Cleopatra is said to be a double character, the dignified tragic queen of the last Act bearing no likeness to the shallow wanton of the previous Acts. This view was largely disregarded by other critics until H. A. Mason developed it further, bringing an acute verbal enquiry equally to bear on the thesis, and suggesting that 'the interest aroused by Cleopatra at the end is too ideal, and that she has ceased to be part and parcel of the real . . . The end does not bring the whole of our minds into play . . . and as it were set a new pattern on our being'. In short, judging the play as a whole, Mason, and less impressively Schücking before him, argued that what Wilson Knight called the unifying theme is almost an excrescence, something foisted onto the intensely realised human predicament. Other critics concerned with the technical presentation of the whole play and noticing many of the same features, have argued that Shakespeare intended an opposition between the dreams (or ideals) of the protagonists and the facts and achievements of their lives; among these are M. N. Proser in his *Heroic Image of Five Shakespearean Tragedies* (1965), Arnold Stein in 'The Image of Antony: Lyric and Tragic Imagination' in the *Kenyon Review* for 1959, and R. A. Foakes in 'Vision and Reality in *Antony and Cleopatra*' in the *Durham University Journal* for 1964. Both John Danby and William Rosen, in *Shakespeare and the Craft of Tragedy* (1960), have noted the prevalence of comment upon both Antony and Cleopatra from other characters, and the incessant use of contrasts and oppositions between one statement and another.

Maurice Charney's *Shakespeare's Roman Plays: the Function of Imagery in the Drama* (1961) is, as its title suggests, in the line of verbal and imagistic analysis, but Charney was also concerned with stage action and, by noting how armour is put on and off, when swords are drawn and how various ceremonies are introduced, and even when and how characters stand or sit, he has shown meaning and purpose in the physical enactment of the stage-business, sometimes as a counterstatement to the words; this is an important book to read beside those that emphasise verbal poetry above all other elements of the drama. It is related to John Holloway's *Story of the Night* (1961) that seeks to re-emphasise the basic action of the tragedies against the incidental, and often ambiguous, suggestions of verbal texture. In *Antony and Cleopatra,* he argued, the protagonists become outcasts from society, and in this lies the fundamental interest of the drama; he also emphasised the oscillating rhythms that suggest, in politics and love alike, a state of flux. Michael Goldman's *Acting and Action in Shakespearean Tragedy* (1985), by focusing on the demands Shakespeare made upon the actors, argued that both Antony and Cleopatra can be considered as performing for the audience of each other; and we, the audience in a theatre, sense that their greatness lies in their command over our imaginations.

The fullest and most illuminating account of the theatrical techniques of the play is still Granville-Barker's *Preface* published in 1930; part of it is reprinted here. He defended the arrangement and sequences of scenes, and so accentuated political themes and a prevailing irony and critical tone; he made practical suggestions for speaking the verse and for arranging battles, messages and deaths – including the hauling aloft of Antony into Cleopatra's monument and the comings and goings of Caesar's emissaries in the last scene. In doing this he proved how continuously alert we must be as readers or spectators if we are to respond adequately to Shakespeare's artifice and his imaginary world.

V

Later developments in study of the play, in the 1970s and 80s, have widened our view of the context in which this tragedy was written. Janet Abelman's *The Common Liar: An Essay on 'Antony and Cleopatra'* (1973) considered its hero and heroine in a long tradition of treating mythological characters – Dido and Aeneas, Mars and Venus – and characters in contemporary comedies. Howard Felperin, in *Shakespearean Representation: Mimesis and Modernity in Eliza-*

bethan Tragedy (1977), examined two separate myths in the play, one heroic and the other romantic, and showed how they are kept in conflict and in interaction. John Leeds Barroll's *Shakespearean Tragedy: Genre, Tradition and Change in 'Antony and Cleopatra'* (1983) took such enquiries still further, viewing the play in a long tradition of playwriting. Michael Long's *The Unnatural Scene* (1976) drew extensively from Nietzsche's ideas in *The Birth of Tragedy* (1872) and other writings, in order to reassess the ageless grounds of the 'furious but generous energies' at work in the creation of *Antony and Cleopatra*.

Psychological studies and feminist criticism have also forwarded our knowledge. The title of L. T. Fitz's article in *Shakespeare Quarterly* for 1977 alerts readers to important distinctions: 'Egyptian Queens and Male Reviewers: Sexist Attitudes in *Antony and Cleopatra* Criticism'. Fitz commented: 'I do not think it would be going too far to suggest that many male critics feel personally threatened by Cleopatra and what she represents to them' (p. 298). Among newer studies have been Carol Thomas Neely's *Broken Nuptials in Shakespeare's Plays* (1985) which points to ambiguities of 'gender roles' in the tragedy and Kay Stockholder's *Dream Works: Lovers and Families in Shakespeare's Plays* (1987) which assumes the protagonist to be the dreamer of the play in which he appears and so brings greater definition to Antony's fears and shames, and to his defences against Cleopatra's power. *Antony and Cleopatra* has become a crucial testing ground for attempts to assess Shakespeare's presentation of sex, gender and the deepest grounds of unconscious thought and feeling.

PART ONE

Critical Reactions before 1900

Seventeenth-century Comment on the Theme and the Play

ROBERT ANTON (1616)

Or why are *women* rather grown so mad,
That their *immodest feet* like *planets* gad
With such *irregular motion* to base *Plays*,
Where all the *deadly sins* keep *holidays*?
There shall they see the *vices* of the *times*,
Orestes' incest, *Cleopatra's* crimes.

SOURCE: From *The Philosopher's Satyrs*, 1616: V 'Of Venus'.

RICHARD BRATHWAIT (1631)

Love's interview betwixt Cleopatra and Mark Antony, promised to itself as much secure freedom as fading fancy could tender; yet the last scene closed all those comic passages with a tragic conclusion.

SOURCE: *The English Gentlewoman*, 1631.

JOHN DRYDEN (1678)

The death of Antony and Cleopatra is a subject which has been treated by the greatest wits of our nation, after Shakespeare; and by all so variously, that their example has given me the confidence to try myself in this bow of Ulysses amongst the crowd of suitors; and, withal, to take my own measures, in aiming at the mark. I doubt not but the same motive has prevailed with all of us in this attempt; I mean the excellency of the moral. For the chief persons represented were famous patterns of unlawful love; and their end accordingly was unfortunate.

SOURCE: From the Preface to *All for Love*, 1678.

NAHUM TATE (1680)

What I have already asserted concerning the necessity of learning to make a complete poet, may seem inconsistent with my reverence for our Shakespeare.

– *Cuius amor semper mihi crescit in Horas.*

I confess I cou'd never yet get a true account of his learning, and am apt to think it more than common report allows him. I am sure he never touches on a Roman Story, but the persons, the passages, the manners, the circumstances, the ceremonies, all are Roman. And what relishes yet of a more exact knowledge, you do not only see a Roman in his hero, but the particular genius of the man, without the least mistake of his character, given him by their best historians. You find his Antony in all the defects and excellencies of his mind, a soldier, a reveller, amorous, sometimes rash, sometimes considerate, with all the various emotions of his mind. . . .

But however it far'd with our author for book-learning, 'tis evident that no man was better studied in men and things, the most useful knowledge for a dramatic writer. He was a most diligent spy upon Nature, trac'd her through her darkest recesses, pictur'd her in her just proportion and colours; in which variety 'tis impossible that all shou'd be equally pleasant, 'tis sufficient that all be proper.

SOURCE: From *The Loyal General, a Tragedy* (1680): Address to Edward Tayler.

Samuel Johnson (1765)

This Play keeps curiosity always busy, and the passions always interested. The continual hurry of the action, the variety of incidents, and the quick succession of one personage to another, call the mind forward without intermission from the first Act to the last. But the power of delighting is derived principally from the frequent changes of the scene; for, except the feminine arts, some of which are too low, which distinguish *Cleopatra*, no character is very strongly discriminated. . . .

The events, of which the principal are described according to history, are produced without any art of connection or care of disposition.

SOURCE: From *Shakespeare's Works*, 1765.

Augustus William Schlegel (1809–11)

In the three Roman pieces, *Coriolanus, Julius Caesar*, and *Antony and Cleopatra*, the moderation with which Shakespeare excludes foreign appendages and arbitrary suppositions, and yet fully satisfies the wants of the stage, is particularly deserving of our admiration. These plays are the very thing itself; and under the apparent artlessness of adhering closely to history as he found it, an uncommon degree of art is concealed. Of every historical transaction Shakespeare knows how to seize the true poetical point of view, and to give unity and rounding to a series of events detached from the immeasurable extent of history without in any degree changing them. The public life of ancient Rome is called up from its grave, and exhibited before our eyes with the utmost grandeur and freedom of the dramatic form, and the heroes of Plutarch are ennobled by the most eloquent poetry. . . .

Antony and Cleopatra, may, in some measure, be considered as a continuation of *Julius Caesar*: the two principal characters of *Antony* and *Augustus* are equally sustained in both pieces. *Antony and Cleopatra* is a play of great extent; the progress is less simple than in *Julius Caesar*. The fulness and variety of political and warlike events, to which the union of the three divisions of the Roman world under one master necessarily gave rise, were perhaps too great to admit of being clearly exhibited in one dramatic picture. In this consists the great difficulty of the historical drama: – it must be a crowded extract, and a living development of history: – the difficulty however has generally been successfully overcome by Shakespeare. But here many things, which are transacted in the background, are merely alluded to, in a manner which supposes an intimate acquaintance with the history; and a work of art should contain every thing necessary for fully understanding it within itself. Many persons of historical importance are merely introduced in passing; the preparatory and concurring circumstances are not sufficiently collected into masses to avoid distracting our attention. The principal personages, however, are most emphatically distinguished by lineament and colouring, and powerfully arrest the imagination. In Antony we observe a mixture of great qualities, weaknesses, and vices; violent ambition and ebullitions of magnanimity: we see him sunk in luxurious enjoyments and nobly ashamed of his own aberrations, – manning himself to resolutions not unworthy of himself, which are always shipwrecked against the seductions of an artful woman. It is Hercules in the chains of Omphale, drawn from the fabulous heroic ages into history, and invested with the Roman costume. The seductive arts of Cleopatra are in no respect veiled over; she is an ambiguous being made up of royal pride, female vanity, luxury, inconstancy, and true attachment. Although the mutual passion of herself and Antony is without moral dignity, it still excites our sympathy as an insurmountable fascination: – they seem formed for each other, and Cleopatra is as remarkable for her seductive charms as Antony for the splendour of his deeds. As they die for each other, we forgive them for having lived for each other. The open and lavish character of Antony is admirably contrasted with the heartless littleness of Octavius Caesar, whom Shakespeare seems to have completely seen through without allowing himself to be led astray by the fortune and the fame of Augustus.

SOURCE: From *Lectures on Dramatic Literature*, 1809–11.

Samuel Taylor Coleridge (1808–19)

The highest praise or rather form of praise, of this play which I can offer in my own mind, is the doubt which its perusal always occasions in me, whether it is not in all exhibitions of a giant power in its strength and vigor of maturity, a formidable rival of the *Macbeth, Lear, Othello* and *Hamlet. Feliciter audax* is the motto for its style comparatively with his other works, even as it is the general motto of all his works compared with those of other poets. Be it remembered too, that this happy valiancy of style is but the representative and result of all the material excellencies so exprest.

This play should be perused in mental contrast with *Romeo and Juliet*: – as the love of passion and appetite opposed to the love of affection and instinct. But the art displayed in the character of Cleopatra is profound in this, especially, that the sense of criminality in her passion is lessened by our insight into its depth and energy, at the very moment that we cannot but perceive that the passion itself springs out of the habitual craving of a licentious nature, and that it is supported and reinforced by voluntary stimulus and sought-for associations, instead of blossoming out of spontaneous emotion.

But of all perhaps of Shakespeare's plays the most wonderful is the *Antony and Cleopatra.* [There are] scarcely any in which he has followed history more minutely, and yet few even of his own in which he impresses the notion of giant strength so much, perhaps none in which he impresses it more strongly. This [is] owing to the manner in which it is sustained throughout – that he *lives* in and through the play – to the numerous momentary flashes of nature counteracting the historic abstraction, in which take as a specimen the [death of Cleopatra.]. . .

SOURCE: From some manuscript notes, 1808–19.

William Hazlitt (1817)

This is a very noble play. Though not in the first class of Shakespear's productions, it stands next to them, and is, we think, the finest of his historical plays, that is, of those in which he made poetry the organ of history, and assumed a certain tone of character and sentiment, in conformity to known facts, instead of trusting to his observations of general nature or to the unlimited indulgence of his own fancy. What he has added to the actual story, is upon a par with it. His genius was, as it were, a match for history as well as nature, and could grapple at will with either. The play is full of that pervading comprehensive power by which the poet could always make himself master of time and circumstances. It presents a fine picture of Roman pride and Eastern magnificence: and in the struggle between the two, the empire of the world seems suspended, 'like the swan's down-feather,

> That stands upon the swell at the full of tide,
> And neither way inclines.'

The characters breathe, move, and live. Shakespear does not stand reasoning on what his characters would do or say, but at once *becomes* them, and speaks and acts for them. He does not present us with groups of stage-puppets or poetical machines making set speeches on human life, and acting from a calculation of problematical motives, but he brings living men and women on the scene, who speak and act from real feelings, according to the ebbs and flows of passion, without the least tincture of pedantry of logic or rhetoric. Nothing is made out by inference and analogy, by climax and antithesis, but every thing takes place just as it would have done in reality, according to the occasion. – The character of Cleopatra is a master-piece. What an extreme contrast it affords to Imogen! One would think it almost impossible for the same person to have drawn both. She is voluptuous, ostentatious, conscious, boastful of her charms, haughty, tyrannical, fickle. The luxurious pomp and gorgeous extravagance of the Egyptian queen are displayed in all their force and lustre, as well as the irregular grandeur of the soul of Mark Antony. Take only the first four lines that they speak as an example of the regal style of love-making.

> *Cleopatra.* If it be love indeed, tell me how much?
> *Antony.* There's beggary in the love that can be reckon'd.
> *Cleopatra.* I'll set a bourn how far to be belov'd.
> *Antony.* Then must thou needs find out new heav'n, new earth.

The rich and poetical description of her person beginning –

> The barge she sat in, like a burnish'd throne,
> Burnt on the water; the poop was beaten gold,
> Purple the sails, and so perfumed, that
> The winds were love-sick –

seems to prepare the way for, and almost to justify the subsequent infatuation of Antony when in the sea-fight of Actium, he leaves the battle, and 'like a doating mallard' follows her flying sails.

Few things in Shakespear (and we know of nothing in any other author like them) have more of that local truth of imagination and character than the passage in which Cleopatra is represented conjecturing what were the employments of Antony in his absence – 'He's speaking now, or murmuring – *Where's my serpent of old Nile?*' Or again, when she says to Antony, after the defeat at Actium, and his summoning up resolution to risk another fight – 'It is my birthday; I had thought to have held it poor; but since my lord is Antony again, I will be Cleopatra.' Perhaps the finest burst of all is Antony's rage after his final defeat when he comes in, and surprises the messenger of Caesar kissing her hand –

> To let a fellow that will take rewards,
> And say 'God quit you,' be familiar with
> My play-fellow, your hand; this kingly seal,
> And plighter of high hearts.

It is no wonder that he orders him to be whipped; but his low condition is not the true reason: there is another feeling which lies deeper, though Antony's pride would not let him shew it, except by his rage; he suspects the fellow to be Caesar's proxy.

Cleopatra's whole character is the triumph of the voluptuous, of the love of pleasure and the power of giving it, over every other consideration. Octavia is a dull foil to her, and Fulvia a shrew and shrill-tongued. What a picture do those lines give of her –

> Age cannot wither her, nor custom steal [*sic*]
> Her infinite variety. Other women cloy
> The appetites they feed, but she makes hungry
> Where most she satisfies.

What a spirit and fire in her conversation with Antony's messenger who brings her the unwelcome news of his marriage with Octavia! How all the pride of beauty and of high rank breaks out in her promised reward to him –

> – There's gold, and here
> My bluest veins to kiss! –

She had great and unpardonable faults, but the grandeur of her death almost redeems them. She learns from the depth of despair the strength of her affections. She keeps her queen-like state in the last disgrace, and her sense of the pleasurable in the last moments of her life. She tastes a luxury in death. After applying the asp, she says with fondness –

> Dost thou not see my baby at my breast,
> That sucks the nurse asleep?
> As sweet as balm, as soft as air, as gentle.
> Oh Antony!

It is worth while to observe that Shakespear has contrasted the extreme magnificence of the descriptions in this play with pictures of extreme suffering and physical horror, not less striking – partly perhaps to place the effeminate character of Mark Antony in a more favourable light, and at the same time to preserve a certain balance of feeling in the mind. Caesar says, hearing of his rival's conduct at the court of Cleopatra,

> – Antony,
> Leave thy lascivious wassels. When thou once
> Wert beaten from [Modena], where thou slew'st
> Hirtius and Pansa, consuls, at thy heel
> Did famine follow, whom thou fought'st against,
> Though daintily brought up, with patience more
> Than savages could suffer. Thou did'st drink
> The stale of horses, and the gilded puddle
> Which beasts would cough at. Thy palate then did deign
> The roughest berry on the rudest hedge,
> Yea, like the stag, when snow the pasture sheets
> The barks of trees thou browsed'st. On the Alps,
> It is reported, thou didst eat strange flesh,
> Which some did die to look on: and all this –
> It wounds thine honour, that I speak it now –
> Was borne so like a soldier, that thy cheek
> So much as lank'd not.

The passage after Antony's defeat by Augustus, where he is made to say –

> Yes, . . . yes; he at Philippi kept
> His sword e'en like a dancer; while I struck
> The lean and wrinkled Cassius, and 'twas I
> That the mad Brutus ended –

is one of those fine retrospections which show us the winding and eventful march of human life. The jealous attention which has been paid to the unities both of time and place has taken away the principle of perspective in the drama, and all the interest which objects derive from distance, from contrast, from privation, from change of fortune, from long-cherished passion; and contrasts our view of life from a strange and romantic dream, long, obscure, and infinite, into a smartly contested, three hours' inaugural disputation on its merits by the different candidates for theatrical applause.

The later scenes of *Antony and Cleopatra* are full of the changes of accident and passion. Success and defeat follow one another with startling rapidity. Fortune sits upon her wheel more blind and giddy than usual. This precarious state and the approaching dissolution of his greatness are strikingly displayed in the dialogue of Antony with Eros.

Antony. Eros, thou yet behold'st me?
Eros. Ay, noble lord.
Antony. Sometimes we see a cloud that's dragonish,
A vapour sometime, like a bear or lion,
A towered citadel, a pendant rock,
A forked mountain, or blue promontory
With trees upon't, that nod unto the world
And mock our eyes with air. Thou hast seen these signs,
They are black vesper's pageants.
Eros. Ay, my lord.
Antony. That which is now a horse, even with a thought
The rack dislimns, and makes it indistinct
As water is in water.
Eros. It does, my lord.
Antony. My good knave, Eros, now thy captain is
Even such a body . . .

This is, without doubt, one of the finest pieces of poetry in Shakespear. The splendour of the imagery, the semblance of reality, the lofty range of picturesque objects hanging over the world, their evanescent nature, the total uncertainty of what is left behind, are just like the mouldering schemes of human greatness. It is finer than Cleopatra's passionate lamentation over his fallen grandeur, because it is more dim, unstable, unsubstantial. Antony's headstrong presumption and infatuated determination to yield to Cleopatra's wishes to fight by sea instead of land, meet a merited punishment; and the extravagance of his resolutions, increasing with the desperateness of his circumstances, is well commented upon by Œnobarbus.

> – I see men's judgments are
> A parcel of their fortunes, and things outward
> Do draw the inward quality after them
> To suffer all alike

The repentance of Œnobarbus after his treachery to his master is the most affecting part of the play. He cannot recover from the blow which Antony's generosity gives him, and he dies broken-hearted, 'a master-leaver and a fugitive'.

Shakespear's genius has spread over the whole play a richness like the overflowing of the Nile.

SOURCE: From *The Characters of Shakespeare's Plays*, 1817.

Mrs Jameson (1833)

Great crimes, springing from high passions, grafted on high qualities, are the legitimate source of tragic poetry. But to make the extreme of littleness produce an effect like grandeur – to make the excess of frailty produce an effect like power – to heap up together all that is most unsubstantial, frivolous, vain, contemptible, and variable, till the worthlessness be lost in the magnitude, and a sense of the sublime spring from the very elements of littleness – to do this belonged only to Shakspeare, that worker of miracles. Cleopatra is a brilliant antithesis, a compound of contradictions, of all that we most hate with what we most admire. The whole character is the triumph of the external over the innate; and yet, like one of her country's hieroglyphics, though she presents at first view a splendid and perplexing anomaly, there is deep meaning and wondrous skill in the apparent enigma, when we come to analyse and decipher it. But how are we to arrive at the solution of this glorious riddle, whose dazzling complexity continually mocks and eludes us? What is most astonishing in the character of Cleopatra is its antithetical construction – its *consistent inconsistency*, if I may use such an expression –

which renders it quite impossible to reduce it to any elementary principles. It will, perhaps, be found, on the whole, that vanity and the love of power predominate; but I dare not say it *is* so, for these qualities and a hundred others mingle into each other, and shift, and change, and glance away, like the colours in a peacock's train.

In some others of Shakspeare's female characters, also remarkable for their complexity (Portia and Juliet, for instance), we are struck with the delightful sense of harmony in the midst of contrast, so that the idea of unity and simplicity of effect is produced in the midst of variety; but in Cleopatra it is the absence of unity and simplicity which strikes us; the impression is that of perpetual and irreconcilable contrast. The continual approximation of whatever is most opposite in character, in situation, in sentiment, would be fatiguing, were it not so perfectly natural: the woman herself would be distracting, if she were not so enchanting.

I have not the slightest doubt that Shakspeare's Cleopatra is the real historical Cleopatra – the 'rare Egyptian' – individualised and placed before us. Her mental accomplishments, her unequalled grace, her woman's wit and woman's wiles, her irresistible allurements, her starts of irregular grandeur, her bursts of ungovernable temper, her vivacity of imagination, her petulant caprice, her fickleness and her falsehood, her tenderness and her truth, her childish susceptibility to flattery, her magnificent spirit, her royal pride, the gorgeous eastern colouring of the character – all these contradictory elements has Shakspeare seized, mingled them in their extremes, and fused them into one brilliant impersonation of classical elegance, Oriental voluptuousness, and gipsy sorcery.

What better proof can we have of the individual truth of the character than the admission that Shakspeare's Cleopatra produces exactly the same effect on us that is recorded of the real Cleopatra? She dazzles our faculties, perplexes our judgment, bewilders and bewitches our fancy; from the beginning to the end of the drama we are conscious of a kind of fascination against which our moral sense rebels, but from which there is no escape. The epithets applied to her perpetually by Antony and others confirm this impression; 'enchanting queen!' – 'witch' – 'spell' – 'great fairy' – 'cockatrice' – 'serpent of old Nile' – 'thou grave* charm!' are only a few of them: and who does not know by heart the famous quotations

* *Grave*, in the sense of mighty or potent.

in which this Egyptian Circe is described, with all her infinite seductions? . . .

Although Cleopatra talks of dying 'after the high Roman fashion', she fears what she most desires, and cannot perform with simplicity what costs her such an effort. That extreme physical cowardice which was so strong a trait in her historical character, which led to the defeat of Actium, which made her delay the execution of a fatal resolve till she had 'tried conclusions infinite of *easy* ways to die', Shakspeare has rendered with the finest possible effect, and in a manner which heightens instead of diminishing our respect and interest. Timid by nature, she is courageous by the mere force of will, and she lashes herself up with high-sounding words into a kind of false daring. Her lively imagination suggests every incentive which can spur her on to the deed she has resolved, yet trembles to contemplate. She pictures to herself all the degradations which must attend her captivity: and let it be observed, that those which she anticipates are precisely such as a vain, luxurious, and haughty woman would especially dread, and which only true virtue and magnanimity could despise. Cleopatra could have endured the loss of freedom; but to be led in triumph through the streets of Rome is insufferable. She could stoop to Caesar with dissembling courtesy, and meet duplicity with superior art; but 'to be chastised' by the scornful or upbraiding glance of the injured Octavia – 'rather a ditch in Egypt!'

> . . . If knife, drugs, serpents, have
> Edge, sting, or operation, I am safe:
> Your wife Octavia, with her modest eyes
> And still conclusion,* shall acquire no honour
> Demuring upon me.
> Now, Iras, what think'st thou?
> Thou, an Egyptian puppet, shalt be shown
> In Rome, as well as I. Mechanic slaves,
> With greasy aprons, rules, and hammers, shall
> Uplift us to the view; in their thick breaths,
> Rank of gross diet, shall we be enclouded
> And forc'd to drink their vapour.
>
> *Iras.* The gods forbid!
>
> *Cleopatra.* Nay, 'tis most certain, Iras: Saucy lictors
> Will catch at us, like strumpets; and scald rhymers
> Ballad us out o'tune. The quick comedians

* i.e. sedate determination. – Johnson.

Extemporally will stage us, and present
Our Alexandrian revels; Antony
Shall be brought drunken forth, and I shall see
Some squeaking Cleopatra boy my greatness.

She then calls for her diadem, her robes of state, and attires herself as if 'again for Cydnus, to meet Mark Antony'. Coquette to the last, she must make Death proud to take her, and die, 'phoenix-like', as she had lived, with all the pomp of preparation – luxurious in her despair.

The death of Lucretia, of Portia, of Arria, and others who died 'after the high Roman fashion', is sublime according to the Pagan ideas of virtue, and yet none of them so powerfully affect the imagination as the catastrophe of Cleopatra. The idea of this frail, timid, wayward woman dying with heroism, from the mere force of passion and will, takes us by surprise.

SOURCE: From *Characteristics of Women*, 1833.

Charles Bathurst (1857)

[*Antony and Cleopatra*] is carelessly written, with no attempt at dignity, considering what great personages are introduced; but with a great deal of nature, spirit, and knowledge of character, in very many parts, and with several most beautiful passages of poetry and imagination; as, for instance, the dream of Cleopatra. It has passages, where he lets his mind loose, and follows his fancy and feeling freely; particularly, perhaps, in the end; and even the verse breaks delightfully out of its trammels, as in the speech about the cloud.

The subject of the play, in fact, was likely often to lead to this looser and softer character; tenderness, even weakness; is its business. It is historical; but it is chiefly the anecdote of history, not the dignity of it. *Plutarch's Lives*, his only authority, is in fact but, in great degree, a collection of anecdotes. But there was no occasion to read Plutarch, to understand the part of Cleopatra. The tenderness of feeling, however, extends itself to other parts than those of the lovers; at least it is most remarkable in the death of Enobarbus – a part which, after the manner of Shakespeare, is made to throw great light on the character of Antony himself, which he meant to elevate as much as possible; notwithstanding his great weakness in all that concerns Cleopatra, and unmistakable misconduct with regard to his wife. He represents him as, what he certainly was not, a man of the most noble and high spirit, capable at times, notwithstanding the luxury he afterwards fell into, of a thoroughly soldier-like life, and full of kind and generous feelings. He seems to delight in supposing the melancholy meditations of a great and active character, when losing his power, and drawing to his end.

SOURCE: From *Remarks on . . . Shakespeare's Versification*, 1857.

Edward Dowden (1875)

The transition from the *Julius Caesar* of Shakspere to his *Antony and Cleopatra* produces in us the change of pulse and temper experienced in passing from a gallery of antique sculpture to a room splendid with the colours of Titian and Paul Veronese. In the characters of the *Julius Caesar* there is a severity of outline; they impose themselves with strict authority upon the imagination; subordinated to the great spirit of Caesar, the conspirators appear as figures of life-size, but they impress us as no larger than life. The demand which they make is exact; such and such tribute must be rendered by the soul to each. The characters of the *Antony and Cleopatra* insinuate themselves through the senses, trouble the blood, ensnare the imagination, invade our whole being like colour or like music. The figures dilate to proportions greater than human, and are seen through a golden haze of sensuous splendour. *Julius Caesar* and *Antony and Cleopatra* are related as works of art rather by points of contrast than by points of resemblance. In the one an ideal of duty is dominant; the other is a divinisation of pleasure, followed by the remorseless Nemesis of eternal law. Brutus, the Stoic, constant, loyal to his ideas, studious of moral perfection, bent upon gaining self-mastery, unsullied and untarnished to the end, stands over against Antony, swayed hither and thither by appetites, interests, imagination, careless of his own moral being, incapable of self-control, soiled with the stains of passion and decay. And of Cleopatra what shall be said? Is she a creature of the same breed as Cato's daughter, Portia? Does the one word woman include natures so diverse? Or is Cleopatra – Antony's 'serpent of old Nile' – no mortal woman, but Lilith who ensnared Adam before the making of Eve? Shakspere has made the one as truly woman as the other; Portia, the ideal of moral loveliness, heroic and feminine; Cleopatra, the ideal of sensual attractiveness, feminine also:

> A bliss in proof, and proved, a very woe;
> Before, a joy proposed; behind, a dream.

We do not once see the lips of Brutus laid on Portia's lips as seal of perfect union, but we know that their beings and their lives had embraced in flawless confidence, and perfect, mutual service. Antony embracing Cleopatra exclaims,

> The nobleness of life
> Is to do thus; when such a mutual pair
> And such a twain can do't, in which I bind,
> On pain of punishment, the world to weet
> We stand up peerless.

Yet this 'mutual pair', made each to fill the body and soul of the other with voluptuous delight, are made also each for the other's torment. Antony is haunted by suspicion that Cleopatra will betray him; he believes it possible that she could degrade herself to familiarity with Caesar's menials. And Cleopatra is aware that she must weave her snares with endless variety, or Antony will escape.

The spirit of the play, though superficially it appear voluptuous, is essentially severe. That is to say, Shakspere is faithful to the fact. The fascination exercised by Cleopatra over Antony, and hardly less by Antony over Cleopatra, is not so much that of the senses as of the sensuous imagination. A third of the world is theirs. They have left youth behind with its slight, melodious raptures and despairs. Theirs is the deeper intoxication of middle age, when death has become a reality, when the world is limited and positive, when life is urged to yield up quickly its utmost treasures of delight. What may they not achieve of joy who have power, and beauty, and pomp, and pleasure all their own? How shall they fill every minute of their time with the quintessence of enjoyment and of glory?

> Let Rome in Tiber melt! and the wide arch
> Of the rang'd empire fall! here is my space.

Only *one* thing they had not allowed for, – that over and above power, and beauty, and pleasure, and pomp, there is a certain inevitable fact, a law which cannot be evaded. Pleasure sits enthroned as queen; there is a revel, and the lords of the earth, crowned with roses, dance before her to the sound of lascivious flutes. But presently the scene changes; the hall of revel is transformed to an arena; the dancers are armed gladiators; and as they advance to combat they pay the last homage to their Queen with the words, *Morituri te salutant.*

The pathos of *Antony and Cleopatra* resembles the pathos of *Macbeth.* But Shakspere like Dante allows the soul of the perjurer and murderer to drop into a lower, blacker, and more lonely circle of Hell than the soul of the man who has sinned through voluptuous self-indulgence. Yet none the less Antony is daily dropping away farther from all that is sound, strong, and enduring. His judgment wanes with his fortune. He challenges to a combat with swords his clear-sighted and unimpassioned rival into whose hands the empire of the world is about to fall. He abandons himself to a senseless exasperation. . . .

Measure things only by the sensuous imagination, and everything in the world of oriental voluptuousness, in which Antony lies bewitched, is great. The passion and the pleasure of the Egyptian queen, and of her paramour, toil after the infinite. The Herculean strength of Antony, the grandeur and prodigal power of his nature, inflate and buoy up the imagination of Cleopatra:

> The demi-Atlas of this earth, the arm
> And burgonet of men.

While he is absent, Cleopatra would, if it were possible, annihilate time, –

Charmain. Why, Madam?
Cleopatra. That I might sleep out this great gap of time,
My Antony is away.

When Antony dies the only eminent thing in the earth is gone, and an universal flatness, an equality of insignificance remains:

> Young boys and girls
> Are level now with men; the odds is gone,
> And there is nothing left remarkable
> Beneath the visiting moon.

We do not mistake this feeling of Cleopatra towards Antony for love; but he has been for her (who had known Caesar and Pompey), the supreme sensation. She is neither faithful to him nor faithless; in her complex nature, beneath each fold or layer of sincerity, lies one of insincerity, and we cannot tell which is the last and inner-most. Her imagination is stimulated, and nourished by Antony's presence. And he in his turn finds in the beauty and witchcraft of the Egyptian, something no less incommensurable and incomprehensible. Yet no one felt more profoundly than Shakspere, – as his Sonnets abundantly testify, – that the glory of strength and of beauty is subject to limit and to time. What he would seem to say to us in this play, not in the manner of a doctrinaire or a moralist, but wholly as an artist, is that this sensuous infinite is but a dream, a deceit, a snare. The miserable change comes upon Antony. The remorseless practice of Cleopatra upon his heart has done him to death. And among things which the barren world offers to the Queen she now finds death, a painless death, the least hateful. Shakspere, in his high impartiality to fact, denies none of the glory of the lust of the eye and the pride of life. He compels us to acknowledge these to the utmost. But he adds that there is another demonstrable fact of the world, which tests the visible pomp of the earth, and the splendour of sensuous passion, and finds them wanting. The glory of the royal festival is not dulled by Shakspere or diminished; but also he shows us in letters of flame the handwriting upon the wall.

This Shakspere effects, however, not merely or chiefly by means of a catastrophe. He does not deal in precepts or moral reflections, or practical applications. He is an artist, but an artist who grasps truth largely. The ethical truth lives and breathes in every part of his work as an artist, no less than the truth to things sensible and presentable to the imagination. At every moment in this play we assist at a catastrophe – the decline of a lordly nature. At every moment we are necessarily aware of the gross, the mean, the disorderly womanhood in Cleopatra, no less than of the witchery and wonder which excite, and charm, and subdue. We see her a dissembler, a termagant, a coward; and yet 'vilest things become her'. The presence of a spirit of *life* in Cleopatra, quick, shifting, multitudinous, incalculable, fascinates the eye, and would, if it could, lull the moral sense to sleep, as the sea does with its endless snakelike motions in the sun and shade. She is a wonder of the world, which we would travel far to look upon. . . .

If we would know how an artist devoted to high moral ideals would treat such a character as that of the fleshy enchantress we have but to turn to the *Samson Agonistes*. Milton exposes Dalila only to drive her explosively from the stage. Shakspere would have studied her with equal delight and detestation. Yet the severity of Shakspere, in his own dramatic fashion, is as absolute as that of Milton. Antony is dead. The supreme sensation of Cleopatra's life is ended, and she seems in the first passionate burst of chagrin to have no longer interest in anything but death. By-and-by she is in the presence of Caesar, and hands over to him a document, the 'brief of money, plate, and jewels' of which she is possessed. She calls on her treasurer Seleucus to vouch for its accuracy:

Speak the truth, Seleucus.
Seleucus. Madam,
I had rather seal my lips than to my peril
Speak that which is not.
Cleopatra. What have I kept back?
Seleucus. Enough to purchase what you have made known.
Caesar. Nay, blush not, Cleopatra; I approve
Your wisdom in the deed.

In her despair, while declaring that she will die 'in the high Roman fashion', Cleopatra yet clings to her plate and jewels. And the cold approval of Caesar, who never gains the power which passion supplies, nor loses the power which passion withdraws and dissipates, the approval of Caesar is confirmed by the judgment of the spectator. It is right and natural that Cleopatra should love her jewels, and practise a fraud upon her conqueror.

Nor is her death quite in that 'high Roman fashion' which she had announced. She dreads physical pain, and is fearful of the ravage which death might commit upon her beauty; under her physician's direction she has 'pursued conclusions infinite of easy ways to die'. And now to die painlessly is better than to grace the triumph of Octavius. In her death there is something dazzling and splendid, something sensuous, something theatrical, something magnificently coquettish, and nothing stern. Yet Shakspere does not play the rude moralist; he needs no chorus of Israelite captives to utter invective against this Dalila. Let her possess all her grandeur, and her charm. Shakspere can show us more excellent things which will make us proof against the fascination of these.

SOURCE: From *Shakespere: A Critical Study of his Mind and Art*, 1875.

Algernon Charles Swinburne (1880)

It would seem a sign or birthmark of only the greatest among poets that they should be sure to rise instantly for awhile above the very highest of their native height at the touch of a thought of Cleopatra. So was it, as we all know, with William Shakespeare: so is it, as we all see, with Victor Hugo. As we feel in the marvellous and matchless verses of *Zim-Zizimi* all the splendour and fragrance and miracle of her mere bodily presence, so from her first imperial dawn on the stage of Shakespeare to the setting of that eastern star behind a pall of undissolving cloud we feel the charm and the terror and the mystery of her absolute and royal soul. Byron wrote once to Moore, with how much truth or sincerity those may guess who would care to know, that his friend's first 'confounded book' of thin prurient jingle ('we call it a mellisonant tingle-tangle', as Randolph's mock Oberon says of a stolen sheep-bell) had been the first cause of all his erratic or erotic frailties: it is not impossible that spirits of another sort may remember that to their own innocent infantine perceptions the first obscure electric revelation of what Blake calls 'the Eternal Female' was given through a blind wondering thrill of childish rapture by a lightning on the baby dawn of their senses and their soul from the sunrise of Shakespeare's Cleopatra.

Never has he given such proof of his incomparable instinct for abstinence from the wrong thing as well as achievement of the right.

He has utterly rejected and disdained all occasion of setting her off by means of any lesser foil than all the glory of the world with all its empires.

SOURCE: From *A Study of Shakespeare*, 1880.

Georg Brandes (1896/1898)

Assuming that it was Shakespeare's design in *Antony and Cleopatra*, as in *King Lear*, to evoke the conception of a world-catastrophe, we see that he could not in this play, as in *Macbeth* or *Othello*, focus the entire action around the leading characters alone. He could not even make the other characters completely subordinate to them; that would have rendered it impossible for him to give the impression of majestic breadth, of an action embracing half of the then known world, which he wanted for the sake of the concluding effect.

He required in the group of figures surrounding Octavius Caesar, and in the groups round Lepidus, Ventidius, and Sextus Pompeius, a counterpoise to Antony's group. He required the placid beauty and Roman rectitude of Octavia as a contrast to the volatile, intoxicating Egyptian. He required Enobarbus to serve as a sort of chorus and introduce an occasional touch of irony amid the high-flown passion of the play. In short, he required a throng of personages, and (in order to make us feel that the action was not taking place in some narrow precinct in a corner of Europe, but upon the stage of the world) he required a constant coming and going, sending and receiving of messengers, whose communications are awaited with anxiety, heard with bated breath, and not infrequently alter at one blow the situation of the chief characters.

The ambition which characterised Antony's past is what determines his relation to this great world; the love which has now taken such entire possession of him determines his relation to the Egyptian queen, and the consequent loss of all that his ambition had won for him. Whilst in a tragedy like Goethe's *Clavigo*, ambition plays the part of the tempter, and love is conceived as the good, the legitimate power, here it is love that is reprehensible, ambition that is proclaimed to be the great man's vocation and duty. . . .

The English critic, Arthur Symons, writes: '*Antony and Cleopatra* is the most wonderful, I think, of all Shakespeare's plays, and it is so mainly because the figure of Cleopatra is the most wonderful of Shakespeare's women. And not of Shakespeare's women only, but perhaps the most wonderful of women.'

This is carrying enthusiasm almost too far. But thus much is true: the great attraction of this masterpiece lies in the unique figure of Cleopatra, elaborated as it is with all Shakespeare's human experience and artistic enthusiasm. But the greatness of the world-historic drama proceeds from the genius with which he has entwined the private relations of the two lovers with the course of history and the fate of empires. Just as Antony's ruin results from his connection with Cleopatra, so does the fall of the Roman Republic result from the contact of the simple hardihood of the West with the luxury of the East. Antony is Rome. Cleopatra is the Orient. When he perishes, a prey to the voluptuousness of the East, it seems as though Roman greatness and the Roman Republic expired with him.

Not Caesar's ambition, not Caesar's assassination, but this crumbling to pieces of Roman greatness fourteen years later brings home to us the ultimate fall of the old world-republic, and impresses us with that sense of *universal annihilation* which in this play, as in *King Lear*, Shakespeare aims at begetting.

This is no tragedy of a domestic, limited nature like the conclusion of *Othello*; there is no young Fortinbras here, as in *Hamlet*, giving the promise of brighter and better times to come; the victory of Octavius brings glory to no one and promises nothing. No; the final picture is that which Shakespeare was bent on painting from the moment he felt himself attracted by this great theme – the picture of a world-catastrophe.

SOURCE: From *William Shakespeare*, Copenhagen, 1896 – translated 1898.

PART TWO

The Play in Performance

Eleanor Glyn and *Samuel Phelps* at Sadler's Wells (October 1849)

On Monday night the long announced Shaksperian 'revival' of *Antony and Cleopatra* was the means of attracting a very full attendance at this theatre – we however must defer any lengthened notice of the performance of this tragedy, until our next number, when we promise to enter fully into particulars. In the meantime suffice it to say, that the loud plaudits which marked its progress, and the deafening approbation which attended the fall of the curtain, testified the unequivocal success of this, in our opinion, somewhat bold venture on the part of the management. Miss Glyn, and Messrs. Phelps and Bennett came forward in obedience to the call of an audience, who were quite enthusiastic in the bestowal of their approbation.

SOURCE: *Literary Review and Stage-Manager*, 25 October 1849.

Shakspere's long winded and certainly tedious tragedy of *Antony and Cleopatra*, was re-represented on Monday evening, at this theatre. The play is admirably mounted, as we have before stated, and the *mise en scene* reflects the highest credit on the management – further than this we will not go. The less said in the way of honesty about Miss Glyn's Cleopatra the better. Mr Phelps will not suffer in reputation, either, by having any portions of his Antony passed over in charitable silence. Decidedly the best played characters in the piece are Mr Bennett's Enobarbus, and Mr Graham's Eros; Mr Dickinson as Octavius Caesar is puny, elocutionary, and effeminate, which by the way he is, in almost every character he attempts to personify. The general company this season at Sadler's Wells smacks shockingly of the amateurish – the female portion particularly.

SOURCE: *Literary Review and Stage-Manager*, 22 November 1849.

On Monday the tragedy of *Antony and Cleopatra* was revived. This magnificent play is a masterpiece of dramatic construction with the most difficult of subjects. Our admiration of it will increase if we compare it with Dryden's *All for Love*, confessedly written in emulation (and a noble emulation it was) of the diviner Shakspeare's. Dryden found it necessary to make *Antony* a weak man, so weak that, as Mr Campbell has rightly observed, 'any wanton might have seduced him'. Shakspeare's Roman required the Egyptian Queen. The *Cleopatra* of Dryden, also, is even such a woman as his hero needed – no more; but the heroine of Shakspeare is a splendid creature, such as history has suggested to the imagination, such as was suitable to the lofty spirit, whose sense of beauty and taste for luxury had been cultivated into heroism. The persons of this wonderful drama are ideas – of voluptuous sublimity and gorgeous pleasure – gifted with almost divine capacities for enjoyment, having, as it were, the patent of heaven itself for the privilege; clothed gloriously in 'barbaric pearl and gold'; and revelling in their own proper Elysium, like spirits delivered from legal restraints, and free to indulge the bent of their genius and the disposition of their nature, without hindrance either from gods or men. To maintain the action at this elevation, and yet to enable it to touch our human sympathies at innumerable points, required the Poet whose myriad-mindedness has been the wonder of philosophers and critics in exact proportion to the competency of their judgment for the due appreciation of the highest creative efforts. We are not surprised that such a work should have proved *caviare* to the general public, and that there was a period when, as Campbell records, Dryden's play was infinitely preferred, having been 'acted ten times oftener than Shakspeare's', though so decidedly inferior.

The management of this theatre have certainly endeavoured to put this 'wonderful tragedy' of *Antony and Cleopatra* on the stage in the spirit in which it was composed. They have done their best to realise the past, and to bring the historic into actual presence. The Egyptian scenes are exceedingly *vraisemblable*; that on board of *Pompey's* galley, with the banquetting sovereigns of the world as drunk as cobblers, is exceedingly life-like. As it is managed, too, on the boards, it is rendered one of the most picturesque and exciting incidents in the representation. Mr Phelps, in particular, aided the pictorial, by his well-studied bacchanalian attitudes, some of which were exceedingly fine. We may here mention that Mr Phelps' make-up of the character of *Antony* was capital. The illusion was almost perfect; the actor could scarcely be recognised through the disguise. He played the character also with great spirit; neither was it lacking in the higher qualifications of histrionic art. *Antony's* passion – his infatuation – his absorption of being for and in that of *Cleopatra* was interpreted 'excellent well'. It was, indeed, a remarkable triumph over difficulties and will go far to raise his reputation as an actor, which must increase just in proportion as he succeeds in delivering himself from mere individualities. Such characters as these break up a performer's mannerisms, and do him accordingly infinite good.

A similar effect was produced on Miss Glyn. In this almost impossible character of *Cleopatra* she put forth new energies, and exhibited a versatility of power which surprised those most acquainted with her style and the scope of her genius. She dared at once at that 'infinite variety' of Cleopatra's character which 'custom could not stale'; and realised the conception to an almost miraculous extent. She combined grace and dignity – all the fascination of a Vestris with the majesty of a Pasta; she was, as it were, the impersonation at once of the sublime and the beautiful. Critics who before doubted her capacity were now astonished at the extent of her resources, and the grandeur of the results. Gorgeous in person, in costume, and in her style of action, she moved, the Egyptian Venus, Minerva, Juno – now pleased, now angry – now eloquent, now silent – capricious, and resolved, according to the situation and sentiment to be rendered. Withal she was classical, and her *poses* severely statuesque. Her death was sublime. With a magnificent smile of triumph, she is, as it were, translated to the shades, there to meet her imperial lover. Altogether, Miss Glyn's performance of *Cleopatra* is the most superb thing ever witnessed on the modern stage. At the end of the play she was called before the curtain; and, led on by Mr Phelps, received the well-merited ovation of an over-crowded house.

SOURCE: *Illustrated London News*, 27 October 1849.

Constance Collier and *Beerbohm Tree* at His Majesty's Theatre (December 1906)

[*Antony and Cleopatra*] is one of the classics of what M. Porto-Riche would call the Theatre de l'Amour. Mr Bernard Shaw would give its theme a less elegant name, 'sexual infatuation'. Cleopatra is the irresistible enchantress, Antony the colossal lover, and the whole play must burn to a white heat with their fire. . . . Nevertheless, if you present *Antony and Cleopatra* at all, you must present it, above everything, as a treatment of 'sexual infatuation' in the grand style. And that is just what Mr Tree has perceived and has done. . . . [Mr Tree] has the supreme quality of thinking out the master-idea of a play, of disengaging its essential essence, and of comprehending the play 'in its quiddity'. To get at the heart of the play, and to exhibit that heart to you, he will boldly lop here and still more boldly add there – and who shall blame him? The pedants, no doubt; but certainly not the great body of playgoers who come to Shakespeare, as they come to any other dramatist, simply and solely to get what pleasure they can out of him, – and whose pleasure is dependent upon the clearness, the unity, of what is put before them. . . . Where is that unity in *Antony and Cleopatra*? Is it in the Imperial Roman *motif*? No; that is merely North's *Plutarch* cut up into blank verse, and taken by itself would be as dull as ditch water. Is it in the Octavia *motif*, the contrast of the ultra-respectable matron, the pattern of domesticity, with the voluptuous orchidaceous Cleopatra? No; that is a mere additional touch of art. It is in the passion-*motif* of Cleopatra and Antony, there and not elsewhere; and it is upon that *motif* that Mr Tree concentrates the whole force of his stage. Hence the scenes in 'Caesar's House' are cut very short indeed. Hence the 'camp' scenes become mere kinematographs. Hence the passionate duologue between Antony and Cleopatra is given all the advantage of scenic magnificence and orchestral illustration. Egypt, not Rome nor Athens nor Misenum, becomes the 'hub' of the play. . . . A dissolving vision of the Sphinx opens and closes the play. Weird nerve-thrilling Oriental strains are in the air. You hear those same strains even in Rome or Athens – on the Wagnerian plan – whenever

Antony's thoughts turn to the far-away Cleopatra. For example, Antony has just parted, not without conjugal tenderness, from Octavia. He seems, for once, to have in him the makings of a model home-loving husband. But there swiftly enters a messenger – Cleopatra's trusty messenger – with a scroll. Antony falls on his couch murmuring 'Cleopatra', and covering his eyes that he may shut out the present scene and dream of her, again to the faint sound of the Oriental music. You will search in vain for any indication of this 'business' in Shakespeare; but it is ingeniously, and quite legitimately, invented; it helps the unity of impression. Another example: in the text Caesar describes Antony's return to Alexandria, how 'I' th' market place on a Tribunal silver'd' [etc. III vi 3 ff]. All this Mr Tree actually shows you in a silent and yet extraordinarily eloquent tableau, which will, perhaps, vex the text-worshippers, but certainly will delight everybody else. . . .

SOURCE: *The Times*, 4 January 1907.

Certainly the piece is very well played. Miss Constance Collier, handsome, dark-skinned, barbaric, dominates the scene wherever she appears. Nor has she ever had a better chance, or more fully availed herself of it, than when in the second act she has to prove how close the tiger's cruelty lies under the sleek skin of the cultivated woman. Mr Tree's Mark Antony was a fine, masculine, resolute rendering of a hero ruined by love. There is not much subtlety or complexity in the part. Antony is the Samson caught by Delilah; a sort of primitive, elemental hero, whose degradation is all the more sure because his intellect is so inferior to his heart. And this is precisely the hero whom Mr Tree so skilfully rendered. Apart from these two principal personages, there were many others who gained a significant success on the boards. Mr Basil Gill was very alert and vivid in the part of Octavius Caesar, saying his lines with that prompt energy which belongs to the nature of the Shakespearian conqueror. Mr Norman Forbes gave adequate presentment of the weakness of Lepidus, an invaluable help in the evolution of the play, keeping the figure within its proper limits, as wholly subordinate, yet illustrative of the increasing degeneracy of the Roman. Mr Lyn Harding's Enobarbus was also a fine performance, picturesque, and varied, done with admirable lightness and no little artistic skill; while Mr Julian L'Estrange, in such brief opportunities as he possessed, gave a firm sketch of Sextus Pompeius. Cleopatra's two attendants, Iras and Charmian, were both excellent – especially, perhaps, Charmian, as played by Miss Alice Crawford, who revealed real dramatic power in the last act, and throughout presented a beautiful picture of Eastern womanhood. Nor ought we to forget the dignified Sooth-sayer of Mr J. Fisher White – a characteristic personage, who at various crises in the story illustrated before our eyes the noiseless steps of on-coming Destiny. . . .

SOURCE: *Daily Telegraph*, 28 December 1906.

Ellen Terry's View of Cleopatra (*c.*1911)

A greater contrast to Cordelia than Cleopatra could hardly be conceived. The moral contrast is sufficiently obvious. I am not referring to that, but to the contrast between Cordelia's reticence and Cleopatra's ebullience. I think Cleopatra is the most expressive of all Shakespeare's heroines. She can put all her emotions into words, and she gives me the impression sometimes of saying more than she feels. I believe Shakespeare conceived her as a woman with a shallow nature, and I should like to see her played as such. If she were not idealized in the theatre, it would be clear to us that Shakespeare has done what no other writer, novelist, dramatist or poet has done – told the truth about the wanton. Yes, Cleopatra is that, and if she is represented as a great woman with a great and sincere passion for Antony, the part does not hang together.

SOURCE: From *Four Lectures on Shakespeare*, *c.* 1911.

Vivien Leigh and *Laurence Olivier* at the St James's Theatre (May 1951)

In the last two acts of *Antony and Cleopatra* Shakespeare wrote as never before or after. To see them performed with a majesty equal to their mighty utterance of desire, ecstasy, despair, and the brave end has been my life's desire in the theatre, and now I have seen it done. Olivier's Antony is a witty piece of work, especially admirable in the earlier scenes of Roman conference; this is a clever Antony rather missing the rich folly of the unlimited sensualist but infinitely tragic when he comes to his end with Eros and to his dream of a lover's immortality with all the ghosts a-gaze at such a peerless pair. But the challenge is to Cleopatra, and Vivien Leigh takes it not only with the necessary beauty, which was certain anyway, but with a technical skill, a range of voice, and an emotional power that are a revelation of developed artistry. She moved me almost beyond endurance at the close when the gipsy wanton has turned marble-constant, now a sovereign in dignity and in fortitude as once 'a daughter of the game', the all-conquering coquette. This noble conclusion is helped, no doubt, by cutting the attempt to trick Octavius over the jewels and 'immoment toys'; it is a questionable liberty to take and purists may grumble. But it is justified in the splendour of the finish, with Cleopatra purged of carnality and making death proud to take her, throned cold and Sphinx-like beside the Sphinx where Shaw discovered his kitten-queen.

SOURCE: Ivor Brown, in the *Observer*, 13 May 1951.

Shakespeare's Cleopatra is hot, bewrinkled, and black-complexioned. Miss Leigh is cold, smooth, pale, and dazzlingly beautiful. She is also extremely intelligent, and intelligence in her performance proves an adequate substitute for heat, duskiness, and even wrinkles. She has not to manifest an interior magnetism the more enslaving for its lack of physical justification; and she speaks her tremendous lines musically, justly, and well.

Sir Laurence's Antony, gracefully bearded, passionately

vacillating, passes with accomplishment from doting amorousness, through gusts of nervous optimism, to fierce despair. This performance is more showy and less impressive than his Caesar [in Shaw's *Caesar and Cleopatra*]. Mr Helpmann's Octavius is a very good shot indeed for a great ballet dancer to make at a man whose joints were of iron. Mr Norman Wooland, as Enobarbus, was given some of the most beautiful lines in the play, but seemed resolved not to share the beauty with us. Mr Roger Furse's dramatic, sun-kissed columns, rising out of the burning sand, are very fine.

SOURCE: Harold Hobson, in the *Sunday Times*, 13 May 1951.

Peggy Ashcroft and *Michael Redgrave* at the Prince's Theatre (November 1953)

In the steady and unswerving pilgrimage towards greatness, Peggy Ashcroft as the serpent of old Nile surely reaches the peak. What a woman is this queen, how generous is her sacrifice to every passion. She is a gipsy, a child, a fury and a great and noble queen in her immortal longings.

Michael Redgrave's Antony is in every way equal in stature, the slave of his queen and of his conscience as a soldier. Harry Andrews is a splendid and lusty Enobarbus.

Glen Byam Shaw's production has a rich and austere beauty, and the 40-odd scenes flow easily one into another to the final climax with a perfect balance of dramatic emphasis.

SOURCE: 'E.F.', in the *News Chronicle*, 5 November 1953.

Though Peggy Ashcroft fails where so many other fine actresses have failed to give completeness to the many-sided character of the Egyptian enchantress, the Stratford production of *Antony and Cleopatra* at the Princes Theatre is one of memorable beauty.

Michael Redgrave's bearded, ruddy-visaged Antony is full of splendid masculine strength, stirring in delivery, forthright in passion and deeply moving in fallen grandeur.

Miss Ashcroft hardly matches the high quality of this performance, though what she does is something of a triumph over the lack of that art which suggests Cleopatra's voluptuous guile, the beauty of voice that should give music to gorgeous lines.

It is also a triumph over an unbecoming make-up of red hair and pallid face. But imperiousness is there as well as fiery passion, and the death scene is touched with genuine pathos.

Marius Goring plays Caesar somewhat in the manner of a prim and chilly high church dignitary. Harry Andrews's bluff and soldierly strength makes Enobarbus a striking performance.

The production is admirable. The fighting is vigorous and the stage is filled with Egyptians who look like Egyptians, and stalwarts who really look like hard-bitten Roman soldiers.

SOURCE: A. E. Wilson, in the *Star*, 5 November 1953.

Peter Brook's *Antony and Cleopatra* at the Royal Shakespeare Theatre (October 1978)

Brook's search for what the play is about has taken him in several directions. First, the Rome/Egypt contrast is made far subtler than in most readings. Jonathan Pryce's Octavius is a pacific, almost priestlike figure, a serious but by no means flinty embodiment of his divine imperial role. The cue for the interpretation is his own view of himself in Act V: 'You shall see/How hardly I was drawn into this still/In all my writings'. His senators are similarly restrained and kindly seeming; shrewd, too, under the surface – their conversation with Enobarbus after the Octavius–Antony rapprochement is played as a skilled piece of diplomatic investigation about the real likelihood of a change in Antony. In all this, Octavius' deeply complicated, part-sexual relationship with Octavia genuinely balances

Antony's with Cleopatra – a dividend of playing the text uncut. The interval comes, not after the party on Pompey's galley (very well done – funny, then orgiastic, then sinister), but after Octavia's return from Antony to her brother.

Some subtle insights are made available in this treatment of the Romans, then – and in David Suchet's playing of Pompey, too, as a dark, impulsive, emotional Corsican. But there are losses. Caesar's grand-scale ceremoniousness isn't on display, for example, and Antony's attraction to Egypt is unusually hard to fathom. The people in Cleopatra's court are sensual but remote – Alexas a sphinx, Mardian a bald, fleshy Buddha, the women, including Cleopatra herself, both volatile and almost eerily suave: one minute Cleopatra is gesturing with her hands and arms in writhing slow-motion, like an Indian dancer, the next she's kicking her messengers around the floor and pulling their hair out. The double-sidedness is true to the character, of course, but Glenda Jackson hadn't found a bridge between the different moments on the first night: she just seemed like Glenda Jackson playing two kinds of woman. All the same, she has a very convincing rapport with Charmian and Iras, and is vocally a match – impressively so – for Alan Howard's throaty Antony.

At his best, Howard is thrillingly operatic; at his worst a tiresome parody of the Stratford voice – Larry the Lamb, or the man with the artificial larynx. He comes over as too young as Antony, though the production goes out of its way to emphasize his age – all his lieutenants are grizzled, balding old troopers, and Brook colours the point in at various moments, none more effective than Antony's arming scene, played by candle-light as an insomniac obsession in the small hours, Cleopatra's 'Sleep a little' not sexy, or even procrastinating, but just exasperated and middle-aged. What the couple manage together is often brilliantly unexpected and effective. They are turned on mainly by shock and violent action. At the beginning of the play their relationship is restrained – almost arrogantly formal. But they are both exhilarated by the news of Fulvia's death, independently bursting into laughter when they hear of it. And Glenda Jackson makes the difficult speeches that follow it ('O! my oblivion is a very Antony/And I am all forgotten' and so on) deeply erotic and complicated. She and Antony get similarly wound up by the prospect of battle; but that they are drawn or driven together not only sexually but in all kinds of psychological ways is brought out by their increasing and moving mutual dependence in the trauma – which is precisely how Brook treats it – of defeat. Separately shattered, they gradually together patch each other up for another gaudy night.

The last hour or so (the production runs for 3¾ hours with the interval) is on the whole more interesting than gripping. One of the big surprises is how funny it is – Antony's grim patience while Eros delays, and finally evades, killing him; his own embarrassment about his botched suicide ('Now my spirit *is going*' he tells Cleopatra at last, with the restrained irritation of someone held up at an airport): and the comedy of the Clown (played by Richard Griffiths in a red nose and slippers) with the asps.

If all this makes the first night sound a piecemeal experience, it was. But Brook is a good director because he probes and dares, and because the questions he asks of a text are difficult and genuine, rather than factitious ones whose answer he has already decided. It's the only *Antony and Cleopatra* I've seen that I've wanted to go back to in a few months' time, to see what's happening.

SOURCE: Jeremy Treglown, in *Plays & Players*, xxvi, 3, December 1978.

Peter Hall's *Antony and Cleopatra* at the National Theatre (April 1987)

Like all great Shakespearean productions, Peter Hall's uncovers meanings in the text that may seem obvious but that have never hit one so penetratingly before. For me this production is rooted in prophesy and dream. From the Soothsayer's first predictions to Enobarbus's tart comment that the new-found amity between Antony and Octavius cannot hold, everything that happens is foreseeable and foreseen. It is all there in Shakespeare. But I have never before been so aware that this is not a tragedy (like *Hamlet*) of constant narrative surprise but one in which a pattern is fulfilled.

But Peter Hall also deliberately heightens the extent to which the characters exist in a state of intoxicated fantasy. When Michael Bryant's admirable Enobarbus begins his famous speech about Cleopatra's barge, it is in the casual tones of an old sweat reporting what he has seen: as he continues, he gets carried into an imaginative trance from which he has to be roused.

Similarly when Judi Dench's Cleopatra describes her Antony ('His legs bestrid the ocean'), she does so with the intensity of someone recounting a dream. 'Nature,' she says, 'wants stuff to vie strange forms with fancy.' I was reminded, strangely, of *A Midsummer Night's Dream* in which Shakespeare also deals with the transubstantiating power of love.

What this means in practice is that the production – played in Jacobean costume against Alison Chitty's circular, blood-red surround with broken columns and fragmented porticoes – is about two chunkily real people living out some epic fantasy.

And no one could be more real than Judi Dench's breathtaking Cleopatra. She is capricious, volatile, the mistress of all moods who in the course of a single scene can switch easily from breathy languour ('O happy horse to bear the weight of Antony') to cutting humour ('How much unlike art thou Mark Antony' to an effeminate messenger) to a pensive melancholy ('My salad days when I was green in judgement') at the frank acknowledgement of the passing years.

Ms Dench ensures that Cleopatra's sexual magnetism lies not in any Centrefold posturing but in emotional extremism: she can be highly funny, as when she rushes for the door in affronted dignity at being told Octavia is 30, and highly dangerous as when she fells a messenger with a right hook.

Ms Dench even gets over the notorious hurdle of the last Act (how often has one waited impatiently for Cleopatra to die) by looking for the precise meaning of each speech and by achieving a kind of fulfilment on 'now the fleeting moon no planet is of mine.' After the boggling inconstancy of her life, Ms Dench goes to her death with single-minded certainty.

She in no way, however, o'ertops Antony Hopkins's magnificent Antony: a real old campaigner (you can believe that he ate 'strange flesh' in the Alps) for whom Alexandria represents escape and fantasy. Mr Hopkins, like many heavyweights, is extraordinarily light on his feet, externalises the conflict in Antony between the soldier and the lover: when recalled to Rome he prowls the stage hungrily like a lion waiting to get back in the arena.

But what I shall remember most is Mr Hopkins's false gaiety – and overpowering inward grief – in the short scene where he bids farewell to his servants. From that point on, the knowledge of death sits on Antony; and when Mr Hopkins says he will contend even with his pestilent scythe it is with a swashbuckling bravura that moves one to tears.

But the strength of this production lies in the way every role has been reconsidered. Tim Pigott-Smith does not play Octavius as the usual cold prig but as a man who combines calculation with passion: it is a superb study of a power-lover who delights in spotting and playing on other men's flaws.

Michael Bryant's Enobarbus is also played, fascinatingly, not as a contrast to Antony but as someone who delights in aping his master's drinking and womanising and who even, as I have indicated, shares in the erotic dream to which he has fallen prey.

I have always, to be honest, had my doubts about this play, feeling that the later stages camouflage in poetic glory what they lack in emotional dynamism. But Hall's production, cinematically dissolving one scene into another and then playing it with due deliberation, banishes my qualms. It is about two middle-aged people – carnal, deceitful, often sad – seeking in love a reality greater than themselves.

SOURCE: Michael Billington, in the *Guardian*, 11 April 1987.

PART THREE

Twentieth-century Criticism

A. C. Bradley Shakespeare's *Antony and Cleopatra* (1905)

Coleridge's one page of general criticism on *Antony and Cleopatra* contains some notable remarks. 'Of all Shakespeare's historical plays,' he writes, '*Antony and Cleopatra* is by far the most wonderful. There is not one in which he has followed history so minutely, and yet there are few in which he impresses the notion of angelic strength so much – perhaps none in which he impresses it more strongly. This is greatly owing to the manner in which the fiery force is sustained throughout.' In a later sentence he refers to the play as 'this astonishing drama'. In another he describes the style: '*feliciter audax* is the motto for its style comparatively with that of Shakespeare's other works'. And he translates this motto in the phrase 'happy valiancy of style'.

Coleridge's assertion that in *Antony and Cleopatra* Shakespeare followed history more minutely than in any other play might well be disputed; and his statement about the style of this drama requires some qualification in view of the results of later criticism as to the order of Shakespeare's works. The style is less individual than he imagined. On the whole it is common to the six or seven dramas subsequent to *Macbeth*, though in *Antony and Cleopatra*, probably the earliest of them, its development is not yet complete. And we must add that this style has certain special defects, unmentioned by Coleridge, as well as the quality which he points out in it. But it is true that here that quality is almost continuously present; and in the phrase by which he describes it, as in his other phrases, he has signalised once for all some of the most salient features of the drama.

It is curious to notice, for example, alike in books and in conversation, how often the first epithets used in reference to *Antony and Cleopatra* are 'wonderful' and 'astonishing'. And the main source of the feeling thus expressed seems to be the 'angelic strength' or 'fiery force' of which Coleridge wrote. The first of these two phrases is, I think, the more entirely happy. Except perhaps towards the close, one is not so conscious of fiery force as in certain other tragedies; but one is astonished at the apparent ease with which extraordinary effects are produced, the ease, if I may paraphrase Coleridge, of an angel moving with a wave of the hand that heavy matter which men find so intractable. We feel this sovereign ease in contemplating Shakespeare's picture of the world – a vast canvas, crowded with figures, glowing with colour and a superb animation, reminding one spectator of Paul Veronese and another of Rubens. We feel it again when we observe (as we can even without consulting Plutarch) the nature of the material; how bulky it was, and, in some respects, how undramatic; and how the artist, though he could not treat history like legend or fiction, seems to push whole masses aside, and to shift and refashion the remainder, almost with the air of an architect playing (at times rather carelessly) with a child's bricks.

Something similar is felt even in the portrait of Cleopatra. Marvellous as it is, the drawing of it suggests not so much the passionate concentration or fiery force of *Macbeth*, as that sense of effortless and exultant mastery which we feel in the portraits of Mercutio and Falstaff. And surely it is a total mistake to find in this portrait any trace of the distempered mood which disturbs our pleasure in *Troilus and Cressida*. If the sonnets about the dark lady were, as need not be doubted, in some degree autobiographical, Shakespeare may well have used his personal experience both when he drew Cressida and when he drew Cleopatra. And, if he did, the story in the later play was the nearer to his own; for Antony might well have said what Troilus could never say,

> When my love swears that she is made of truth,
> I do believe her, though I know she lies.

But in the later play, not only is the poet's vision unclouded, but his whole nature, emotional as well as intellectual, is free. The subject no more embitters or seduces him than the ambition of Macbeth. So that here too we feel the angelic strength of which Coleridge speaks. If we quarrelled with the phrase at all, it would be because we fancied we could trace in Shakespeare's attitude something of the irony of superiority; and this may not altogether suit our conception of an angel.

I have still another sentence to quote from Coleridge: 'The highest praise, or rather form of praise, of this play which I can offer in my own mind, is the doubt which the perusal always occasions in me, whether the *Antony and Cleopatra* is not, in all exhibitions of a giant power in its strength and vigour of maturity, a formidable rival of *Macbeth, Lear, Hamlet*, and *Othello*.' Now, unless the clause here about the 'giant power' may be taken to restrict the rivalry to the quality of angelic strength, Coleridge's doubt seems to show a lapse in critical judgment. To regard this tragedy as a rival of the famous four, whether on the stage or in the study, is surely an error. The world certainly has not so regarded it; and, though the world's reasons for its verdicts on works of art may be worth little, its mere verdict is worth much. Here, it seems to me, that verdict must be accepted. One may notice that, in calling *Antony and Cleopatra* wonderful or astonishing, we appear to be thinking first of the artist and his activity, while in the case of the four famous tragedies it is the product of this activity, the thing presented, that first engrosses us. I know that I am stating this difference too sharply, but I believe that it is often felt; and, if this is so, the fact is significant. It implies that, although *Antony and Cleopatra* may be for us as wonderful an achievement as the greatest of Shakespeare's plays, it has not an equal value. Besides, in the attempt to rank it with them there is involved something more, and more important, than an error in valuation. There is a failure to discriminate the peculiar marks of *Antony and Cleopatra* itself, marks which, whether or no it be the equal of the earlier tragedies, make it decidedly different. If I speak first of some of these differences it is because they thus contribute to the individuality of the play, and because they seem often not to be distinctly apprehended in criticism.

I

Why, let us begin by asking, is *Antony and Cleopatra*, though so wonderful an achievement, a play rarely acted? For a tragedy, it is not painful. Though unfit for children, it cannot be called indecent; some slight omissions, and such a flattening of the heroine's part as might confidently be expected, would leave it perfectly presentable. It is, no doubt, in the third and fourth Acts, very defective in construction. Even on the Elizabethan stage, where scene followed scene without a pause, this must have been felt; and in our theatres it would be felt much more. There, in fact, these two and forty scenes could not possibly be acted as they stand. But defective construction would not distress the bulk of an audience, if the matter presented were that of *Hamlet* or *Othello*, of *Lear* or *Macbeth*. The matter, then, must lack something which is present in those tragedies; and it is mainly owing to this difference in substance that *Antony and Cleopatra* has never attained their popularity either on the stage or off it.

Most of Shakespeare's tragedies are dramatic in a special sense of the word, as well as in its general sense, from beginning to end. The story is not merely exciting and impressive from the movement of conflicting forces towards a terrible issue, but from time to time there come situations and events which, even apart from their bearing on this issue, appeal most powerfully to the dramatic feelings – scenes of action or passion which agitate the audience with alarm, horror, painful expectation, or absorbing sympathies and antipathies. Think of the street fights in *Romeo and Juliet*, the killing of Mercutio and Tybalt, the rapture of the lovers, and their despair when Romeo is banished. Think of the ghost-scenes in the first Act of *Hamlet*, the passion of the early soliloquies, the scene between Hamlet and Ophelia, the play-scene, the sparing of the King at prayer, the killing of Polonius. Is not *Hamlet*, if you choose so to regard it, the best melodrama in the world? Think at your leisure of *Othello*, *Lear*, and *Macbeth* from the same point of view; but consider here and now even the two tragedies which, as dealing with Roman history, are companions of *Antony and Cleopatra*. Recall in *Julius Caesar* the first suggestion of the murder, the preparation for it in a 'tempest dropping fire', the murder itself, the speech of Antony over the corpse, and the tumult of the furious crowd; in *Coriolanus* the bloody battles on the stage, the scene in which the hero attains the consulship, the scene of rage in which he is banished. And remember that in each of these seven tragedies the matter referred to is contained in the first three Acts.

In the first three Acts of our play what is there resembling this? Almost nothing. People converse, discuss, accuse one another, excuse themselves, mock, describe, drink together, arrange a marriage, meet and part; but they do not kill, do not even tremble or weep. We see hardly one violent movement; until the battle of Actium is over we witness scarcely any vehement passion; and that battle, as it is a naval action, we do not see. Even later, Enobarbus, when he dies, simply dies; he does not kill himself.[1] We hear wonderful talk; but it is not talk, like that of Macbeth and Lady Macbeth, or that of Othello and Iago, at which we hold our breath. The scenes that we remember first are those that portray Cleopatra; Cleopatra coquetting, tormenting, beguiling her lover to stay;

Cleopatra left with her women and longing for him; Cleopatra receiving news of his marriage; Cleopatra questioning the messenger about Octavia's personal appearance. But this is to say that the scenes we remember first are the least indispensable to the plot. One at least is not essential to it at all. And this, the astonishing scene where she storms at the messenger, strikes him, and draws her dagger on him, is the one passage in the first half of the drama that contains either an explosion of passion or an exciting bodily action. Nor is this all. The first half of the play, though it forebodes tragedy, is not decisively tragic in tone. Certainly the Cleopatra scenes are not so. We read them, and we should witness them, in delighted wonder and even with amusement. The only scene that can vie with them, that of the revel on Pompey's ship, though full of menace, is in great part humorous. Enobarbus, in this part of the play, is always humorous. Even later, when the tragic tone is deepening, the whipping of Thyreus, in spite of Antony's rage, moves mirth. A play of which all this can truly be said may well be as masterly as *Othello* or *Macbeth*, and more delightful; but, in the greater part of its course, it cannot possibly excite the same emotions. It makes no attempt to do so; and to regard it as though it made this attempt is to miss its specific character and the intention of its author.

That character depends only in part on Shakespeare's fidelity to his historical authority, a fidelity which, I may remark, is often greatly exaggerated. For Shakespeare did not merely present the story of ten years as though it occupied perhaps one fifth of that time, nor did he merely invent freely, but in critical places he effected startling changes in the order and combination of events. Still it may be said that, dealing with a history so famous, he could not well make the first half of his play very exciting, moving, or tragic. And this is true so far as mere situations and events are concerned. But, if he had chosen, he might easily have heightened the tone and tension in another way. He might have made the story of Antony's attempt to break his bondage, and the story of his relapse, extremely exciting, by portraying with all his force the severity of the struggle and the magnitude of the fatal step.

And the structure of the play might seem at first to suggest this intention. At the opening, Antony is shown almost in the beginning of his infatuation; for Cleopatra is not sure of her power over him, exerts all her fascination to detain him, and plays the part of the innocent victim who has yielded to passion and must now expect to be deserted by her seducer. Alarmed and ashamed at the news of the results of his inaction, he rouses himself, tears himself away, and speeds to Italy. His very coming is enough to frighten Pompey into peace. He reconciles himself with Octavius and, by his marriage with the good and beautiful Octavia, seems to have knit a bond of lasting amity with her brother, and to have guarded himself against the passion that threatened him with ruin. At this point his power, the world's peace, and his own peace, appear to be secured; his fortune has mounted to its apex. But soon (very much sooner than in Plutarch's story) comes the downward turn or counter-stroke. New causes of offence arise between the brothers-in-law. To remove them Octavia leaves her husband in Athens and hurries to Rome. Immediately Antony returns to Cleopatra and, surrendering himself at once and wholly to her enchantment, is quickly driven to his doom.

Now Shakespeare, I say, with his matchless power of depicting an inward struggle, might have made this story, even where it could not furnish him with thrilling incidents, the source of powerful tragic emotions; and, in doing so, he would have departed from his authority merely in his conception of the hero's character. But he does no such thing till the catastrophe is near. Antony breaks away from Cleopatra without any strenuous conflict. No serious doubt of his return is permitted to agitate us. We are almost assured of it through the impression made on us by Octavius, through occasional glimpses into Antony's mind, through the absence of any doubt in Enobarbus, through scenes in Alexandria which display Cleopatra and display her irresistible. And, finally, the downward turn itself, the fatal step of Antony's return, is shown without the slightest emphasis. Nay, it is not shown, it is only reported; and not a line portrays any inward struggle preceding it. On this side also, then, the drama makes no attempt to rival the other tragedies; and it was essential to its own peculiar character and its most transcendent effects that this attempt should not be made, but that Antony's passion should be represented as a force which he could hardly even desire to resist. By the very scheme of the work, therefore, tragic impressions of any great volume or depth were reserved for the last stage of the conflict; while the main interest, down to the battle of Actium, was directed to matters exceedingly interesting and even, in the wider sense, dramatic, but not overtly either terrible or piteous: on the one hand, to the political aspect of the story; on the other, to the personal causes which helped to make the issue inevitable.

II

The political situation and its development are simple. The story is taken up almost where it was left, years before, in *Julius Caesar*. There Brutus and Cassius, to prevent the rule of one man, assassinate Caesar. Their purpose is condemned to failure, not merely because they make mistakes, but because that political necessity which Napoleon identified with destiny requires the rule of one man. They spill Caesar's blood, but his spirit walks abroad and turns their swords against their own breasts; and the world is left divided among three men, his friends and his heir. Here *Antony and Cleopatra* takes up the tale; and its business, from this point of view, is to show the reduction of these three to one. That Lepidus will not be this one was clear already in *Julius Caesar*; it must be Octavius or Antony. Both ambitious, they are also men of such opposite tempers that they would scarcely long agree even if they wished to, and even if destiny were not stronger than they. As it is, one of them has fixed his eyes on the end, sacrifices everything for it, uses everything as a means to it. The other, though far the greater soldier and worshipped by his followers, has no such singleness of aim; nor yet is power, however desirable to him, the most desirable thing in the world. At the beginning he is risking it for love; at the end he has lost his half of the world, and lost his life, and Octavius rules alone. Whether Shakespeare had this clearly in his mind is a question neither answerable nor important; this is what came out of his mind.

Shakespeare, I think, took little interest in the character of Octavius, and he has not made it wholly clear. It is not distinct in Plutarch's 'Life of Antony'; and I have not found traces that the poet studied closely the 'Life of Octavius' included in North's volume. To Shakespeare he is one of those men, like Bolingbroke and Ulysses, who have plenty of 'judgment' and not much 'blood'. Victory in the world, according to the poet, almost always goes to such men; and he makes us respect, fear, and dislike them. His Octavius is very formidable. His cold determination half paralyses Antony; it is so even in *Julius Caesar*. In *Antony and Cleopatra* Octavius is more than once in the wrong; but he never admits it; he silently pushes his rival a step backward; and, when he ceases to fear, he shows contempt. He neither enjoys war nor is great in it; at first, therefore, he is anxious about the power of Pompey, and stands in need of Antony. As soon as Antony's presence has served his turn, and he has patched up a union with him and seen him safely off to Athens, he destroys first Pompey and next Lepidus. Then, dexterously using Antony's faithlessness to Octavia and excesses in the East in order to put himself in the right, he makes for his victim with admirable celerity while he is still drunk with the joy of reunion with Cleopatra. For his ends Octavius is perfectly efficient, but he is so partly from his limitations. One phrase of his is exceedingly characteristic. When Antony in rage and desperation challenges him to single combat, Octavius calls him 'the old ruffian'. There is a horrid aptness in the phrase, but it disgusts us. It is shameful in this boy, as hard and smooth as polished steel, to feel at such a time nothing of the greatness of his victim and the tragedy of his victim's fall. Though the challenge of Antony is absurd, we would give much to see them sword to sword. And when Cleopatra by her death cheats the conqueror of his prize, we feel unmixed delight.

The doubtful point in the character is this. Plutarch says that Octavius was reported to love his sister dearly; and Shakespeare's Octavius several times expresses such love. When, then, he proposed the marriage with Antony (for of course it was he who spoke through Agrippa), was he honest, or was he laying a trap and, in doing so, sacrificing his sister? Did he hope the marriage would really unite him with his brother-in-law; or did he merely mean it to be a source of future differences; or did he calculate that, whether it secured peace or dissension, it would in either case bring him great advantage? Shakespeare, who was quite as intelligent as his readers, must have asked himself some such question; but he may not have cared to answer it even to himself; and, in any case, he has left the actor (at least the actor in days later than his own) to choose an answer. If I were forced to choose, I should take the view that Octavius was, at any rate, not wholly honest; partly because I think it best suits Shakespeare's usual way of conceiving a character of the kind; partly because Plutarch construed in this manner Octavius's behaviour in regard to his sister at a later time, and this hint might naturally influence the poet's way of imagining his earlier action.[2]

Though the character of Octavius is neither attractive nor wholly clear, his figure is invested with a certain tragic dignity, because he is felt to be the Man of Destiny, the agent of forces against which the intentions of an individual would avail nothing. He is represented as having himself some feeling of this sort. His lament over Antony, his grief that their stars were irreconcilable, may well be genuine, though we should be surer if it were uttered in soliloquy. His austere words to Octavia again probably speak his true mind:

> Be you not troubled with the time, which drives
> O'er your content these strong necessities;
> But let determined things to destiny
> Hold unbewailed their way.

In any case the feeling of fate comes through to us. It is aided by slight touches of supernatural effect; first in the Soothsayer's warning to Antony that his genius or angel is overpowered whenever he is near Octavius; then in the strangely effective scene where Antony's soldiers, in the night before his last battle, hear music in the air or under the earth:

> 'Tis the god Hercules, whom Antony loved,
> Now leaves him.

And to the influence of this feeling in giving impressiveness to the story is added that of the immense scale and world-wide issue of the conflict. Even the distances traversed by fleets and armies enhance this effect.

And yet there seems to be something half-hearted in Shakespeare's appeal here, something even ironical in his presentation of this conflict. Its external magnitude, like Antony's magnificence in lavishing realms and gathering the kings of the East in his support, fails to uplift or dilate the imagination. The struggle in Lear's little island seems to us to have an infinitely wider scope. It is here that we are sometimes reminded of *Troilus and Cressida*, and the cold and disenchanting light that is there cast on the Trojan War. The spectacle which he portrays leaves Shakespeare quite undazzled; he even makes it appear inwardly small. The lordship of the world, we ask ourselves, what is it worth, and in what spirit do these 'world-sharers' contend for it? They are no champions of their country like Henry V. The conqueror knows not even the glory of battle. Their aims, for all we see, are as personal as if they were captains of banditti; and they are followed merely from self-interest or private attachment. The scene on Pompey's galley is full of this irony. One 'third part of the world' is carried drunk to bed. In the midst of this mock boon-companionship the pirate whispers to his leader to cut first the cable of his ship and then the throats of the two other Emperors; and at the moment we should not greatly care if Pompey took the advice. Later, a short scene, totally useless to the plot and purely satiric in its purport, is slipped in to show how Ventidius fears to pursue his Parthian conquests because it is not safe for Antony's lieutenant to outdo his master.[3] A painful sense of hollowness oppresses us. We know too well what must happen in a world so splendid, so false, and so petty. We turn for relief from the political game to those who are sure to lose it; to those who love some human being better than a prize, to Eros and Charmian and Iras; to Enobarbus, whom the world corrupts, but who has a heart that can break with shame; to the lovers, who seem to us to find in death something better than their victor's life.

This presentation of the outward conflict has two results. First, it blunts our feeling of the greatness of Antony's fall from prosperity. Indeed this feeling, which we might expect to be unusually acute, is hardly so; it is less acute, for example, than the like feeling in the case of Richard II, who loses so much smaller a realm. Our deeper sympathies are focused rather on Antony's heart, on the inward fall to which the enchantment of passion leads him, and the inward recovery which succeeds it. And the second result is this. The greatness of Antony and Cleopatra in their fall is so much heightened by contrast with the world they lose and the conqueror who wins it, that the positive element in the final tragic impression, the element of reconciliation, is strongly emphasised. The peculiar effect of the drama depends partly, as we have seen, on the absence of decidedly tragic scenes and events in its first half; but it depends quite as much on this emphasis. In any Shakespearean tragedy we watch some elect spirit colliding, partly through its error and defect, with a superhuman power which bears it down; and yet we feel that this spirit, even in the error and defect, rises by its greatness into ideal union with the power that overwhelms it. In some tragedies this latter feeling is relatively weak. In *Antony and Cleopatra* it is unusually strong; stronger, with some readers at least, than the fear and grief and pity with which they contemplate the tragic error and the advance of doom.

III

The two aspects of the tragedy are presented together in the opening scene. Here is the first. In Cleopatra's palace one friend of Antony is describing to another, just arrived from Rome, the dotage of their great general; and, as the lovers enter, he exclaims:

> Look, where they come:
> Take but good note, and you shall see in him
> The triple pillar of the world transformed
> Into a strumpet's fool: behold and see.

With the next words the other aspect appears:

> *Cleopatra.* If it be love indeed, tell me how much.
> *Antony.* There's beggary in the love that can be reckoned.
> *Cleopatra.* I'll set a bourne how far to be beloved.
> *Antony.* Then must thou needs find out new heaven, new earth.

And directly after, when he is provoked by reminders of the news from Rome:

> Let Rome in Tiber melt, and the wide arch
> Of the ranged empire fall! Here is my space.
> Kingdoms are clay: our dungy earth alike
> Feeds beast as man: the nobleness of life
> Is to do thus.

Here is the tragic excess, but with it the tragic greatness, the capacity of finding in something the infinite, and of pursuing it into the jaws of death.

The two aspects are shown here with the exaggeration proper in dramatic characters. Neither the phrase 'a strumpet's fool', nor the assertion 'the nobleness of life is to do thus', answers to the total effect of the play. But the truths they exaggerate are equally essential; and the commoner mistake in criticism is to understate the second. It is plain that the love of Antony and Cleopatra is destructive; that in some way it clashes with the nature of things; that, while they are sitting in their paradise like gods, its walls move inward and crush them at last to death. This is no invention of moralising critics; it is in the play; and any one familiar with Shakespeare would expect beforehand to find it there. But then to forget because of it the other side, to deny the name of love to this ruinous passion, to speak as though the lovers had utterly missed the good of life, is to mutilate the tragedy and to ignore a great part of its effect upon us. For we sympathise with them in their passion; we feel in it the infinity there is in man; even while we acquiesce in their defeat we are exulting in their victory; and when they have vanished we say,

> the odds is gone,
> And there is nothing left remarkable
> Beneath the visiting moon.

Though we hear nothing from Shakespeare of the cruelty of Plutarch's Antony, or of the misery caused by his boundless profusion, we do not feel the hero of the tragedy to be a man of the noblest type, like Brutus, Hamlet, or Othello. He seeks power merely for himself, and uses it for his own pleasure. He is in some respects unscrupulous; and, while it would be unjust to regard his marriage exactly as if it were one in private life, we resent his treatment of Octavia, whose character Shakespeare was obliged to leave a mere sketch, lest our feeling for the hero and heroine should be too much chilled. Yet, for all this, we sympathise warmly with Antony, are greatly drawn to him, and are inclined to regard him as a noble nature half spoiled by his time.

It is a large, open, generous, expansive nature, quite free from envy, capable of great magnanimity, even of entire devotion. Antony is unreserved, naturally straightforward, we may almost say simple. He can admit faults, accept advice and even reproof, take a jest against himself with good-humour. He is courteous (to Lepidus, for example, whom Octavius treats with cold contempt); and, though he can be exceedingly dignified, he seems to prefer a blunt though sympathetic plainness, which is one cause of the attachment of his soldiers. He has none of the faults of the brooder, the sentimentalist, or the man of principle; his nature tends to splendid action and lusty enjoyment. But he is neither a mere soldier nor a mere sensualist. He has imagination, the temper of an artist who revels in abundant and rejoicing appetites, feasts his senses on the glow and richness of life, flings himself into its mirth and revelry, yet feels the poetry in all this, and is able also to put it by and be more than content with the hardships of adventure. Such a man could never have sought a crown by a murder like Macbeth's, or, like Brutus, have killed on principle the man who loved him, or have lost the world for a Cressida.

Beside this strain of poetry he has a keen intellect, a swift perception of the lie of things, and much quickness in shaping a course to suit them. In *Julius Caesar* he shows this after the assassination, when he appears as a dexterous politician as well as a warm-hearted friend. He admires what is fine, and can fully appreciate the nobility of Brutus; but he is sure that Brutus's ideas are moonshine, that (as he says in our play) Brutus is mad; and, since his mighty friend, who was incomparably the finest thing in the world, has perished, he sees no reason why the inheritance should not be his own. Full of sorrow, he yet uses his sorrow like an artist to work on others, and greets his success with the glee of a successful adventurer. In the earlier play he proves himself a master of eloquence, and especially of pathos; and he does so again in the later. With a few words about his fall he draws tears from his followers and even from the caustic humorist Enobarbus. Like Richard II, he sees his own fall with the eyes of a poet, but a poet much greater than the young Shakespeare, who could never have written Antony's marvellous speech about the sunset clouds. But we listen to Antony, as we do not to Richard, with entire sympathy, partly because he is never unmanly, partly because he himself is sympathetic and longs for sympathy.

The first of living soldiers, an able politician, a most persuasive orator, Antony nevertheless was not born to rule the world. He enjoys being a great man, but he has not the love of rule for rule's sake. Power for him is chiefly a means to pleasure. The pleasure he wants is so huge that he needs a huge power; but half the world, even a third of it, would suffice. He will not pocket wrongs, but he shows not the slightest wish to get rid of his fellow Triumvirs and reign alone. He never minded being subordinate to Julius Caesar. By women he is not only attracted but governed; from the effect of Cleopatra's taunts we can see that he had been governed by Fulvia. Nor has he either the patience or the steadfastness of a born ruler. He contends fitfully, and is prone to take the step that is easiest at the moment. This is the reason why he consents to marry Octavia. It seems the shortest way out of an awkward situation. He does not intend even to try to be true to her. He will not think of the distant consequences.

A man who loved power as much as thousands of insignificant people love it would have made a sterner struggle than Antony's against his enchantment. He can hardly be said to struggle at all. He brings himself to leave Cleopatra only because he knows he will return. In every moment of his absence, whether he wake or sleep, a siren music in his blood is singing him back to her; and to this music, however he may be occupied, the soul within his soul leans and listens. The joy of life had always culminated for him in the love of women: he could say 'no' to none of them: of Octavia herself he speaks like a poet. When he meets Cleopatra he finds his Absolute. She satisfies, nay glorifies, his whole being. She intoxicates his senses. Her wiles, her taunts, her furies and meltings, her laughter and tears, bewitch him all alike. She loves what he loves, and she surpasses him. She can drink him to his bed, out-jest his practical jokes, out-act the best actress who ever amused him, out-dazzle his own magnificence. She is his playfellow, and yet a great queen. Angling in the river, playing billiards, flourishing the sword he used at Philippi, hopping forty paces in a public street, she remains an enchantress. Her spirit is made of wind and flame, and the poet in him worships her no less than the man. He is under no illusion about her, knows all her faults, sees through her wiles, believes her capable of betraying him. It makes no difference. She is his heart's desire made perfect. To love her is what he was born for. What have the gods in heaven to say against it? To imagine heaven is to imagine her; to die is to rejoin her. To deny that this is love is the madness of morality. He gives her every atom of his heart.

She destroys him. Shakespeare, availing himself of the historic fact, portrays, on Antony's return to her, the suddenness and the depth of his descent. In spite of his own knowledge, the protests of his captains, the entreaties even of a private soldier, he fights by sea simply and solely because she wishes it. Then in mid-battle, when she flies, he deserts navy and army and his faithful thousands and follows her. 'I never saw an action of such shame,' cries Scarus; and we feel the dishonour of the hero keenly. Then Shakespeare begins to raise him again. First, his own overwhelming sense of shame redeems him. Next, we watch the rage of the dying lion. Then the mere sally before the final defeat – a sally dismissed by Plutarch in three lines – is magnified into a battle, in which Antony displays to us, and himself feels for the last time, the glory of his soldiership. And, throughout, the magnanimity and gentleness which shine through his desperation endear him to us. How beautiful is his affection for his followers and even for his servants, and the devotion they return! How noble his reception of the news that Enobarbus has deserted him! How touchingly significant the refusal of Eros either to kill him or survive him! How pathetic and even sublime the completeness of his love for Cleopatra! His anger is born and dies in an hour. One tear, one kiss, outweighs his ruin. He believes she has sold him to his enemy, yet he kills himself because he hears that she is dead. When, dying, he learns that she has deceived him once more, no thought of reproach crosses his mind: he simply asks to be carried to her. He knows well that she is not capable of dying because he dies, but that does not sting him; when, in his last agony, he calls for wine that he may gain a moment's strength to speak, it is to advise her for the days to come. Shakespeare borrowed from Plutarch the final speech of Antony. It is fine, but it is not miraculous. The miraculous speeches belong only to his own hero:

> I am dying, Egypt, dying; only
> I here importune death awhile, until
> Of many thousand kisses the poor last
> I lay upon thy lips;

or the first words he utters when he hears of Cleopatra's death:

> Unarm, Eros: the long day's task is done,
> And we must sleep.

If he meant the task of statesman and warrior, that is not what his words mean to us. They remind us of words more familiar and less great –

> No rest but the grave for the pilgrim of love.

And he is more than love's pilgrim; he is love's martyr.

IV

To reserve a fragment of an hour for Cleopatra, if it were not palpably absurd, would seem an insult. If only one could hear her own remarks upon it! But I had to choose between this absurdity and the plan of giving her the whole hour; and to that plan there was one fatal objection. She has been described (by Ten Brink) as a courtesan of genius. So brief a description must needs be incomplete, and Cleopatra never forgets, nor, if we read aright, do we forget, that she is a great queen. Still the phrase is excellent; only a public lecture is no occasion for the full analysis and illustration of the character it describes.

Shakespeare has paid Cleopatra a unique compliment. The hero dies in the fourth Act, and the whole of the fifth is devoted to the heroine.[4] In that Act she becomes unquestionably a tragic character, but, it appears to me, not till then. This, no doubt, is a heresy; but as I cannot help holding it, and as it is connected with the remarks already made on the first half of the play, I will state it more fully. Cleopatra stands in a group with Hamlet and Falstaff. We might join with them Iago if he were not decidedly their inferior in one particular quality. They are inexhaustible. You feel that, if they were alive and you spent your whole life with them, their infinite variety could never be staled by custom; they would continue every day to surprise, perplex, and delight you. Shakespeare has bestowed on each of them, though they differ so much, his own originality, his genius. He has given it most fully to Hamlet, to whom none of the chambers of experience is shut, and perhaps more of it to Cleopatra than to Falstaff. Nevertheless, if we ask whether Cleopatra, in the first four Acts is a tragic figure like Hamlet, we surely cannot answer 'yes'. Naturally it does not follow that she is a comic figure like Falstaff. This would be absurd; for, even if she were ridiculous like Falstaff, she is not ridiculous to herself; she is no humorist. And yet there is a certain likeness. She shares a weakness with Falstaff – vanity; and when she displays it, as she does quite naïvely (for instance, in the second interview with the Messenger), she does become comic. Again, though like Falstaff she is irresistible and carries us away no less than the people around her, we are secretly aware, in the midst of our delight, that her empire is built on sand. And finally, as his love for the Prince gives dignity and pathos to Falstaff in his overthrow, so what raises Cleopatra at last into pure tragedy is, in part, that which some critics have denied her, her love for Antony.

Many unpleasant things can be said of Cleopatra; and the more that are said the more wonderful she appears. The exercise of sexual attraction is the element of her life; and she has developed nature into a consummate art. When she cannot exert it on the present lover she imagines its effects on him in absence. Longing for the living, she remembers with pride and joy the dead; and the past which the furious Antony holds up to her as a picture of shame is, for her, glory. She cannot see an ambassador, scarcely even a messenger, without desiring to bewitch him. Her mind is saturated with this element. If she is dark, it is because the sun himself has been amorous of her. Even when death is close at hand she imagines his touch as a lover's. She embraces him that she may overtake Iras and gain Antony's first kiss in the other world.

She lives for feeling. Her feelings are, so to speak, sacred, and pain must not come near her. She has tried numberless experiments to discover the easiest way to die. Her body is exquisitely sensitive, and her emotions marvellously swift. They are really so; but she exaggerates them so much, and exhibits them so continually for effect, that some readers fancy them merely feigned. They are all-important, and everybody must attend to them. She announces to her women that she is pale, or sick and sullen; they must lead her to her chamber but must not speak to her. She is as strong and supple as a leopard, can drink down a master of revelry, can raise her lover's helpless heavy body from the ground into her tower with the aid only of two women; yet, when he is sitting apart sunk in shame, she must be supported into his presence, she cannot stand, her head droops, she will die (it is the opinion of Eros) unless he comforts her. When she hears of his marriage and has discharged her rage, she bids her women bear her away; she faints; at least she would faint, but that she remembers various questions she wants put to the Messenger about Octavia. Enobarbus has seen her die twenty times upon far poorer moment than the news that Antony is going to Rome.

Some of her feelings are violent, and, unless for a purpose, she does not dream of restraining them; her sighs and tears are winds and waters, storms and tempests. At times, as when she threatens to give Charmian bloody teeth, or hales the luckless Messenger up and down by the hair, strikes him and draws her knife on him, she resembles (if I dare say it) Doll Tearsheet sublimated. She is a mother; but the threat of Octavius to destroy her children if she takes her own life passes by her like the wind (a point where Shakespeare contradicts Plutarch). She ruins a great man, but shows no sense of the tragedy of his ruin. The anguish of spirit that appears in his language to his servants is beyond her; she has to ask Enobarbus what he means. Can we feel sure that she would not have sacrificed him if she could have saved herself by doing so? It is not even certain that she did not attempt it. Antony himself believes that she did – that the fleet went over to Octavius by her orders. That she and her people deny the charge proves nothing. The best we can say is that, if it were true, Shakespeare would have made that clear. She is willing also to survive her lover. Her first thought, to follow him after the high Roman fashion, is too great for her. She would live on if she could, and would cheat her victor too of the best part of her fortune. The thing that drives her to die is the certainty that she will be carried to Rome to grace his triumph. That alone decides her.[5]

The marvellous thing is that the knowledge of all this makes hardly more difference to us than it did to Antony. It seems to us perfectly natural, nay, in a sense perfectly right, that her lover should be her slave; that her women should adore her and die with her; that Enobarbus, who foresaw what must happen, and who opposes her wishes and braves her anger, should talk of her with rapture and feel no bitterness against her; that Dolabella, after a minute's conversation, should betray to her his master's intention and enable her to frustrate it. And when Octavius shows himself proof against her fascination, instead of admiring him we turn from him with disgust and think him a disgrace to his species. Why? It is not that we consider him bound to fall in love with her. Enobarbus did not; Dolabella did not; we ourselves do not. The feeling she inspires was felt then, and is felt now, by women no less than men, and would have been shared by Octavia herself. Doubtless she wrought magic on the senses, but she had not extraordinary beauty, like Helen's, such beauty as seems divine.[6] Plutarch says so. The man who wrote the sonnets to the dark lady would have known it for himself. He goes out of his way to add to her age, and tells us of her wrinkles and the waning of her lip. But Enobarbus, in his very mockery, calls her a wonderful piece of work. Dolabella interrupts her with the cry, 'Most sovereign creature', and we echo it. And yet Octavius, face to face with her and listening to her voice, can think only how best to trap her and drag her to public dishonour in the streets of Rome. We forgive him only for his words when he sees her dead:

> She looks like sleep,
> As she would catch another Antony
> In her strong toil of grace.

And the words, I confess, sound to me more like Shakespeare's than his.

That which makes her wonderful and sovereign laughs at definition, but she herself came nearest naming it when, in the final speech (a passage surpassed in poetry, if at all, only by the final speech of Othello), she cries,

> I am fire and air; my other elements
> I give to baser life.

The fire and air which at death break from union with those other elements, transfigured them during her life, and still convert into engines of enchantment the very things for which she is condemned. I can refer only to one. She loves Antony. We should marvel at her less and love her more if she loved him more – loved him well enough to follow him at once to death; but it is to blunder strangely to doubt that she loved him, or that her glorious description of him (though it was also meant to work on Dolabella) came from her heart. Only the spirit of fire or air within her refuses to be trammelled or extinguished; burns its way through the obstacles of fortune and even through the resistance of her love and grief; and would lead her undaunted to fresh life and the conquest of new worlds. It is this which makes her 'strong toil of grace' unbreakable; speaks in her brows' bent and every tone and movement; glorifies the arts and the rages which in another would merely disgust or amuse us; and, in the final scenes of her life, flames into such brilliance that we watch her entranced as she struggles for freedom, and thrilled with triumph as, conquered, she puts her conqueror to scorn and goes to meet her lover in the splendour that crowned and robed her long ago, when her barge burnt on the water like a burnished throne, and she floated to Cydnus on the enamoured stream to take him captive for ever.[7]

Why is it that, although we close the book in a triumph which is more than reconciliation, this is mingled, as we look back on the story, with a sadness so peculiar, almost the sadness of disenchantment? Is it that, when the glow has faded, Cleopatra's ecstasy comes to appear, I would not say factitious, but an effort strained and prodigious as well as glorious, not, like Othello's last speech, the final expression of character, of thoughts and emotions which have dominated a whole life? Perhaps this is so, but there is something more, something that sounds paradoxical: we are saddened by the very fact that the catastrophe saddens us so little; it pains us that we should feel so much triumph and pleasure. In *Romeo and Juliet, Hamlet, Othello*, though in a sense we accept the deaths of hero and heroine, we feel a keen sorrow. We look back, think how noble or beautiful they were, wish that fate had opposed to them a weaker enemy, dream possibly of the life they might then have led. Here we can hardly do this. With all our admiration and sympathy for the lovers we do not wish them to gain the world. It is better for the world's sake, and not less for their own, that they should fail and die. At the very first they came before us, unlike those others, unlike Coriolanus and even Macbeth, in a glory already tarnished, half-ruined by their past. Indeed one source of strange and most unusual effect in their story is that this marvellous passion comes to adepts in the experience and art of passion, who might be expected to have worn its charm away. Its splendour dazzles us; but, when the splendour vanishes, we do not mourn, as we mourn for the love of Romeo or Othello, that a thing so bright and good should die. And the fact that we mourn so little saddens us.

A comparison of Shakespearean tragedies seems to prove that the tragic emotions are stirred in the fullest possible measure only when such beauty or nobility of character is displayed as commands unreserved admiration or love; or when, in default of this, the forces which move the agents, and the conflict which results from these forces, attain a terrifying and overwhelming power. The four most famous tragedies satisfy one or both of these conditions; *Antony and Cleopatra*, though a great tragedy, satisfies neither of them completely. But to say this is not to criticise it. It does not attempt to satisfy these conditions, and then fail in the attempt. It attempts something different, and succeeds as triumphantly as *Othello* itself. In doing so it gives us what no other tragedy can give, and it leaves us, no less than any other, lost in astonishment at the powers which created it.

SOURCE: Extract from *Oxford Lectures on Poetry* (London, 1909) pp. 279–305.

NOTES

1. We are to understand, surely, that Enobarbus dies of 'thought' (melancholy or grief), and has no need to seek a 'swifter mean'. Cf. IV vi 34 ff, with the death-scene and his address there to the moon as the 'sovereign mistress of true melancholy (IV ix). Cf. also III xiii, where, to Cleopatra's question after Actium, 'What shall we do, Enobarbus?' he answers, 'Think, and die.' The character of Enobarbus is practically an invention of Shakespeare's. The death-scene, I may add, is one of the many passages which prove that he often wrote what pleased his imagination but would lose half its effect in the theatre. The darkness and moonlight could not be represented on a public stage in his time.

2. 'Now whilest Antonius was busie in this preparation, Octauia his wife, whom he had left at Rome, would needs take sea to come vnto him. Her brother Octauius Caesar was willing vnto it, not for his respect at all (as most authors do report) as for that he might haue an honest colour to make warre with Antonius if he did misuse her, and not esteeme of her as she ought to be.' – *Life of Antony* (North's translation) sec. 29. The view I take does not, of course, imply that Octavius had no love for his sister.

3. The scene is the first of the third Act. Here Ventidius says:

> Caesar and Antony have never won
> More in their officer than person: Sossius,
> One of my place in Syria, his lieutenant,
> For quick accumulation of renown,
> Which he achieved by the minute, lost his favour.

Plutarch (North, sec. 19) says that 'Sossius, one of Antonius' lieutenants in Syria, did notable good service,' but I cannot find in him the further statement that Sossius lost Antony's favour. I presume it is Shakespeare's invention, but I call attention to it on the bare chance that it may be found elsewhere than in Plutarch, when it would point to Shakespeare's use of a second authority.

4. The point of this remark is unaffected by the fact that the play is not divided into acts and scenes in the folios.

5. Since this lecture was published (*Quarterly Review*, April 1906) two notable editions of *Antony and Cleopatra* have been produced. Nothing recently written on Shakespeare, I venture to say, shows more thorough scholarship or better judgment than Mr Case's edition in the Arden series; and Dr Furness has added to the immense debt which students of Shakespeare owe to him, and (if that is possible) to the admiration and respect with which they regard him, by the appearance of *Antony and Cleopatra* in his New Variorum edition.

On one question about Cleopatra both editors, Mr Case more tentatively and Dr Furness very decidedly, dissent from the interpretation given in the last pages of my lecture. The question is how we are to understand the fact that, although on Antony's death Cleopatra expresses her intention of following him, she does not carry out this intention until she has satisfied herself that Octavius means to carry her to Rome to grace his triumph. Though I do not profess to feel certain that my interpretation is right, it still seems to me a good deal the most probable, and therefore I have not altered what I wrote. But my object here is not to defend my view or to criticise other views, but merely to call attention to the discussion of the subject in Mr Case's Introduction and Dr Furness's Preface.

6. Shakespeare, it seems clear, imagined Cleopatra as a gipsy. And this, I would suggest, may be the explanation of a word which has caused much difficulty. Antony, when 'all is lost', exclaims (IV x 38):

> O this false soul of Egypt! this grave charm, –
> Whose eye beck'd forth my wars, and call'd them home,

Whose bosom was my crownet, my chief end, –
Like a right gipsy, hath, at fast and loose,
Beguil'd me to the very heart of loss.

Pope changed 'grave' in the first line into 'gay'. Other conjecture 'great' and 'grand'. Steevens says that 'grave' means 'deadly', and that the word 'is often used by Chapman' thus; and one of his two quotations supports his statement; but certainly in Shakespeare the word does not elsewhere bear this sense. It could mean 'majestic', as Johnson takes it here. But why should it not have its usual meaning? Cleopatra, we know, was a being of 'infinite variety', and her eyes may sometimes have had, like those of some gipsies, a mysterious gravity or solemnity which could exert a spell more potent than her gaiety. Their colour, presumably, was what is called 'black'; but surely they were not, like those of Tennyson's Cleopatra, '*bold* black eyes'. Readers interested in seeing what criticism is capable of may like to know that it has been proposed to read, for the first line of the quotation above, 'O this false fowl of Egypt! haggard charmer.' (Though I have not cancelled this note I have modified some phrases in it, as I have not much confidence in my suggestion, and am inclined to think that Steevens was right.)

7. Of the 'good' heroines, Imogen is the one who has most of this spirit of fire and air; and this (in union, of course, with other qualities) is perhaps the ultimate reason why for so many readers she is, what Mr Swinburne calls her, 'the woman above all Shakespeare's women'.

Harley Granville-Barker The Play's Construction (1930)

We should never, probably, think of Shakespeare as sitting down to construct a play as an architect must design a house, in the three dimensions of its building. His theatre did not call for this, as the more rigorous economics of modern staging may be said to do. He was liker to a musician, master of an instrument, who takes a theme and, by generally recognised rules, improvises on it; or even to an orator, so accomplished that he can carry a complex subject through a two-hour speech, split it up, run it by divers channels, digress, but never for too long, and at last bring the streams abreast again to blend them in his peroration. Clarity of statements, a sense of proportion, of the value of contrast, justness of emphasis – in these lie the technique involved; and these, it will be found, are the dominant qualities of Shakespeare's stagecraft – of the craft merely, be it understood.

He is apt to lay the main lines of his story very firmly and simply, and to let us see where we are going from the start, to cut the complexities from borrowed plots, and if any side-issue later promises distraction, to make (literally) short work of it. Here he reduces the actual story to simplicity itself. Antony breaks from Cleopatra to patch up an insincere peace with Ceasar, since Pompey threatens them both; he marries Octavia, and deserts her to return to Cleopatra; war breaks out, Caesar defeats them and they kill themselves. That is the plot; and every character is concerned with it and hardly a line is spoken that does not relate to it. There is no under-plot, nor any such obvious relief as Falstaff, Nym, Bardolph, Pistol and Fluellen give to the heroics of the Henriad.

But, for a broad picturesque contrast, Roman and Egyptian are set against each other; and this opposition braces the whole body of the play, even as conflict between character and character will sustain each scene. He asserts this contrast at once; for we assemble expectant in a theatre, therefore first impressions cut deep and a first stretch of action will be of prime importance. We have the two indignant, hard-bitten Roman campaigners, who must stand aside while the procession passes – '*Cleopatra, her ladies, the train, with Eunuchs fanning her*' – and see Antony in the toils. Their bitter comments follow it. Next, we have a taste of the chattering, shiftless, sensual, credulous Court, with its trulls and wizards and effeminates.[1] Then we see Antony, with Rome, the 'garboils' of his wife's making and the threats of Pompey calling him, breaking his toils for a time; and the statement of the theme is complete.

Do events now proceed (we ask Dr Johnson) 'without any art of connection or care of disposition'? We are shown Caesar, the passionate Antony's passionless rival, correct and charmless, in conference with Lepidus – that third and very feeble pillar of the world! – upon their poor prospects, while Antony's 'lascivious wassails' hold him in Egypt. The action then swings back to a Cleopatra sighing after an Antony, who is already travelling Romeward; then to Pompey, questionably confident in his rising star.

> If the great gods be just, they shall assist
> The deeds of justest men.

Much virtue – and some risk – in such an if! And we pass at once to the knitting up of the alliance that is to eclipse him.

Caesar and Antony (when he is in his senses) are realists both, and there is neat wary work all round before their bargain is made, with the marriage to Octavia for a seal to it. A long passage, comparatively; but how artfully it is proportioned and modulated! First comes the straight dispute between the rivals. This must, of course, be given full importance, for here is the play's main clash. But it is salted by the ironies of Enobarbus, lightened by Lepidus and his fussiness, eased by Maecenas and Agricola and their tact. Now, the dispute over and the alliance made, the worth of it will be shown us. The great men depart to the sound of trumpets; the three pillars of the world, mutual in its support again. And while Antony does his brisk wooing Enobarbus talks to the gloating Agrippa, and the somewhat shocked Maecenas – of Cleopatra! Note that the famous panegyric comes from a coarse-mouthed cynic; he, too, can feel her witchery.

Maecenas. Now Antony must leave her utterly.
Enobarbus. Never! He will not.
Age cannot wither her, nor custom stale
Her infinite variety. Other women cloy
The appetites they feed: but she makes hungry
Where most she satisfies; for vilest things
Become themselves in her, that the holy priests
Bless her when she is riggish.

With this in our ears, '*Enter Antony, Caesar, Octavia between them*', and we hear Octavia, with her gentle gravity, saying

Before the gods my knee shall bow my prayers
To them for you.

So Shakespeare weaves his pattern – to find yet another simile – as he goes along, setting colour against colour, coarse thread by fine. And certainly the thing is done with such seeming ease and natural subtlety that we hardly note the artistry involved. We should feel the flat poverty of its absence soon enough.

Now another thread is woven in. The soothsayer, very symbol of the East, comes shadowing Antony, weakening and poisoning his will.[2] Then follows (contrast again) a touch of Roman energy; Ventidius is despatched to Parthia. Then we are flung back to Egypt and to Cleopatra; and in redoubled contrast – for Shakespeare has now begun to bite upon the ironies of his theme – to a Cleopatra most unlike the golden vision of Cydnus, a spitting fury that hales the messenger of Antony's faithlessness up and down by the hair of his head.

> Age cannot wither her, [truly!] nor custom stale
> Her infinite variety.

We return to Caesar and his policies, to the successful manoeuvring of Pompey to a peace, thanks to Antony and his prestige. What the worth of this also will be we learn as before when the great men have done and their followers talk things over (harsh truths are heard in anterooms). Or we might judge it for ourselves by its crowning in a drinking bout. The wretched Lepidus cannot last this out; and that first bitter outbreak at the sight of the 'strumpet fool' has its derisive echo in Enobarbus', 'There's a strong fellow, Menas . . . a' bears the third part of the world, man: seest not?' And the chivalrous Pompey, we find, would be glad to have his guests' throats cut – by someone less chivalrous than he! Caesar alone keeps his head; but we hardly like him the better for that. Then, sharp upon the crapulous business, Shakespeare shows us '*Ventidius, as it were in triumph, the dead body of Pacorus borne before him*'. He has beaten back the Parthians. But now he dare not, for his own safety's sake, do Rome better service still, with such masters – hers and his – jealously watching him.

> Oh Silius, Silius,
> I have done enough; a lower place, note well,
> May make too great an act: for learn this, Silius;
> Better to leave undone, than by our deed
> Acquire too high a fame when him we serve's away.

Here is so notable and typical a piece of stagecraft that it is worth while to try and see the full effect of it. There is, of course, the subtler aspect, which the reader easily discovers: the contrasting of the soldiers at their duty with the rulers at their drinking bout.[3] But we must keep Shakespeare's stage well in mind if we are to realise the dramatic value to the spectator of the quick shift from singing and dancing and the confusion of tipsy embracings to the strict military march that brings Ventidius '*as in triumph*' upon the stage. There was no pause at all; Enobarbus and Menas would hardly have vanished, their drunken halloos would still be echoing when Ventidius and his procession appeared. This set the contrast at its sharpest; yet, since change of scene did not mean change of scenery, there was no distracting of mind or eye, a unity of effect was kept, and the action flowed on unchecked.

With one more interweaving of the pattern we shall be halfway through the play. Enobarbus' and Agrippa's mockeries give an acrid after-taste to feast, treaty, and marriage, all three; and we are to guess that poor Lepidus – so spendthrift of good nature! – will be made bankrupt soon. Antony and Octavia take their loving farewell of Caesar and lovingly depart. An instant after we see Cleopatra, recovered from her fury, having Octavia's attractions picked to pieces for her comfort by the much repentant messenger.

> Dull of tongue and dwarfish! . . .
> Widow! Charmian, hark! . . .
> Why, methinks by him
> This creature's no such thing. . . .
> The man hath seen some majesty, and should know. . . .
> All may be well enough.

And, watching her smile, we need have little doubt but that it will be. Very little; for as she leaves the stage (yet again only upon an Elizabethan stage will the effect fully count), '*Enter Antony and Octavia*', with the rift that is to part them already showing.

Thus (if Johnson still needs answering, we can turn his own words against him now) curiosity has been kept busy and the passions interested, and the continual hurry of the action, the variety of incidents and the quick succession of one personage to another have called the mind forward without intermission . . . which is what Shakespeare has set out to do. He has told his story, woven his pattern, kept conflict alive and balance true, character prompting action, and action elucidating character, neither made to halt for the other. This really is the be-all and end-all of his stagecraft – and might well be said to be of any stagecraft; it is only the application of the method that will differ from stage to stage.

We may note in passing how he turns one small technical difficulty that he stumbles on to his profit (he has always had the faculty of doing this), and thereafter how he cuts his way out of another. Throughout this first part of the play he has more Roman than Egyptian material to deal with. Somehow he must keep the balance true and Cleopatra pretty constantly in our minds; but all the story asks is that she should be left by Antony and then sit waiting, patiently or impatiently, for his return. A more mechanically minded playwright would have begun, then, with Caesar and Pompey, and so have accounted for some of the overplus at once; would have made, consequently, a mild beginning, and given a minor interest precedence. With Shakespeare what most matters will have pride of place, nor will he, when he has it, abate a chance; and, as we see, he lets the impulse of his opening carry him to the point of Antony's departure, over a stretch of three hundred and sixty-five lines, abundant in life and colour (it is actually a tenth of the entire play), till he has his story's master motive made fertile in our minds. But now he must eke out the rest of the Egyptian material very carefully. The glimpse of Cleopatra pursuing her Antony before he is well away from her with 'twenty several messengers' could (if the need were rather for compression) be dispensed with; but it is true and significant Cleopatra, so this may fill up a space. What next? When the news of her lover's treachery has been brought her the material will have run out; so this episode is split up and spread over two scenes. And at once Shakespeare sees and seizes the chance to show us, first the savage and suffering Cleopatra; next, on the rebound, the colder, baser-natured woman, feeding on deceit. The story is moulded to the development of character. Each scene of Cleopatra's, throughout this first part of the play, adds a specific something to our knowledge of her that will inform the tragedy of her end.

But now, though the two themes are abreast (Antony's concord with Caesar seen on the wane, while Cleopatra, spider-like, sits spinning a new web for him), it is clear, both that the Roman political material still out-measures the Egyptian and that it may lengthen this part of the play into dangerous monotony. The Antony–Octavia theme might be elaborated for a variation. Shakespeare decides against this; it would still leave Cleopatra in the air. There is no more for her to do, that's evident, till Antony returns to her. Roman politics, then, must suffer compression. The wars upon Pompey and his murder, Caesar's new quarrel with Antony, the extinction of Lepidus, are reported in a scene or so.

But neither are we shown Antony's return to Cleopatra; Caesar recounts it to Octavia and his friends. There were other reasons against this. Shakespeare is not, as we have argued, writing a mere love-story, he is transplanting history to the stage; the causes and circumstances of the quarrel and the war that is to end at Actium are, at this juncture, the more important matter to him, and they must be given the widest significance words can give them, a wider if vaguer significance than concrete action will give. He could have shown us effectively enough how

> In Alexandria . . .
> I' the market-place, on a Tribunal silvered
> Cleopatra and himself [Antony] in chairs of gold
> Were publicly enthroned . . .

But in Caesar's

> No, my most wronged sister, Cleopatra
> Hath nodded him to her. He hath given his Empire
> Up to a whore; who now are levying
> The kings o' the earth for war. He hath assembled
> Bocchus, the king of Libya; Archelaus,
> Of Cappadocia; Philadelphos, King
> Of Paphlagonia; the Thracian king, Adallas;
> King Manchus of Arabia; King of Pont;
> Herod of Jewry; Mithridates, King
> Of Comagene; Polemon and Amyntas,
> The Kings of Mede and Lycaonia,
> With a more larger list of sceptres.

a threat to the whole Roman world seems sounded.

Besides, the play's crisis is to come. These scenes are preparation for it, no more; they must be kept tense, but low in tone. The rivals are still only strengthening themselves for the struggle, with indignation as with arms.

Incidentally, Shakespeare will be glad to avoid a scene of reconciliation if it is to involve his boy-actress in any sort of 'amorous transports'. The play is dominated by sexual passion, no bones are made about the carnality of it either; yet how carefully he avoids writing any scene which a boy could not act without unpleasantness or in fear of ridicule! The fatal reunion is far more significantly marked by her spitfire quarrel with Enobarbus.

> *Cleopatra.* I will be even with thee, doubt it not . . .
> Thou hast forspoke my being in these wars,
> And sayst it is not fit. . . .
> *Enobarbus.* Well, is it, is it? . . .
> Your presence needs must puzzle Antony,
> Take from his heart, take from his brain, from 's time

What should not then be spared. He is already
Traduced for levity, and 'tis said in Rome,
That Photinus an Eunuch, and your maids
Manage this war.

For from this springs disaster; this is the beginning of the end.

Yet we are but half-way through the play; and here is another sign that a larger theme than the love story is being worked out. Would Shakespeare otherwise be giving, against all precedent, half his play's length to its catastrophe? Now, it is the craft and art of this long ending that have been most distorted by editors, its intention most grievously misunderstood by critics. A producer must not only start afresh from the untouched text, he must read it in the light of a clear understanding of the stage of its origin.[4]

THE QUESTION OF ACT DIVISION

To begin with he must free the play from act and scene divisions. The Folio gives none. The first five-act division was Rowe's. Johnson thought the first scene of his second act might better be the last scene of his first, but added 'it is of small importance, where these unconnected and desultory scenes are interrupted'. Pope made the first scene of Rowe's fifth act into the last scene of Act IV, and after this all the later editors seem to have fallen unquestioningly into line. A five-act division for any play has, of course, its sanctions. The editors of the Folio indulge in it when they think they will. They (they or their printer for them) start out each time with an *Actus Primus, Scaena Prima*; a schoolboy's heading for his copybook. Sometimes they keep this up, once or twice they get half-way through the play and give it up; sometimes, as with *Antony and Cleopatra*, they just leave it at that. Now, whatever other dramatists may have done, whatever Shakespeare may have done in other plays, whatever may have been the custom of the public and private theatres for which he wrote – and it was probably a differing and a changing one – in the matter of making pauses during a performance, and whether those pauses were formal or prolonged, in this play there is no *dramatically* indicated act-division at all. There is, that is to say (as far as I can discover), no juncture where the play's acting will be made more effective by a pause. On the contrary, each scene has an effective relation to the next, which a pause between them will weaken or destroy. There may have been four pauses in the original performing, or three, two, or one; there may have been none at all, though that is hardly likely. But it would always (again, as far as I can discern) be a question of custom or convenience, not of dramatic effect.

Granted five acts, a case can be made for Rowe's choice of them, or Johnson's, or Pope's, or for half a dozen others, doubtless; and as good a one perhaps for a four-act division or a three. And if, pleading weakness of the flesh in actors or audience, a producer thinks it well to split the play into two, he can call a convenient halt, he'll find, at the turn of the action when Antony's drift back to Cleopatra is plainly to be seen. He may pause with some effect after that 'All may be well enough', or pass on a little further before he pauses and begins again (perhaps with better) with the news that 'Caesar and Lepidus have made wars on Pompey', or with Caesar's own outburst of indignation and the return of Octavia; or, more forcibly still, with the squabble between Cleopatra and Enobarbus and the launching of the war. But let him plead convenience merely; for any halt hereabouts must mean rather the loss of an effect than the making one. And this will be as true of any other pauses in any other places; and the lengthier they are the worse it will be.

For the fact is that Shakespeare's work never parcels up very well. He was not among those writers who industriously gather material, sort and arrange and re-arrange it before they fit it together. When his mood is operative he creates out of an abundance of vitality, and it is no good service to him to start obstructing the flow of it. He keeps, for all his fervour, a keen sense of form; it is largely in this marriage of impulse and control that his genius as pure playwright lies. When inspiration flags, he must come to contriving. He is business-like at that, quite callously business-like sometimes. But even to the most work-a-day stuff he gives a certain force. And should carelessness – for he can be wickedly careless – land him in a tight place, there is, to the practised observer, a sort of sporting interest in seeing him so nimbly and recklessly get out of it.

He does not (*pace* Dr Johnson) write haphazard; it is not that. He plans – and more spaciously than those that have need to plan. He is seldom to be found following a formula, even a proved one of his own. Incidental devices he'll use again and again, as we all repeat words and phrases – and the deeper (one notices) the feelings beneath them the simpler these are apt to be. He is the last man we should look to find submitting himself to an arbitrary scheme, whatever its sanction, a five-act scheme or any other. Custom might even be imposing this on a play's performance and impose it no further on him. And by now he has brought much to the theatre, broken much new ground, has the medium very plastic in his hands. With such a task as this before him, and his imagination fired, he will be out to do it as effectively as he can. There will be no other question. He will have to muster all his resources, and he will need full freedom for the use of them.

The Three Days' Battle

We are plunged, for a beginning to the business, amid the squabbling distractions of Antony's counsels. Enobarbus, level-headed, caustic of tongue, does what he can to stem the tide of folly. Antony stands, weakly obstinate, under Cleopatra's eye. Against all reason, he will meet the enemy at sea – 'For that he dares us to 't'. The news accumulates of Caesar's swift, unchecked advance. We have the veteran legionary breaking all bounds of discipline in a last desperate protest.

> O noble Emperor, do not fight by sea,
> Trust not to rotten planks. Do you misdoubt
> This sword, and these my wounds . . .?

Then, as they disappear, '*Enter Caesar, with his army, marching*'.

The first day's fighting is compressed into the symbolism (it is little else) of a dozen lines of dialogue and business. This is a sort of variation upon the old dumb-show, to an Elizabethan audience a familiar and pregnant convention. But note the niceties of effect. Caesar enters '*with his army, marching*'; a formal processional entrance, capping the news of his approach that has threaded the preceding scene. In two sentences he shows us his strategy and his quality in command. Next, Antony and Enobarbus appear alone on the emptied stage. Antony speaks four hurried and half-purposed lines, Enobarbus never a word, but his glum looks will be eloquent; and they vanish. Then comes the marching and counter-marching of the armies that are not to fight (pure symbolism!), each with its subordinate general in command. The stage empties again, and its emptiness holds us expectant. Then of a sudden, comes the climax, the significant event; '*the noise of a sea-fight*' is heard.[5] Then, actual drama reasserting itself, Enobarbus, with alarums to reinforce his fury, bursts upon us, tongue-tied no more, to interpret disaster with

> Naught, naught, all naught! I can behold no longer;
> Th' Antoniad, the Egyptian Admiral
> With all their sixty fly, and turn the rudder. . . .

He is reinforced by Scarus, younger and fierier still:[6]

> Gods and goddesses, all the whole synod of them! . . .
> The greater cantle of the world is lost
> With very ignorance; we have kissed away
> Kingdoms and provinces.

This symbolism of war is not in itself dramatic, one sees. Shakespeare could hardly make it so, but he hardly needs it to be. He gives us, however, very little of it. His drama lies in the consequences of the fighting, as these are reflected in the conduct of his characters. We are shown, it is to be remarked, no actual fighting at all, come no nearer to it than the sight of young Scarus and his fresh wounds. He is marked out for us as the gallant warrior, and Antony gives him generous praise. Antony's own valour we may take for granted. But his challenge to Caesar to fight him single-handed is stressed, and as a ridiculous thing. Says Enobarbus:

> Caesar, thou hast subdued
> His judgment too.

This is stressed because in it and all it implies lie his failure and his tragedy.

The sequel to the first battle is shown us at length. Scarus' boyish wrath spends itself; Enobarbus, shame rankling deeper in him, relapses to his gibing; Canidius cooly plans to make his peace with Caesar, and departs, no man hindering him; Antony appears. The gradation from the convention of the battle to the actuality of the scene to come between the broken Antony and Cleopatra, all repentance, is nicely adjusted. First we have had the angry agony of defeat, which needs human expression; next, the few lines Canidius speaks give us an abstract of many happenings; then Antony, in the exhaustion of despair, sums up against himself and tells to the end the chapter of disaster. Here is Plutarch's

> and so Antonius . . . went and sat down alone in the prowe of his ship, and said never a word, clapping his head between both his hands . . . and so

lived three days alone without speaking to any man. But when he arrived at the head of Taenarus there Cleopatra's women first brought Antonius and Cleopatra to speak together, and afterwards to sup and lie together. . . . Now for himself he determined to crosse over into Africk and toke one of his carects or hulks loden with gold and silver and other rich cariage, and gave it unto his friends, commanding them to depart, and to seeke to save themselves. They answered him weeping, that they would nether doe it nor yet forsake him. Then Antonius very curteously and lovingly did comfort them. . . .

And it is interesting to see how Shakespeare, contracting the circumstances, can yet keep the sense and temper of the events, can even, by the tune and rhythm of a dozen lines of verse, and by a suggestive phrase or so, give us the slack sense of days of breathing-space following on the blow.

The encounter with Cleopatra brings us back to matter more his own, and of more immediacy, closer therefore in tension. It is to be the first of three in which Antony will face perforce the truth of what is between them, mounting the scale of suffering to madness at the last. This one, then, must be in a low key (Shakespeare even skirts the edge of the comic at its start, with the leading of Cleopatra, spectacularly pitiful, up to the weeping hero), and it holds no contest; he is but too ready with his

> Fall not a tear, I say; one of them rates
> All that is won and lost . . .

We pass to Caesar's diplomatic exploiting of his victory, his curt rejection of Antony's overtures, the sending of Thidias to wean Cleopatra from him. Antony rises to nobility again, with his 'Let her know't' for sole comment upon the offer of peace to Cleopatra if she will yield him up. But with his next breath he falls to the fatuity of the challenge to Caesar.

There follows Cleopatra's ignoble reception of Thidias. Enobarbus can have at least one taste of revenge upon her, and Antony is fetched to see her smiling on Caesar's messenger.

> 'Tis better playing with a lion's whelp
> Than with an old one dying.

The savage outburst, which sends the glib fellow back, dumb and bleeding from his stripes, is as futile – and is meant to seem so – as were the heroics of the challenge; so is the moral stripping and lashing of Cleopatra. For, his rage glutted and appeased by the sight of the wretch half-slaughtered at his feet, he can turn back to her, open-eyed to the truth about her, and, listening to the easy lies, can end them with an easier – and such a hopeless 'I am satisfied'.

After this we may be sure that he is doomed. Enobarbus is sure of it, and Caesar's comment is contemptuous and brief. Shakespeare adds, for the ending of the day, the strange little hysterical passage in which, by

> . . . one of those odd tricks which sorrow shoots
> Out of the mind,

we find him melting his followers to tears as he pathetically paints the prospect of his defeat and death – to show us yet again, one supposes, how helplessly off the rails the man has run.[7]

Now comes, to mark the passing of the night, the episode of the sentries on their watch. It is, as we have noted, the one piece of scene-painting in the play; a developing of atmosphere, rather – for the single line, 'Heard you of nothing strange about the streets?' is the only hint of locality – of the ominous atmosphere of a night of reprieve between the battles. The means to it are merely a few whispering voices and the '*Music of the hoboyes . . . under the stage*'. It is after the couples have met, gossipped a moment and parted with 'good-night', that they hear this:

> *4th Soldier.* Peace! what noise?
> *1st Soldier.* List, list!
> *2nd Soldier.* Hark!
> *1st Soldier.* Music i' the air!
> *3rd Soldier.* Under the earth.
> *4th Soldier.* It signs well, does it not?
> *3rd Soldier.* No.
> *1st Soldier.* Peace, I say.
> What should this mean?
> *2nd Soldier.* 'Tis the god Hercules, whom Antony loved,
> Now leaves him.

They feel their way towards each other and whisper confusedly in the darkness, their nerves a little ragged.

> *2nd Soldier.* How now, masters!
> *All together.* How now? how now? do you hear this?
> *1st Soldier.* Ay: is't not strange?

3rd Soldier. Do you hear, masters? do you hear?
1st Soldier. Follow the noise so far as we have quarter.
Let's see how it will give off.
All. Content! 'Tis strange.

And, holding all together as the music dies into distance, they vanish. The entire effect, simple in itself, is made with masterly economy. The scene has two uses: it preserves the continuity of the action, and is gloom before the bright beginning of the second day.

Antony has not slept. He comes jovial and confident from night-long revelry, calling for his squire. Cleopatra, seeming a lissom girl again, beneath the spell of this still magnificent spendthrift of fortune, plays at buckling on his armour; and with shouts and the flourish of trumpets and the clangour of the gathering of armed men Shakespeare rings up the dawn. Trumpets sound again; it is as if they set out to sure victory. Two notes of doubt are struck: by a shrewder Cleopatra with her

That he and Caesar might
Determine this great war in single fight!
Then, Antony – ! But now – ?

– before she retires to her chamber to recover what she may of her lost night's rest; and by the news, greeting Antony as he marches forth, that Enobarbus – Enobarbus! – has deserted. He puts the treason behind him with a gentle magnanimity which comes strangely – does it? – from a man who could have his enemy's ambassador half flayed alive. But this is Antony.

Next we see Caesar, an over-confident Caesar, by no means the cautious general of the earlier battle. And between the brilliant opening and the brilliant end of Antony's day we have, for contrast, Enobarbus repentant. There is, of course, no strict measuring out of time; and we return to some degree of symbolism when, after alarum, drums and trumpets, Agrippa enters with

Retire, we have engaged ourselves too far:
Caesar himself has work, and our oppression
Exceeds what we expected.[8]

He and his staff pass, unflurried, across the stage. Antony and Scarus pursue them, the youthful elation of Scarus a foil to Antony's self-possession. He is the potent general still, one might believe – set him free from Cleopatra! Drums and alarums subsiding in the distance give us the battle's ending. The emptied stage here is the equivalent of a line of asterisks on a printed page. Then with '*Enter Antony again in a march*' comes the brilliant consummation of this last day of good fortune that he is to see. It ends as it began, with trumpets sounding; and it has shown us Antony at his best, generous, gallant, a born leader of men.

Caesar's sentries on their watch mark the second night's passing; and our sight of Enobarbus, sick of his ague, broken in spirit, crawling out into the misty moonlight to die, gives it a dreary colouring. The dawn breaks dully.

Drums afar off.

Hark, the drums
Demurely wake the sleepers....

The armies parade again. First Antony leads his across. He is smiling grimly, yet there is a desperate edge to his

I would they'd fight i' the fire, or i' the air,
We'd fight there too...

Then we see Caesar, sober caution itself this time. He passes, heading his men, and the stage stays empty a moment.

Antony and Scarus appear alone. No tokens of fighting so far, and Antony is in suspense. With

Yet they are not joined: where yond pine does stand
I shall discover all: I'll bring thee word
Straight, how 'tis like to go.

he vanishes, leaving Scarus to turn suspense to misgiving with

Swallows have built
In Cleopatra's sails their nests: the augurers
Say they know not, they cannot tell; look grimly,
And dare not speak their knowledge. Antony
Is valiant and dejected, and by starts
His fretted fortunes give him hope and fear
Of what he has and has not.

Through this comes sounding an '*Alarum afar off, as at a sea-fight*' – to our remembrance, a most ominous sound. And hard upon it, transformed, wrought to a grand climacteric of fury, Antony reappears.

All is lost!
This foul Egyptian hath betrayed me:
My fleet hath yielded to the foe; and yonder
They cast their caps up and carouse together
Like friends long lost. Triple-turned whore! 'tis thou
Hast sold me to this novice; and my heart
Makes only wars on thee.[9]

From now till he is carried exhausted and dying to the Monument Antony's passion dominates the action. Eros, Mardian, the Guard, Dercetas, Diomedes are caught distractedly in the wind of it; we see nothing of Caesar; panic quickly obliterates Cleopatra. It is a long passage and highly charged; but Shakespeare can find all the change and variety he needs in its own turbulent ebb and flow. Nor, when the medium is rhetoric raised to such a pitch and given such colouring, could any competition be admitted; the audience must be caught and rapt in the mood. The shock of the first outburst should capture us. Then, the brilliant Scarus, Enobarbus' successor, Antony's new right hand, having been sent packing like a lackey (and as ready to go: or do we wrong him?) we are held by the simple magnificence of

Oh, sun, thy uprise shall I see no more:
Fortune and Antony part here; even here
Do we shake hands. All come to this? The hearts
That spanieled me at heels, to whom I gave
Their wishes, do discandy, melt their sweets
On blossoming Caesar; and this pine is barked
That over-topped them all.

His fury soon begins to work again; it is like yeast in him; and when he turns, expectant of Eros coming to his call, to find Cleopatra herself, he chokes for a moment, long enough for her smooth incongruity, 'Why is my lord enraged against his love?' to give a fresh twist to his torture. In this babyish line, and in her flabbergasted, tongue-tied, sudden, very un-queen-like bolting, in his frenzied pursuit of her, Shakespeare again skirts the ridiculous; and closely enough this time to provoke in us a sort of half-hysteria which will attune us to his next shift of key – into the delirium which brings Antony, exhausted, to a pause. We must picture the actor, transfigured to the terms of

The shirt of Nessus is upon me: teach me,
Alcides, thou mine ancestor, thy rage:
Let me lodge Lichas on the horns o' th' moon . . .

and storming from the stage. While we still hear him we see Cleopatra with her scared women and her sapless eunuch scurrying across like rabbits. And as they vanish he follows, vertiginous, insensate! It is a wild, roundabout chase, hazardously raised to poetic power.

If we were not first thrown off our emotional balance we might find the fantasy that follows – for all its beauty – too much an intellectual conceit, and too long-drawn-out.

Antony. Eros, thou yet behold'st me?
Eros. Ay, noble lord.
Antony. Sometime we see a cloud that's dragonish,
A vapour sometime, like a bear or lion,
A tower'd citadel, a pendant rock,
A forked mountain, or blue promontory
With trees upon't, that nod unto the world
And mock our eyes with air: thou hast seen such signs;
They are black vesper's pageants.
Eros. Ay, my lord.
Antony. That which is now a horse, even with a thought
The rack dislimns and makes it indistinct,
As water is in water.
Eros. It does, my lord.
Antony. My good knave Eros, now thy captain is
Even such a body. . . .

But now we should feel with Antony the relief this strange sense of dissolution brings from the antics of passion, and how, as he does, one would prolong the respite, playing with these fancies that the half-freed spirit conceives!

From this he sinks to quiet grief. The sight of the 'saucy eunuch' on tiptoe with his glib tale, sets fury glowing for a moment again. Then comes the news, worded as piteously as ever Cleopatra, safe now in her Monument, could desire – the news that she is dead. He greets them as Antony must.[10] The fact that they are false is of a piece with the other futilities of these three days that have gone to his undoing. Yet another is to follow when he stands waiting for the merciful sword-stroke which Eros turns on himself; yet another when he bungles his own, and has to lie there, begging the guard to dispatch him – and off they go and let him lie![11]

With his carrying to the Monument this long phase of particularly 'unlocalised' action, germane to the three days of fighting, ends. We have been ideal spectators, we know what happened, and why; and just such an impression has been made on us as the reality would leave behind. It is a great technical achievement, and one of great artistry too.

Cleopatra against Caesar

Antony dead, the domination of the play passes at once to Cleopatra. She asserts it in the lament over him; a contrast to his stoic greeting of the news of her death. And from now to the end, the action (but for one short scene) is definitely localised in the Monument. As fitting, this, to the intensity and cunning of Cleopatra's battle with Caesar as diversity was to the chances and changes of the other; and by contrast made more telling.

But Antony's death leaves Shakespeare to face one obvious problem: how to prevent Cleopatra's coming as an anti-climax. Though Plutarch is still lavish of material, it will need some choosing and moulding.

Caesar is surprised by the news – here is one risk of slackening tension avoided – and shocked into more feeling than we expect of him. Then at once the last round of the play's contest is opened, and we see what the struggle is to be. A humble anonymous messenger comes from Cleopatra, his message as humble. Caesar sends him back with fair words; and promptly thereafter –

> Come hither, Proculeius; go and say
> We purpose her no shame: give her what comforts
> The quality of her passion shall require,
> Lest in her greatness by some mortal stroke
> She do defeat us; for her life in Rome
> Would be eternal in our triumph. . . .

It is to be Caesar's wits against Cleopatra's pride and despair. He fought Antony to the death; it may take more generalship to save Cleopatra alive. Proculeius, we notice, is sent; the one man about Caesar, said Antony, that Cleopatra was to trust. Is it in some distrust of him that Caesar sends Gallus too; and, on second thoughts, Dolabella to watch them both, lest Cleopatra wheedle her way round them? It turns out to be Dolabella that needs watching. But here, unfortunately, the text, as we have it, plays us false. There has been cutting and botching, and the niceties of the business we can now only guess at. The main trend of it is clear, though. In their

Roman fashion, Gallus and Proculeius add force to diplomacy and manage to capture Cleopatra in her Monument. Proculeius finds a few moments with this tiger in a trap quite enough for him, and gladly gives place to Dolabella.

The passage that follows is a notable one. He fancies himself, does Dolabella; he is a ladies' man, and quite the gaoler, surely, for this most wonderful of wantons. 'Most noble Empress, you have heard of me?' is his ingratiating beginning. From a Roman there is flattery in the very title; it owns her Antony's widow and ignores Octavia. She is far from responsive. She sulks and snarls, gives him half a glance, and forthwith breaks into invidious praise of her dead hero. But she knows she can twist the conceited fellow round her finger. She has only to turn to him with a smile, with an 'I thank you, sir' and a 'Nay, pray you, sir', and he promptly betrays his master to her, blurts out that, for all these comforting messages, Caesar does mean to lead her chained in his Triumph. At which point Caesar himself appears.

He comes in full state and circumstance, his staff surrounding him, guards clearing the way. And if Cleopatra thinks to impress him in turn, his opening sally might well damp her somewhat. For he faces this marvel among women as she stands there with her mere maids beside her, and coolly asks which of them is the Queen of Egypt. Which? And once it was

Remember
If e'er thou look'st on majesty.

The duel of lies that follows – a pretty piece of fighting! – epitomises this second and subtler struggle. We have Egyptian against Roman now, neither with much simplicity left to shed; but Cleopatra, passionate and unstable, shows a very child beside Caesar. She kneels, and he raises her. He repeats his smooth promise, and she smiles her gratitude, alive to the worth of them – had she ever doubted it! – thanks to coxcomb Dolabella. (But, surely, for a man so indifferent to her, he is a little anxious to be gone. Had she any hope of winning him? It is second nature to her to be wily with men – and to lie.) Seleucus and the false inventory of 'money, plate and jewels' make illuminating matter of dispute. These barbarians can be bribed, surely, and tricked as easily. Caesar is not to be tricked – nor shocked by the attempt on him. And as for her raging and her nobly pathetic attitudes, he counters them, her lies and her flatteries too, with the same cold smile. She is beaten. She cannot even terrify Seleucus now; it is he, contemptuously considerate, who orders the man off. She is helpless in his clutches, but for the one sure escape. And he thinks, does he, to lure her from that with his lies? She fawns on him as he leaves her; let him think he has!

> He words me, girls, he words me;
> That I should not be noble to myself...

If any doubt were left, any chance of yet another noble conquest, Dolabella – the paltry proof that she still can conquer – comes back to disperse it.

> *Dolabella.* Madam, as thereto sworn by your command,
> Which my love makes religion to obey,
> I tell you this: Caesar through Syria
> Intends his journey, and within three days
> You and your children will he send before:
> Make your best use of this: I have performed
> Your pleasure and my promise.
> *Cleopatra.* Dolabella,
> I shall remain your debtor.[12]

She again makes his name sound beautiful in his ears (it is a name that can be lingered on), perhaps gives him her hand to kiss (he does not pay Thidias' price for the honour) and he goes. Her way is clear now to death.

But she has still to be lifted to that nobility, with which the sight of the dead Antony inspired her.

> ...and then, what's brave, what's noble,
> Let's do it after the high Roman fashion,
> And make death proud to take us...

She climbs there by no straight path. The longing to die never leaves her; but we all long to die at times, and there is much protesting, a stealthy look or so for chances of escape, some backsliding into the old twisted passions; and she must at last lash herself – with, for company, poor frail Iras – through agony and beyond it before she can repose upon

> My resolution's placed, and I have nothing
> Of woman in me: now from head to foot
> I am marble-constant....

Then, for one more mitigation before the play's last tragic height is reached, Shakespeare gives us the countryman and his figs. By now (here is the art of it) Cleopatra is past bitterness or fear, and can smile and take the simple pleasure in his simplicity that we do. She jokes with him. This must have been, if one comes to think of it, not the least of her charms. When she would royally 'Hop forty paces through the public street' how the people – the common people, so despised by Caesar and the politicians – how evidently they would adore her! It is very right that one of them should bring her the comfort of death in a basket slung on his arm, and that she should trust him, and joke with him, a great lady at her ease.

From this she turns to a queenliness unapproached before.

> Give me my robe, put on my crown; I have
> Immortal longings in me . . .

Long ago, we learn, a dead king's servants would be slaughtered around him. This is a still more royal death; for Iras' heart breaks silently at the sight of it, and Charmian only lags behind to set a crooked crown straight once again, and to send triumphant mockery echoing to Caesar's ears.

He accepts his defeat like a gentleman, let us own. The ceremony of his coming matches the ceremony of her dying; and the end of the play, we should note, is sensibly delayed while they stand gazing – tough soldiers that they are – at a queen so strangely throned:

> . . . she looks like sleep,
> As she would catch another Antony
> In her strong toil of grace.

SOURCE: Extract from *Prefaces to Shakespeare*, 2: *Antony and Cleopatra* (London, ed. 1970) pp. 87–119.

NOTES

1. There was possibly more matter in the scene at one time. Lamprius, Rannius and Lucillius, whose entrance survives, will hardly have been brought on, this first and last time, for nothing. Was there chaffing between Romans and Egyptians? Nothing is left of it, if so, but Enobarbus' 'Mine, and most of our fortunes to-night shall be drunk to bed.' Or did Shakespeare, having written the stage directions, discover he could make enough effect without them?

2. The Romans had their soothsayers too; but this one, by costume and

association, would recall us to Cleopatra's court. What modern playwright would so opulently employ him – bring him from Egypt too, even by Plutarch's permission – to such seemingly small purpose? Here we see the extravagant ease of Elizabethan stagecraft. But the episode yields the exact effect needed, not an iota more.

3. Easily discovered by reading the folio. But Rowe made an act-division between the scenes, and later editors have copied him (of which more on pp. 93–5), so that even this much of the effect may pass unnoticed.

4. The Folio text itself may have been edited, I know; but not to the measure of another stage than Shakespeare's.

5. I cannot pretend to say how the 'noise of a sea-fight' was made. Professor Stuart-Jones (who speaks with authority upon one aspect of the matter) suggests that what one heard was the breaking of the sweeps of the galleys. But is that – would it have been to Shakespeare's audience – a recognisable sound? I fancy that a hurly-burly flavoured with Avasts, Belays and other such sea-phrases from the landsman's vocabulary would be a likelier refuge in a difficulty for the prompter and his staff. But there may have been some recognised symbolism of a sea-fight.

6. There is no authority (that I know of) for Scarus' age. But the dramatic value of the contrast between his keen youth and Antony's waning powers is indubitable.

7. Shakespeare elaborates this from a couple of sentences in Plutarch; and the suggestion (from Enobarbus) that Antony almost deliberately 'makes a scene', is all his own.

8. The Folio's stage-direction brings Agrippa on alone, but this, his speech pretty clearly shows, must be an error. He may have Dolabella or Maecenas with him. It will hardly, however, be a symbolic army in retreat. All the disorder of battle Shakespeare is giving us by sound, its thrills through individuals; and his massed entries are processional. The stage-directions hereabouts are all rather cursory.

9. The Folio gives the stage-direction '*Alarum farre off, as at a sea fight*' in the interval between Caesar's exit with his army and Antony's entrance with Scarus. This is almost certainly wrong. Antony would not enter upon an alarum with a 'Yet they are not joined'. But it does not as certainly follow that the editors (from 1778 onwards, according to Furness) are right in transferring it to the instant before his re-entrance with 'All is lost'. They may be. But it is an 'alarum afar off', and might come more effectively before, or even during, Scarus' speech. The point is not a very important one. It is hard to tell what sheer dramatic value there was for the Elizabethans in these symbolic alarums and the like, and what variety of effect could be given them. Some without doubt; they speak a language, if a simple one. The effect of that first *noise of a sea-fight* which precipitated Enobarbus' outburst of 'Naught, naught, all naught' is evidently not precisely the same – nor meant to be – as this *alarum afar off* which brings Antony on to the greater crisis of 'All is lost'. We may note that, besides the 'symbolism' Shakespeare gives about a dozen illustrative lines of dialogue to each of the first two battles, to the third about twenty.

10. If we remember his 'On:/Things that are past are done with me'.

11. Eros is despatched from the stage for a moment or so by an apparently motiveless 'From me awhile'. The practical need is probably to dispose of Antony's armour; for soon there will be both Antony and the body of Eros himself to be carried off by *'four or five of the guard'*, Diomedes and (more doubtfully) Dercetas. But Shakespeare, by merely leaving it unexplained, lets it seem part of the general slack confusion.

12. He made no promise. Here is an interesting instance either of the way in which Shakespeare intensifies an effect by an over-statement, which he knows will pass muster, or of a subtlety in character-drawing by which Dolabella, in thrall to Cleopatra, feels he did promise. The critic may take his choice.

John Middleton Murry *Antony and Cleopatra* (1936)

We all remember – nobody ever forgets; for, although the words may elude his recollection, the impression, the quality, the music: these remain – Cleopatra's description of the dead Antony:

> His legs bestrid the ocean: his rear'd arm
> Crested the world: his voice was propertied
> As all the tunèd spheres, and that to friends;
> But when he meant to quail and shake the orb,
> He was as rattling thunder. For his bounty,
> There was no winter in't; an autumn 'twas
> That grew the more by reaping: his delights
> Were dolphin-like; they showed his back above
> The element they lived in: in his livery
> Walk'd crowns and crownets; realms and islands were
> As plates dropped from his pocket. (v.ii. 82–92)

Having thus marvellouly pictured her dead lord, Cleopatra drops her voice. For a moment she wakes wistfully out of her dream. She has spoken as one inspired, like a Sybil or a Pythonissa: so that Dolabella, to whom she speaks, can cry only, in dumb astonishment: 'Cleopatra!' Now she comes down to earth: her closed and dreaming eyes are opened; and she asks Dolabella, in a voice of apprehension, Was it only a dream?

> Think you there was, or might be, such a man
> As this I dreamed of? (v.ii. 93–4)

For a moment, she is all a woman, all a girl, all a child, even. In a little while, she will proclaim and prove that there is no more woman in her.

> I have nothing
> Of woman in me: now from head to foot
> I am marble-constant; now the fleeting moon
> No planet is of mine. (V.ii. 238–41)

But for this instant, she is a child lost in a dark forest, wavering and timorous: caught between her vision of a world made magnificent by Antony, and her knowledge of a world made dead by his death. She is wistful and afraid. She wakes out of her trance, and reaches for a hand.

> Think you there was, or might be such a man
> As this I dreamed of?

And Dolabella speaks to her condition. He reaches out the hand she gropes for: tenderly, like a true man. 'Gentle madam – no!' The word, so softly spoken, is only the harsher for its tenderness. Cleopatra starts back, thrusts him away, cries shrilly, like one caught in the toils of reality. 'You lie – up to the hearing of the gods!' The sudden frenzy dies. She sinks back into her dream – the dream that is not a dream. She speaks to herself again. Dolabella is, as he was before, only an eavesdropper, while she murmurs:

> But if there be, nor ever were one such,
> It's past the size of dreaming: nature wants stuff
> To vie strange forms with fancy; yet to imagine
> An Antony, were nature's piece 'gainst fancy,
> Condemning shadows quite. (V.ii. 95–100)

This dream was real. This man she had loved and known, played false and adored. To him she had been 'a right gipsy'; and his very voice, propertied like all the tuned spheres, had said to her: 'Where's now my serpent of old Nile?'

To her dream that was no dream, to her Antony who was, and is, her 'man of men', she henceforward turns. She thrusts away reality; but first she looks upon it for what it is, and what it will be. She will be the brooch to the purple cloak of Caesar's triumph.

> Nay, 'tis most certain, Iras: saucy lictors
> Will catch at us like strumpets; and scald rhymers
> Ballad us out o' tune: the quick comedians

Extemporally will stage us, and present
Our Alexandrian revels; Antony
Shall be brought drunken forth, and I shall see
Some squeaking Cleopatra boy my greatness
I' the posture of a whore. (V.ii. 214–21)

And that, let us remember, was what was actually happening when those lines were first spoken. The reality, which Cleopatra thrusts away, thus becomes doubly real. It is not some imagined or apprehended degradation which she can avoid: it has already overtaken her.

This is, of course, a dramatic device of Shakespeare, which he had employed already in *Julius Caesar* (III.i. 111–17), but there more clumsily. Now Shakespeare is a master indeed. This sudden, deliberate shattering of the dramatic illusion by Cleopatra's words, comes out of the very substance of the character. That is to say, this dramatic device of Shakespeare's is really an anti-dramatic device; perhaps it would be more exact to say a super-dramatic device. And the word 'device', moreover, begs an important question. 'Device' suggests a very deliberate and conscious technical cunning, which indeed Shakespeare possessed in plenty; but I should say that Shakespeare's method here is quite intuitive.

He challenges the dramatic illusion, because he can, and because he must. First, because he can: he has created the imaginative reality of his Antony and his Cleopatra. For us, they *are*. Second, because he must. In the confidence, in the ecstasy, in the 'intensity' of his own creativeness, he must seize the opportunity that has offered itself naturally of directly confronting the order of reality which he has created with the order of actuality which is.

This triumph of art seems to me so wonderful that I must, at the risk of displaying my own clumsiness, enlarge upon it. Let the magnificent and memorable scene between Cleopatra and Dolabella, with which we began, be our starting point. I have tried to indicate the contrast between the ecstasy of Cleopatra's imaginative dream, and the tenderness of Dolabella's human sympathy, which yet springs from and is rooted in the world of actuality. I am sure that I have not read into Shakespeare's text more than is there. Dolabella stands by the Queen – gentle with a man's gentleness, wondering, anxious, eager to comfort and reassure. But she, in her ecstasy, is beyond his ken. He admits it in so many words. He, too, has loved Antony; he grieves for him and he grieves for her. But the region where her mind and heart are wandering is strange to him. At the nature of her grief he must conjecture; yet the vibration of it strikes him to the heart.

> Hear me, good madam.
> Your loss is as yourself, great; and you bear it
> As answering to the weight: would I might never
> O'ertake pursued success,but I do feel
> By the rebound of yours a grief that smites
> My very heart at root. (v.ii. 100–5)

It is the incommensurability of Cleopatra's loss, the incommensurability of her suffering, which Dolabella thus registers. It is, in respect of the world which he inhabits and represents – the real world – superhuman. Shakespeare finds a word for it – a word indeed which, taken from its context in this great play, is nothing: but, in this context, is truly a symbol of the magnificence he communicates to us. It is the word 'royal'. In *Antony and Cleopatra* the word 'royal' is royal because it is made royal. Therefore it crowns the close – twice in a dozen lines.

> Now boast thee, death, in thy possession lies
> A lass unparallel'd. Downy windows, close;
> And golden Phoebus never be beheld
> Of eyes again so royal. (v.ii. 317–21)

What lines are these! If poetry ever *played* with the universe, it is here. From the bottom to the top of the gamut, Shakespeare moves infallible. 'A *lass* unparallel'd.' Who dare risk it? Who but the man to whom these things were no risk at all? Every other great poet the world has known, I dare swear, would have written, would have been compelled to write: 'A queen unparallel'd.' But Shakespeare's daimon compels him otherwise: compels him not indeed consciously to remember, but instinctively to body forth in utterance, the Cleopatra who dreams, and is a girl: the Cleopatra who is superhuman and human: the Cleopatra who has already answered to the challenge of this same word – 'royal'.

> *Iras.* Royal Egypt!
> Empress! . . .
> *Cleopatra.* No more, but e'en a woman, and commanded
> By such poor passion as the maid that milks
> And does the meanest chares. (IV.xv. 70 ff)

Yet the same Cleopatra who proclaims:

> My resolution's placed, and I have nothing
> Of woman in me: now from head to foot
> I am marble-constant; now the fleeting moon
> No planet is of mine. (V.ii. 238–41)

And all this, which is Cleopatra, is (as I say) not remembered, but bodied forth anew in Charmian's words: 'A lass unparallel'd.' There is the harmony between 'Royal Egypt!' – and 'the maid that milks'. These two are blent in one in the phrase.

Then the music rises again. Somehow, by the words 'golden Phoebus' Cleopatra herself is suffused with a sunset glow, and her dignity in death is endued with the majesty of the heavens. The order of the words is magical. It gives point and meaning to Coleridge's definition of poetry as 'The best words in the best order'.

> Downy windows, close!
> And golden Phoebus never be beheld
> Of eyes again so royal.

This order is such that every significance is gathered up into the one word, 'royal'. Now we know what 'royalty' means – it means all that has gone before – all that was gathered up, before, into the 'lass unparallel'd', – all this, moreover, bathed in the majesty of 'bright Phoebus in his strength'. For we shall not have forgotten Perdita's

> Pale primroses,
> That die unmarried ere they can behold
> Bright Phoebus in his strength – a malady
> Most incident to maids. (*Winter's Tale*, IV.iv. 122–5)

Cleopatra had not died unmarried – far from it. She had beheld 'bright Phoebus in his strength', with the eyes of a peer – royal eyes. And as the phrase glances forward to the probably yet unwritten *Winter's Tale*, so it glances backward to the scene with which we began.

> *Cleopatra*. I dreamed there was an Emperor Antony:
> O, such another sleep, that I might see
> But such another man.
> *Dolabella*. If it might please ye, –
> *Cleopatra*. His face was as the heavens; and therein stuck
> A sun and moon, which kept their course, and lighted
> The little O, the earth. (V.ii. 76–81)

Poetry is not a matter of crude equivalents and equations; and I am not suggesting that the sun and moon, which were the eyes of the Antony of Cleopatra's vision, *were* also Antony and Cleopatra. But a flicker of that suggestion is there: enough to bring new depth, and add a new glancing reflection to the final 'royalty'. Cleopatra is moon to Antony's sun, while they are alive together. When the sun is set, then Cleopatra leaves the moon –

> the fleeting moon
> No planet is of mine –

to take upon her the strength and majesty of the sun. And so what we have called her final royalty is totally suffused by the glory of 'golden Phoebus'.

That is, I know, to make a mechanism of the natural alchemy of the supreme poetic imagination. But rather than it should go unregarded, I have risked the sacrilege of a momentary anatomy. It is performed only in order that it may be forgotten; only in order that we may be aware of the several glories that have blended their rays into the splendour of this sunset glow. There she lies, 'the lass unparallel'd' who has beheld bright Phoebus in his strength, nay, who was married to him. The downy windows close, as the sun sinks below the horizon. She is bathed in glory, she radiates the glory, she is the glory – and this is 'royal'.

We cannot escape the word; it is the music of that magic, the great phrase pealed from the golden trumpets, when the sun sets over the waste of waters – the phrase that can never be uttered, otherwise than as it is uttered here, by the plenary instrument of poetry – the phrase after which William Blake was groping when he cried: '"What," it will be questioned, "When the sun rises, do you not see a round disk of fire somewhat like a Guinea?" O no, no, I see an Innumerable company of the Heavenly host, crying, "Holy, Holy, Holy is the Lord God Almighty."' And that is also 'royal'. But the miracle of Shakespeare is that the unutterable glory is uttered, not symbolised. It is, so to speak, incarnate. It is not we who must stretch and rack our imaginations to conceive what 'royal' may mean. We know the meaning, before we know the word; the various, rich and infinite significance is first given to us, then at last the word which captures and crowns it. Crowns it indeed, but not with a circle of gold that descends, but with a halo of glory which arises – this is, and this it is to be, 'royal'.

Nor can we escape it, or its meaning. The golden trumpets sound once more. The guards rush in upon the sleeping queen, 'the lass unparallel'd'.

> *First Guard.* What work is here! Charmian, is this well done?
> *Charmian.* It is well done, and fitting for a princess
> Descended of so many royal kings. (V.ii. 328–30)

The touch itself comes almost bodily from North's Plutarch, where Shakespeare read and marked:

> But when they had opened the doors, they found Cleopatra stark dead, laid upon a bed of gold, attired and arrayed in her royal robes, and one of her two women which was called Iras, dead at her feet: and her other woman called Charmian half dead and trembling, trimming the diadem which Cleopatra wore upon her head. One of the soldiers seeing her, angrily said unto her: Is that well done Charmian? Very well said she again, and meet for a princess descended of so many noble kings.

All that Shakespeare has changed in the final phrase itself is the word 'noble' to the word 'royal'. There was no need. 'Descended of so many noble kings' is, in itself, as fine a verse as 'Descended of so many royal kings'; but not here, not now, when we know what 'royal' means. By that simple change the phrase is surcharged with the great music that still rings in our spiritual ear, and its very substance is transmuted.

Into this word 'royal', as we have tried to show, Shakespeare crams the sense of the superhuman, standing over against the human, which Dolabella recognises and salutes in his scene with Cleopatra: what I have called the incommensurability of her experience and his. In that scene the contrast takes the form of dream against actuality, trance against waking, inspiration (almost in the literal sense) against reason. It is the contrast, the contraposition of two orders. They are not set in conflict. Dolabella is gentle towards the Queen's ecstasy; it strikes him with awe and wonder and also with sympathy. With Dolabella and Cleopatra at this moment we may compare Enobarbus and Antony in an earlier scene (IV ii), when Antony, before his last fight, commands one final feast. When the serving-men come in to set the banquet, he takes them by the hand, one by one.

> Give me thy hand,
> Thou hast been rightly honest; – so hast thou –
> Thou – and thou – and thou: – you have served me well
> And kings have been your fellows. (IV.ii. 10–13)

There is the double touch, which makes Antony Antony – the simple humanity of his handshake with his servants and the reminder that kings have done him the like office. In comparison with Antony, and in his own accustomed sight, servants and kings are one. If kings were his servants, so his servants are now made kings. It is, if I may dare to put it thus, the Last Supper of Antony – sacramental, simple and strange. But Cleopatra does not understand it. 'What means this?' she whispers to Enobarbus; and Enobarbus replies:

> 'Tis one of those odd tricks which sorrow shoots
> Out of the mind. (IV.ii. 14–15)

Enobarbus half understands. So might an unknown – or may be a known – disciple have said that the Last Supper itself was 'one of those odd tricks which sorrow shoots out of the mind'. An 'odd trick': the words come from Enobarbus' desire to master by bluntness the emotion within himself. Enobarbus does not understand – Antony himself does not understand – but he feels the meaning of the gesture.

Then Antony returns to the theme again.

> Well, my good fellows, wait on me to-night:
> Scant not my cups; and make as much of me
> As when mine empire was your fellow too,
> And suffered my command. (IV.ii. 20–3)

It is the same thought as before. They serve him now, where kings served him before; and by the change it is not Antony that is declined, but they who are advanced. They are become kings: fellows of empire. A pathetic illusion, some may call it. But it is something rather different from this. Royalty – it is the great burden of this play – is no external thing; it is a kingdom and conquest of the human spirit, an achieved greatness. It is like that which

> becomes
> The throned monarch better than his crown;
> His sceptre shows the force of temporal power,
> The attribute to awe and majesty,

> Wherein doth sit the dread and fear of kings;
> But mercy is above this sceptred sway;
> It is enthroned in the hearts of kings,
> It is an attribute to God himself;
> And earthly power doth then show likest God's
> When mercy seasons justice.
>
> (*Merchant of Venice*, IV.i. 188–97)

Shakespeare wrote that some ten years before he wrote *Antony and Cleopatra*; and mercy is not in question now. But the spiritual essence of royalty is. And Shakespeare, who has written the tragedies, knows more about it. It is still something which lifts man towards the divine, by driving man to be more than man. And this royal essence is a grace of communion between men. By their recognition of, and devotion to, this essence, they also become royal. Thus Antony, at this moment, when there are no more throned monarchs to serve him, invites his servants into royalty. By serving him now, they become kings of the spirit.

Something of all this is in this tiny and wonderful scene between Antony and his servants. It is not the pathos of it, but the royalty of it that strikes Enobarbus to the heart. But Cleopatra, at this moment, does not understand. 'What does he mean?' she whispers to Enobarbus again. And he replies gruffly: 'To make his followers weep.' That is, of course, not what he means at all, as Enobarbus well knows. He knows what Antony means, but he cannot say. We know what Antony means, but we cannot say. As well ask what Jesus of Nazareth *meant* by his gesture in the upper-room, at the brink of death. So Antony goes on:

> Tend me to-night;
> May be it is the period of your duty;
> Haply you shall not see me more; or if,
> A mangled shadow: perchance to-morrow
> You'll serve another master. I look on you
> As one that takes his leave. Mine honest friends,
> I turn you not away; but like a master
> Married to your good service, stay till death.
>
> (IV.ii. 24–31)

The glance at the great marriage-service – 'to have and to hold from this day forward, for better for worse, for richer for poorer, in sickness and in health, to love, cherish, and obey, till death us do part' – is neither accidental nor calculated: it is just natural – the spontaneous expression of the sacramental essence of the scene. Antony is 'inspired'.

In this scene it is Cleopatra herself who does not understand. She plays the part towards Antony which bewildered Dolabella will play towards her afterwards, when she, remembering Antony, is likewise 'inspired'. She has yet, crowned queen though she is, to achieve her 'royalty'; and she will achieve it by her resolution to follow her 'man of men' to death.

Let us see now whether we can enter a little more deeply into the secret of this 'royal' essence. There is a moment when Cleopatra, confronted with this 'royal' essence in the Antony she loves, does not understand it: it is, in the simple and literal sense, beyond her. It is not beyond Enobarbus. To Enobarbus, therefore, we must go. A little time before the scene between Antony and the servants, when Antony has been beaten in the sea-fight to which he was persuaded against his better judgment, and in a fit of passion has challenged Caesar to single combat, Enobarbus is torn within himself. He knows, now – none better – that the itch of Antony's affection has nicked his captainship, and that final defeat is certain. What is the use of loyalty, he asks himself?

> Mine honesty and I begin to square.
> The loyalty well held to fools does make
> Our faith mere folly. (III.xiii. 41–3)

To that it seems there is no answer. Reason declares that it is unanswerable. But Enobarbus has an answer.

> Yet he that can endure
> To follow with allegiance a fall'n lord
> Does conquer him that did his master conquer,
> And earns a place i' the story. (III.xiii. 43–6)

There, in imperishable phrase, is the proclamation of the two orders. Spiritual victory can be wrung out of bodily defeat. 'He that can endure . . .' Again we are reminded of the New Testament: 'He that can endure to the end.' Loyalty is an essence of itself, that somewhere, somehow, can be triumphant over earthly vicissitude; and exists, not merely unscathed by temporal defeat, but because of it. Yet the question is: to whom shall such loyalty be given? What is the secret point of change, where on the one side faith becomes folly, and on the other folly becomes faith? And to that no answer in words can be given. Here the servant must trust himself, or rather the God within him. Is the man he serves worthy of this final allegiance? That only the heart, not the mind, of the servant can declare. And that inward struggle, between the mind and the heart, we see resolved in Enobarbus. Led by his mind, he does forsake Antony; and the mind of the world applauds him, making question only of why he waited so long.

And what is Antony's reaction? Not, as the mind would expect, one of fury.

> Go, Eros, send his treasure after; do it.
> Detain no jot, I charge thee: write to him –
> I will subscribe – gentle adieus and greetings;
> Say that I wish he never find more cause
> To change a master. O, my fortunes have
> Corrupted honest men! (IV. v. 12–17)

The speech is of the heart, and of that heart which Enobarbus' own heart knew. In response to it, there is an upsurge in Enobarbus' heart. 'Throw my heart', he cries to the darkness,

> Against the flint and hardness of my fault;
> Which, being dried with grief, will break to powder,
> And finish all foul thoughts. O Antony,
> Nobler than my revolt is infamous,
> Forgive me in thine own particular;
> But let the world rank me in register
> A master-leaver and a fugitive. (IV.ix. 14–22)

Is it not, imagination asks, the story of Judas, told as it might have been told had a Shakespeare been there to tell it? Enobarbus lives in our memory not as 'the master-leaver and the fugitive' of which he claimed the reputation for his punishment, but as the thing his heart bade him be – one that could endure to follow with allegiance a fall'n lord. His loyalty is final and secure: he earned his place i' the story.

What is it that compels this final loyalty? The heart in him responsive to the heart in Antony, the thing which made him weep while Antony bade farewell to his servants. But what was that? That royalty in Antony which made his servants kings: that power which was in Antony to say to them simply: 'I am I', and trust to their love of that; the manhood in him which disdained a compelled allegiance, and when allegiance was withdrawn from him, sought instantly, by a natural motion, to find the cause within himself. This is the point at which the superhuman becomes human. The royalty that draws loyalty to it, that compels loyalty indeed, but by an internal, not an external compulsion, whereby the servant is at once the lover and the friend, and knows that he becomes his own true self only in serving his lord – this royalty is, in the lord himself, superhuman. It cannot be acquired by taking thought: it *is*. It expects allegiance, as the earth expects rain. This is the simple mystery that one star differs from another in glory; but in the company where this difference of glory is acknowledged, all are stars. And this is human: and this also is to worship God where he is manifest, as William Blake declared:

> Go, tell them that the Worship of God is honouring his gifts
> In other men and loving the greatest men best, each according
> To his Genius which is the Holy Ghost in Man; there is no other
> God than that God who is the intellectual fountain of Humanity.

Royalty and loyalty, then, go hand in hand; and the man who is loyal by his loyalty, becomes royal.

That, if I were required to state it in so many words, is the true theme of Shakespeare's *Antony and Cleopatra*. And Shakespeare's prodigious art consists first and foremost in convincing us of Antony's royalty. In the last resort, as I have already hinted, and as I shall seek to show further, the great motion of the drama derives from that. That is the *primum mobile*. And it operates in the very first scene. There the conflict and the contrast are posited, between the judgment of the mind and the impulse of the heart, between Reason and Energy (as Blake distinguished them). Reason first:

> *Philo*. Nay, but this dotage of our general's
> O'erflows the measure: those his goodly eyes,
> That o'er the files and musters of the war
> Have glowed like plated Mars, now bend, now turn,
> The office and devotion of their view
> Upon a tawny front: his captain's heart,
> Which in the scuffles of great fights hath burst
> The buckles on his breast, reneges all temper,
> And is become the bellows and the fan
> To cool a gipsy's lust. (I.i. 1–10)

That charge Shakespeare must overcome. We must be convinced, straightway, that this is false, or rather that its truth is of another and a lower order than that to which Antony belongs. And Shakespeare does it. We see Antony ignoring the messengers from Rome: he daffs the world aside:

> Let Rome in Tiber melt, and the wide arch
> Of the ranged empire fall! Here is my space.
> Kingdoms are clay: our dungy earth alike
> Feeds beast as man: the nobleness of life
> Is to do thus: when such a mutual pair
> And such a twain can do't, in which I bind,
> On pain of punishment, the world to weet
> We stand up peerless. (I.i. 33–9)

'The nobleness of life is to do thus.' There is the challenge. And the magic of the poetry is that the challenge is won. The potency of language which can cram imperial Rome, its arenas and its aqueducts, its roads and its provinces, into a single phrase and topple it over – 'let the wide arch of the ranged empire fall!' – has won the challenge in a dozen words. For the power of the poet becomes the power of Antony. It is he, not the poetic genius of Shakespeare, that can build up Rome and lay it in ruins in a moment of the imagination, which is 'spiritual sensation'.

If you look for a description of what has happened in this initial triumph of Energy over Reason, we shall find no better one than the paragraph of Blake's *Marriage of Heaven and Hell*, where he says:

> The giants who formed this world into its sensual existence and now seem to live in it in chains, are in truth the causes of its life and the sources of all activity; but the chains are the cunning of weak and tame minds which have power to resist energy; according to the proverb, the weak in courage is strong in cunning.
>
> Thus one portion of being is the Prolific, the other the Devouring: to the Devourer it seems as if the Producer was in his chains; but it is not so, he only takes portions of existence and fancies that the whole.

In this sense Antony is a Giant, a Prolific: he operates by what Shakespeare elsewhere calls 'sovereignty of nature'. And we are convinced of this, primarily, by the power of utterance which Shakespeare lends him; next, by the power of utterance which Shakespeare lends to those who describe him; then, by the actions which he does; then, by the effect of those actions upon others. And let us remember that, in this kind, we cannot distinguish between act and utterance. What Antony says to his servants, what he bids Eros write to Enobarbus, – the words are his gesture; just as, in the main, their words are the gesture by which they in turn respond to his.

What I am driving at is the power of poetry, as it was used by Shakespeare in this play. It overrides drama; it overrides psychology. The ultimate and enduring structure of the play is in the poetry. Its life, its inward progression, derive from the response of poetry to poetry. That overpowering dynamic, that impression of cumulative growth, of which, from another angle, we have discerned the law as the creation of royalty by loyalty, can be simply reduced to the response of poetry to poetry. Not that we should gain much by so reducing it; but it would at least serve to remind us that we cannot judge such a play as this as a record of action merely; if we do, its essence escapes our judgment. And by essence here, I do not mean something vague, such as we might call the 'soul of the play'; but its vital inward unity. Thus, Antony must be set before our imaginations as one to whom the final sacrifice of Enobarbus and Eros is a natural duty paid, which he receives 'by sovereignty of nature'; he has to be felt by us as belonging to an order of beings who can declare 'he that loseth his life for my sake, the same shall save it'. It is true that he becomes what he is in our imaginations partly by reason of those sacrifices. When they have happened, we recognise that he is such a man that he can call them forth. But no less, he must already be such that we feel no misgiving, no tremor of a doubt lest their sacrifice should be wasted on an unworthy object: and this, in spite of all we know and see of the havoc his will is working on his reason. To this end two things are necessary. One is that the passion to which he yields should seem to us overwhelming and elemental, a force of nature and a power of destiny. The other is that we should be convinced of his essential nobility. And of these two the second is more important than the first: for once the latter is established, we are bound to take the former for granted, by that logic of humanity which tells us that if a noble nature acts in a way which is contrary to our reason, it is our reason which is at fault.

This is, as we have said, the secret of Shakespeare's method in the great plays. He builds the character of royal nature. We say to ourselves: 'the man *is* noble!' If then he does monstrous things, as Macbeth and Othello do, we can but ascribe it to his falling into the clutches of some superhuman power. And so it is in *Antony and Cleopatra*. Cleopatra, judged by herself alone, as she is presented to us in the earlier acts of the play, is not of power to make Antony 'the ruin of her magic'; though Cleopatra, as she is described, might be. It is her effect upon the Antony we know that convinces us of her witchcraft: she is, so to speak, only a partial embodiment of the power which has overwhelmed him. And it has often been remarked that the Cleopatra of the last act is a far greater figure than the Cleopatra who has been shown to us before. That immediate impression is true enough; but it is due to the fact that up to the death of Antony it is from him that the life of the play has been derived. She is what she is to the imagination, rather in virtue of the effect we see in Antony, than by virtue of herself. He is magnificent: therefore she must be. But when he dies, her poetic function is to maintain and prolong, to reflect and reverberate, that achieved royalty of Antony's.

We have tried to indicate how subtly, yet how simply Shakespeare suggests the gulf between them, as Antony's life draws to an end. When he is inspired to his royal gesture to his servants, Cleopatra is uncomprehending, where Enobarbus comprehends. The supreme relation of royalty and loyalty has not been established in her. Antony upbraids her:

> I made these wars for Egypt; and the queen,
> Whose heart I thought I had, for she had mine;
> Which whilst it was mine had annex'd unto't
> A million more, now lost, – she, Eros, has
> Pack'd cards with Caesar and false-play'd my glory
> Unto an enemy's triumph. (IV.xiv. 15–20)

Whether she played him, indeed, as false as this, we cannot tell: but she played with him. She plays, desperately, with him now, when she bids Mardian tell him the false news of her death, to turn aside his anger at her cowardice, or her treachery. She is, as yet, neither royal nor loyal.

But, with his death, straightway her nature and her utterance change. She lifts her voice in an imperishable lament:

The crown o' the earth doth melt. My lord!
O, wither'd is the garland of the war,
The soldier's pole is fall'n: young boys and girls
Are level now with men: the odds is gone
And there is nothing left remarkable
Beneath the visiting moon. (IV.xv. 63–7)

And that, in the order of poetry and the imagination, is our instant security that Antony, being dead, yet liveth. When he breathed out his soul, it found an abiding place in Cleopatra's body. There it must needs struggle, but it will prevail. She, as it were, picks up the note. Antony's last words had been: 'A Roman by a Roman valiantly vanquished.' Cleopatra echoes them:

Good sirs, take heart:
We'll bury him; and then what's brave, what's noble,
Let's do it after the high Roman fashion
And make death proud to take us. (IV.xv. 85–9)

Roman, here, is the same as royal. Cleopatra wavers in her resolution, and steels herself to it by the thought of the indignities that await her in Rome. But more, though less consciously, by the thought that death is as a sleep, in a kindly bosom. Death is 'the beggar's nurse and Caesar's'; at whose breast the tired child 'sleeps and never palates more the dug'. And again she prolongs the note:

Where art thou, death?
Come hither, come! come, come and take a queen,
Worth many babes and beggars. (V.ii. 46–8)

And this note, as of a musing dream, is sustained: so that it seems to us as though Cleopatra henceforward moves in a trance, governed by some secret music of the kind that marked the passing of God from Antony. As in a dream she speaks to Dolabella the wonderful words with which we began. They are visionary words. Some would call them rhetorical; but to me the epithet seems quite meaningless. They are, of course, full of hyperbole: but hyperbole is an empty grammatical label. The point, and the only relevant point about them, is that they do body forth, against a mighty background, the nature and the meaning of Antony. He is manifested as the force of nature we knew him to be; and it is done with the magnificent ease of nature – that implicit power of the greatest poetry which Keats, who had the like gift, once bodied forth in a like fashion as 'Might, half-sleeping [*sic*] on its own right arm'. Poetry of this kind, I grow more convinced as I grow older, is the very consummation of human utterance; it is the creative power of life made audible and visible: and one is certain, I know not how, that such poetry can only come, as Keats said it must come, 'naturally, as the leaves to a tree'. Think only of the four lines:

> For his bounty
> There was no winter in't: an autumn 'twas
> That grew the more by reaping: his delights
> Were dolphin-like; they showed his back above
> The element they lived in. (V.ii. 86–90)

In those lines, simply and strangely, Antony is made incorporate with Nature, with the riches of harvest, and the golden splendour of a stubble-field; but no less than with this quiet opulence, incorporate also with the gleam and flash and strong impetuosity of the dolphin. And all this we feel to be true. This is Antony. It is as though his essence had been made plain, his secret revealed to Cleopatra in her vision. And this again is true to the deeps of human experience: we do know those we have loved better after their death than we knew them while they lived; and sometimes the deepening of knowledge is so profound that we could almost say that, in comparison with the knowledge we now possess, our former knowledge was ignorance. The difference between us and Shakespeare is that Shakespeare can express the kind of knowledge which remains unutterable and unuttered in the hearts of us ordinary folk.

Now in very deed, Cleopatra loves Antony: now she discerns his royalty, and loyalty surges up in her to meet it. Now we feel that her wrangling with Caesar and her Treasurer which follows is all external to her – as it were a part which she is still condemned to play 'in this vile world': a mere interruption, an alien interlude, while the travail of fusion between the order of imagination and love, and the order of existence and act is being accomplished: till the flame of perfect purpose breaks forth:

> Now Charmian!
> Show me, my women, like a queen: go fetch
> My best attires: I am again for Cydnus,
> To meet Mark Antony. (V.ii. 226–9)

No, not *again* for Cydnus: but now for the first time, indeed. For that old Cydnus, where the wonder pageant was, was but a symbol and prefiguration of this. That was an event in time; this is an event in eternity. And those royal robes were then only lovely garments of the body, now they are the integument of a soul. They must show her like a queen, now, because she *is* a queen, as she never was before.

It is at this moment, of suspense, while the queenly soul in travail of its own royalty awaits the flash of incandescence, that Shakespeare makes the extreme challenge to reality.

> The quick comedians
> Extemporally will stage us, and present
> Our Alexandrian revels; Antony
> Shall be brought drunken forth, and I shall see
> Some squeaking Cleopatra boy my greatness
> I' the posture of a whore. (V.ii. 214–21)

I am not maintaining that this supreme stroke of art was conscious or deliberate: indeed, I do not believe that art of this order ever can be conscious or deliberate. It just happens, and 'inspiration' is as good a name for what happens as any other I know: for at least it excludes the fatal suggestion that the calculating mentality devises and determines such master-strokes as this. It is the nature and quality of its effect which is our concern.

From the beginning of the play we have been gradually raised, by means such as I have tried to describe, to a height far above that of ordinary dramatic illusion: we have been lifted from the human to the superhuman. We have watched Antony ennoble the sacrifice of his friends, and be the more ennobled by that sacrifice; and we have watched him die royally. Then we have watched the mysterious transfusion of his royal spirit into the mind and heart of his fickle queen. And all this we have watched, not merely with the bodily, but with the spiritual, eye; we have heard it, not merely with the bodily, but with the spiritual, ear. The prime instrument of this sustained and deepening enchantment has been a peculiar quality of poetry, of such a kind that it is the reverberation of the noble deeds which our bodily eyes have seen enacted; and more than the reverberation of them. This quality of poetry conditions those acts; gives them a quality of significance, over and above and distinguishable from the declared intention of the acts: so that the quality of 'inspiration', which our dividing minds would attribute to the poetry alone, envelops and suffuses the acts which it accompanies. The poetic utterance passes, without jolt or jar, into the dramatic deed, as though utterance and act were but a single kind of expression.

Indeed, one might say that the inward life and creative process of such a drama as this is the gradual invasion and pervasion of the characters by the poetry of their own utterance. Their acts gradually, and reluctantly, move into harmony with their utterance; and, as the acts slowly change their nature, so the quality of the utterance becomes more rich and rare. To this process of attunement of deed to poetry, there is, it seems, but one inevitable end. The total suffusion of the character by poetry is death. The nature of this law is spiritual; it derives from the strange logic of the imagination, which finds response in the hearts of all men when it takes the form: 'Greater love hath no man than this, that he lay down his life for his friend.' That means, that the total self-sacrifice of one human being for another in death, is the only true symbol we have and can recognise for Love. Hence, the inextinguishable significance of the Crucifixion. Without this symbol, Love would remain unuttered and unutterable: in this symbol, which is a simple human act, directly comprehensible by all men, Time is suffused and made incandescent by Eternity.

Of the same kind is the spiritual law of Shakespeare's drama here. The total self-surrender of chosen or self-inflicted death is the only symbol of the complete suffusion of the character by poetry. Whether or not Shakespeare consciously conceived it thus, is no matter. It may well be that, as a fact of the history of his poetic creation, the deaths were foreordained. They came first, in Shakespeare's mind, no doubt. His task was to load the particular act of death with all the significance it could contain; and poetry is the means by which he does it. This is Shakespeare's supreme dramatic 'device': he entangles his characters in the compulsive magic of poetic utterance, and submits them to that alchemy. They change:

they needs must change. The process of change in Cleopatra we have tried a little to follow and to understand. It is at the very instant when she is in travail of her final transfiguration that the impulse comes to Shakespeare to shatter the dramatic illusion – to compel us to see, if we can, in the great queen in travail of her own royalty a squeaking boy Cleopatra in the posture of a whore.

We cannot see it; we should not, even if we were watching now the actual play. But when those words were first spoken at the Globe, the audience, if they had been able to use their bodily eyes alone, would have seen just that. Did they, could they? I do not know. But if they did, as I can imagine that they did, I cannot doubt that there were some among them, who dumbly understood, as I do, why Shakespeare made the fear of the very catastrophe he compelled them to behold the final motive in the great queen's mind: why he made that the spark to set her soul ablaze with perfect purpose:

I am again for Cydnus
To meet Mark Antony.

That sudden break: that sudden flash is the inrush of the eternal moment.

The great drama was to be played, not again, not once more, but for the first time – 'all breathing human passion far above' – in the fields of Eternity, where there is no more Time.

SOURCE: Extract from *Shakespeare* (London, 1936), pp. 352–79.

Franklin M. Dickey The Elizabethans' *Antony and Cleopatra* (1957)

First of the saints' lives in Chaucer's *Legend of Good Women* is the martyrdom of Cleopatra, who marches naked into a pit of serpents. Without any of Chaucer's irony, modern critics praise *Antony and Cleopatra* as an Eliabethan 'Seintes Legende of Cupyde'. True, many concede that among Shakespeare's themes are the torments of love and the incompatibility of politics with private desire. However, few would agree that Shakespeare takes any moral stand, and many of the most eloquent contend that the play hymns a love beyond good and evil. If the lovers have lost a kingdom, they have gained a more 'ethereal diadem of love'. For life on earth they have traded an eternal passion.[1]

But Chaucer speaks for a very small minority of those who from classical times to the end of the seventeenth century wrote of the lovers. When Dryden revised Shakespeare in 1678 to make him square with neo-classical theory, the story had long been an *exemplum*. 'I doubt not,' he apologises, 'but the same Motive has prevailed with all of us in this attempt; I mean the excellency of the Moral; for the chief persons represented, were famous patterns of unlawful love; and their end accordingly was unfortunate.'

Most critics since Dryden have preferred to dismiss the 'excellency of the Moral'. Almost without exception they agree that Shakespeare's tragedy is expressed by Dryden's sub-title – 'The World Well Lost'. Because the tradition which makes Antony and Cleopatra 'famous patterns of unlawful love' and modern criticism are so much at odds, it is worth our time to look again at the early literary portraits of the lovers for what Shakespeare's audience might have expected when they attended the first performance.

Needless to say Shakespeare was under no compulsion to give them what they expected. Romantic critics argue that he did not; that in fact Shakespeare is unique because he 'dares to defend the illicit passion that set the halves of the world at war and destroyed its possessors'.[2] The critical parties are lined up, and their views are absolute, or nearly so.

1. THE CLASSICAL VIEW OF THE LOVERS

From Antony's political enemy Cicero, through Horace, Virgil, Velleius Paterculus, Lucan, Josephus, Suetonius, Plutarch, Pliny the Elder, Appian, Dion Cassius, and Sidonius – from the lovers' contemporaries, in short, to the fifth century, Antony and Cleopatra appear as most extraordinarily degenerate. Horace may admire Cleopatra's manly suicide, but in life she is a 'mad queen . . . / With her scabb'd Troop of men effeminate' who in turn makes Antony strive 'her with'red Eunuchs to content'.[3]

All reiterate that Cleopatra's love destroyed Antony and led him into monstrous crimes.

Shakespeare's principal source, Sir Thomas North's translation of Amyot's French Plutarch (1579), interprets the *Parallel Lives* as *exempla* written to profit and delight. There is no doubt about the lessons to be learned from the lovers. Although Plutarch praises Antony generously as commander and warrior, he condemns him as cruel and wanton, a man made uxorious first by Fulvia and then by Cleopatra, 'and if any sparke of goodnesse or hope of rising were left him, Cleopatra quenched it straight and made it worse than before'. Finally the 'sweete poyson' of love and the 'unreyned lust of concupiscence' end 'Antonius abominable life'.

Pliny is shocked by Cleopatra's drinking of a valuable pearl while 'Antony looked wistly upon her' and claims that Antony wrote a book '*Of his owne drunkennesse* . . . and thereby approved . . . all those miseries and calamities that hee brought upon the whole world'.[4]

Another of Shakespeare's sources, Appian's *Auncient Historie*, anonymously translated in 1578, and its continuation based on Plutarch embody classical and Elizabethan attitudes toward the lovers. Antony loved 'like a young man, though he were fourty yeeres of age' and 'did all things as Cleopatra would have him, without respecte of God or mannes law' so that his love for her 'was the beginning of his troubles, and the ende of his life'.[5]

From the classics, then, the Elizabethans might have learned how to judge Antony and Cleopatra: whatever virtues the lovers had, they were notorious for the luxury and extravagance which feminised Antony and tied his soldier's heart to the Egyptian queen. It would have taken 'small Latine and lesse Greeke' to find out these facts, for the most important accounts had appeared in English before Shakespeare wrote.

2. THE MEDIEVAL TRADITION

Medieval writers embroidered the legend of Antony and Cleopatra freely. A tradition known to the Renaissance makes Cleopatra author of books on cosmetics and gynaecology. In all the major accounts before Chaucer she is an *exemplum* to warn of the end of those who live for pleasure. Dante places her in the second circle of hell, swirled about with carnal Semiramis, Helen, and Dido, in whose lives 'Reason by lust is swayed'. Boccaccio devotes sections of *De casibus virorum illustrium* and *De claris mulieribus* to Antony, who became Cleopatra's creature and 'let himself be dragged into greatest infamy by unbridled lust'. Cleopatra robs and murders, tries vainly to seduce Octavius, applies the asps to her breasts and dies. Her soft limbs, the pleasure of so many men, were in the end the pleasure of serpents. The *De claris mulieribus* is, possibly, a shade more severe.[6]

In the *Fall of Princes* Lydgate apologises to his master Chaucer, 'cheefe poete of Breteyne', but retains the moral condemnation of Boccaccio. And in his amusing poem 'Beware of Doublenesse' neither eels nor winds are as slippery or inconstant as the minds of women, among them Cleopatra.

Thus the medieval tradition known to the Elizabethans follows the classical, but adds Christian, moralisation. The concept of God's justice makes the punishment fit the crime as in Dante's and in Boccaccio's treatment of carnal sinners. Save for Chaucer's, most of the medieval Cleopatras are very wicked indeed.

3. RECEIVED OPINION: RENAISSANCE *EXEMPLA*

The Elizabethan reader of English, French, or Latin would have found almost unanimous authority from classical times to his own day condemning the lovers for their 'lustis foul & abhominable'. Popular books of moral philosophy and the equally popular commonplace books cite them regularly as examples of extravagant behaviour. Poets from the anonymous author of *The Fable of Ovid treting of Narcissus* (1560)[7] to Spenser take similar views. In book I of the *Faerie Queene* the lovers are Lucifera's captives, exemplifying those who 'Through wastfull Pride, and wanton Riotise' are condemned 'to live in woe, & die in wretchednesse' (I.v. 46). Cleopatra shares her dungeon with licentious Semiramis and the Amazon Sthenoboea – 'Proud wemen, vaine, forgetfull of their yoke' (I.v. 50).

In book V, devoted to the allegory of Justice, Artegal, forced to wear women's clothes and spin, is one with Samson, Hercules, and Antony, heroes who could not be conquered by strong men made effeminate by 'beauties louely baite':

> that doth procure
> Great warriours oft their rigour to represse,
> And mighty hands forget their manlinesse . . .
> And so did warlike *Antony* neglect
> The worlds whole rule for *Cleopatras* sight.
>
> (V.viii. 1–2)

The aspiring reader who turned to Thomas Hoby's translation of Castiglione's *Courtier* (1560) would have found Cleopatra among queens who 'gave themselves to all their appetites' (p. 248). Or if he knew his Montaigne (1603) or his Burton (1621) or any of a long list stretching from the middle of the sixteenth to well into the seventeenth century, he would have recognised the lovers as examples of the destruction caused by profligacy. Nowhere does an author hint that their love enriched and ennobled their lives.[8]

Mature Renaissance tragedy, while often full of references to fortune, dealt with the problem of evil by linking the fate of the mighty to their actions. Those whom the gods would destroy they first made passionate.[9] Building upon Aristotle and Horace, Renaissance literary theory saw tragedy as an imitation of an action that would both teach and delight. The delight comes from the liveliness of the imitation; the teaching from the plot, which shows by example rather than mere precept what happens to those whose passions carry them off. Since Antony and Cleopatra were great and since they were unfortunate because their own passion destroyed them, they were ideal dramatic subjects.

4. SENECAN DRAMATISTS

Some knowledge of how these playwrights dramatised the sadly flawed love of Antony and Cleopatra will help us to understand Shakespeare's lovers, different as they may be. Etienne Jodelle's *Cleopatre Captive* (1552) uneasily combines responsibility for passion with the harsh fate bound up with it. Although both lovers reproach themselves at length for their downfall, the Chorus laments the instability of fortune and the mutability of the earth. Jodelle has spared nothing to make us feel for the lovers, but our understanding of the meanings of the play remains confused. Two commonplaces are certain, in addition to the inexorability of fate – that Cleopatra's love ruined Antony and that there is no happiness except in virtue.

Garnier's *Marc Antoine* (1578), translated by the Countess of Pembroke as *Antonius* (1592), is the first drama of the lovers in English. Superior to Jodelle's play it comes much closer to harmonising personal responsibility and blind fate. Antonius is seen struggling to free himself from the love which is destroying him but cannot live apart from Cleopatra's 'guilefull semblant'. Cleopatra assumes sole blame for the defeat at Actium though Charmian tempts her to blame destiny. The gods are good, she tells her maid, and

> leave to mortall men to be dispos'd
> Freelie on earth what ever mortall is.
> If we therin sometimes some faultes commit,
> We may them not to their hight majesties,
> But to our selves impute: whose passions
> Plunge us each day in all afflictions.
> Wherewith when we our soules do thorned feele,
> Flatt'ring our selves we say they dest'nies are.
>
> (473–80)[10]

And Antonius has a parallel speech in which he absolves fortune and blames pleasure alone for his 'strange disastre' (1138 ff). Act V is taken up entirely with Cleopatra's self-reproach for having destroyed Antony.

The Countess's *Antonius* then is more effective than Jodelle's play despite its repetitious moralising. It moves one step closer to Shakespeare's conception because, despite passages on fate, it places the blame for the tragedy on the lovers and relates politics to ethics on an imperial scale. Yet despite these sophisticated accomplishments, so much of the action is taken up by self-recrimination that our feeling for Antony and Cleopatra is, if sympathetic, no catharsis.

Samuel Daniel's *Cleopatra* (1594), a companion piece to the Countess's translation, imitates its French models all too closely. Still it is an extremely interesting philosophical poem if not completely successful drama. As Willard Farnham and others have pointed out, Shakespeare seems to have been familiar with Daniel's work.[11] But aside from any evidence that Shakespeare remembered the play when he wrote his own, Daniel's play is interesting because Cleopatra's motives remain mixed until she rises to nobility in death.

Samuel Brandon's *The Virtuous Octavia* (1598) and the thundering academic *Caesar's Revenge* (*c.* 1606) repeat the commonplaces that the delicious poison of love ruined Antony and Cleopatra and feminised the warlike Antony.

To generalise, classical and medieval authorities, Elizabethan moral philosophers, and Senecan playwrights show us a similar pair of doomed lovers. The Senecan dramatists, however, build up our pity for the lovers by pathetic accounts of their miseries. Shakespeare's queen, despite her magnificent eloquence as she dies, never reaches the moral stature of either Garnier's or Daniel's penitent. The earlier plays, for this reason among many, are paradoxically duller and weaker than Shakespeare's, in which Cleopatra is consistently sensual and passionate. Applaud final virtuous resolves as we may, there is nothing very attractive about the Senecans' reformed sinners and their wordy rejection of their basic nature.

By minimising the part of fortune Shakespeare has moved still farther from the *de casibus* theme which dominates Jodelle's *Cleopatre* and has a place in the later Senecans. We find little in *Antony and Cleopatra* on the insecurity of high estate, but we find a great deal on the consequences of indecorum on the part of princes and on the terrible suffering of excessive love.

5. SHAKESPEARE

Shakespeare's lovers are so much more complex and appealing than their predecessors that modern criticism, as we have seen, cannot admit that so rapturous a love can be degenerative. This somewhat Nietzschean interpretation is exciting, and when Antony challenges conventional morality we share in his tremendous exaltation a temporary freedom from the workaday conventions. Nevertheless that we watch with increasing fascination and sympathy the decline of the lovers' fortunes does not justify calling the play a manifesto in defence of passion. Love here is in more than one sense superb, but that Shakespeare presents it as a pattern of excellence can be held only by overlooking a great many contrary actions and statements in the play. The structure of the plot is further supported by the traditional characterisation of the lovers with which Shakespeare and his audience were familiar. Shakespeare did not have to labour the obvious; his audience would have understood outlines, hints, and epitomes of familiar attitudes. A line is all that is needed to characterise Herod (cf. *Hamlet*, III.ii. 15).

On the other hand, had he wished to present a reversed image, he would have had to labour like Shaw to make clear the contrast between what appeared and what was expected. But Shavian irony, it seems to me, is alien to Shakespeare's plot. Traditionally Antony and Cleopatra threw away a kingdom for lust, and this is how, despite the pity and terror that Shakespeare makes us feel, they appear in the play.

No scenes better illustrate Shakespeare's manner than those at the opening which foreshadow the whole action. Philo promises that we shall see

> The triple pillar of the world transform'd
> Into a strumpet's fool (I.i. 11–12)

Now how a 'eunuch' was presented in the theatre I do not know, but the stage direction from the Folio describes the entrance of Cleopatra 'with Eunuchs fanning her', and it seems clear that Shakespeare meant the procession to further the exposition. During the play Cleopatra feminises Antony, and it is not far-fetched to find the eunuchs, if not symbols, singularly appropriate in the iconography of the theatre.

The last of the introductory scenes laid in Egypt shows in action what North called 'the flickering enticements' of Cleopatra who is a superb showman. Having directed Charmian to find out Antony's mood so that she may act contrarily, she stages a grand 'scene', a magnificent burlesque. We can feel little tenderness at this exquisite scene of Cleopatra's attempt to keep her lord captive. Picturing her as 'cunning past man's thought', Shakespeare keeps his ironic detachment. While we are taken with the pageantry of the court and amused by Cleopatra's art and stirred by Antony's audacious defiance of duty, we understand the justness of Philo's commentary.

Curiously enough, if Shakespeare wanted to present an exalted passion, the most important character after Octavius (I.iv. 2–7) to call our attention to Antony's fall from the decorum of man and prince is Cleopatra, when she exults in having subdued her lover and confirms Octavius' judgment that lust has made Antony 'womanly'. 'That time', she laughs,

> I drunk him to his bed;
> Then put my tires and mantles on him, whilst
> I wore his sword Philippan. (II.v. 21–3)

Equally odd if Shakespeare wished to present an exalted love are Cleopatra's luxurious musings on her past conquests when during Caesar's lifetime she was

> A morsel for a monarch; and great Pompey
> Would stand and make eyes grow in my brow.
> (I.v. 29–30)

Act II only emphasises the food and brothel images which form a leitmotive throughout the play.[12] Pompey puts us in mind of her medieval reputation as sorceress and lavish hostess, 'Let witchcraft join with beauty, lust with both' (II.i. 22). Even in Enobarbus' glowing description of Antony's first meeting with Cleopatra Shakespeare introduces the analogy between eating and lust as Antony

> for his ordinary pays his heart
> For what his eyes eat only. (II.ii. 230–1)

He equates sexual satisfaction with repletion at table:

> Other women cloy
> The appetites they feed, but she makes hungry
> Where most she satisfies . . . (II.ii. 241–3)

And Cleopatra's earlier sexual triumphs are never far away. As Agrippa says of this 'Royal wench',

> She made great Caesar lay his sword to bed.
> He plough'd her, and she cropp'd. (II.ii. 232–3)

On Pompey's galley Enobarbus brings up the old story of bringing 'A certain queen to Caesar in a mattress' (II.vi. 71).

If the complex relationship between Antony and Cleopatra is not to be found in these and other unflattering references to both, they form an antidote to the criticism which sees Enobarbus' picture of Cleopatra in her barge as the whole story. Like Shakespeare's Venus, Cleopatra must be fascinating if her power over Antony is to intrigue us. But along with her allure we see her faults, and as the action progresses, the flaws in the love of Antony and Cleopatra become more evident and Antony's defection from himself more ominous, until at the end both lovers die of the passion they have lived by.

Octavius, not popular even with critics who see him as the

political ideal of Elizabethan authors, admires the Antony he remembers before Cleopatra met him (I.v. 55–71). Nor is there any reason in view of his repeated and generous comments on Antony to suppose that he is cynical in offering his beloved Octavia to Antony for his wife. Certainly his comments on Antony's defeat are not empty rhetoric. At the opening of Act IV, after Antony has whipped Octavius' messenger and sent an insulting challenge, a double affront, Caesar exclaims, 'Poor Antony!' And at the news of Antony's suicide he weeps, even though Antony's defeat is a political and military necessity (V.i. 27–9, 35–49), remembering Antony as 'my brother, my competitor'.

Antony's love has caused him considerable anguish even in the first part of the play as he tries to free himself. Octavia, though not glamorous, is presented as the ideal wife, but Cleopatra has spoiled Antony for marriage. (Cf. II.vi. 131 ff and III.xiii. 105–9.) Cleopatra strikes the messenger from Rome who tells her that Octavia has married Antony; Cleopatra suffers extremes of rage which Alexas remarks are characteristic of her. This fury is Shakespeare's invention. Though Cleopatra never suffers the remorseful agonies that Antony suffers, this rage is part of the perturbation which the Renaissance found to be the inevitable consequence of violent passion. Passions are rewarded by more passions. Cleopatra's unquiet mind is part payment for guilty love. 'In praising Antony I have dispraised Caesar . . . I am paid for't now.' If the course of true love never did run smooth, the course of lust is yet rougher.

In the first two Acts we have seen the sumptuous and occasionally comic side of Antony's and Cleopatra's love. From Act III on we see more and more clearly the miseries of love. Actium makes Antony realise how love has caused him to fail to observe the decorum of both man and ruler. The battle itself is presented only by a few marching men and the off-stage noises 'of a sea-fight'. But the literal and symbolic importance of Antony's fleeing after Cleopatra warrants several bitter and eloquent speeches. At the end of the Act both Antony and Enobarbus believe that Cleopatra is teetering on the edge of surrendering Antony to Octavius. So does the audience.

When Antony, filled with Dutch courage, commands 'one other gaudy night' and ironically challenges the world, 'The next time I do fight, / I'll make Death love me', Enobarbus at last sees him as desperate and, to his own mortal shame, deserts him. When

Cleopatra's navy deserts, Antony's rage and pain mount to near madness. His thoughts are 'murd'rous, bloody, full of blame':

> The shirt of Nessus is upon me. Teach me,
> Alcides, thou mine ancestor, thy rage . . .
> The witch shall die. (IV.xii. 43–5)

Antony's desperate courage as well as his madness are allied with his consuming dotage. Cleopatra too pays for her wantonness. Not only do both lose their kingdoms and their lives, but both suffer as their love turns to ashes before the play is over. Antony's passion turns to hate after his final defeat, and Cleopatra is haunted to the end by Antony's furious hope that Octavia will mock her in the Roman triumph.

Most bitter of all is that Cleopatra's last stratagem causes his death. Just as she has schooled Antony in life, now she teaches him to die. For the last time Antony sees himself as less than a woman (IV.xiv. 55–62).

Succeeding where his Senecan predecessors failed, Shakespeare works on our pity for the lovers in their last hours. In no other treatment of the love story can we find anything to match the magnificent lines of Antony's farewell to life (IV.xiv. 35–54). Yet we may not assume that Antony's momentary vision of Elysium is identical with Shakespeare's view of his love. He still must suffer. Ironically his agonies are not over. Cleopatra is not dead for love; to save herself she has tricked him again. Nor is she ready to die. When Antony is carried all bloody to her monument and asks for a kiss before he dies, she thinks more of herself than of him, 'I dare not, dear,' she falters, 'Lest I be taken.'

Only after nine lines of rhetorical concern for her honour does she draw Antony up into the monument. To his eloquent 'I am dying, Egypt, dying,' she answers with a tirade not half so moving. More concerned with her safety than with himself, he dies consoling her with thoughts of former glory. Like the Senecans, Shakespeare has given Antony a nobility in death which he has equalled only sporadically in life.

And like Daniel's Cleopatra, Shakespeare's only realises true devotion when schooled by Antony's death. After her magnificent lines, 'The crown o'th'earth doth melt . . .', she faints, and when she revives sees herself no longer as queen of Egypt, but as a mortal torn 'By such poor passion as the maid that milks / And does the meanest chares.' Shakespeare did not need to preach the fall of the mighty and the vanity of human wishes: the action alone demonstrates these truisms.

Yet although Shakespeare's Cleopatra, like Daniel's, is schooled by adversity, her motives for death remain wavering. Unlike Daniel's heroine she does not die for pure love; her memories of Antony alternate with visions of her humiliation in Rome. She attempts to trick Octavius out of half her treasure and only after learning from Dolabella that Caesar will surely show her in his triumph does she make the final resolve to end her life.

Anticipation of her disgrace in Rome is part of the torments which she suffers and the means by which Shakespeare creates pity for her. Horrified by the mockery she will endure, she gives no thought to Antony except as he is involved in her disgrace:

> The quick comedians
> Extemporally will stage us, and present
> Our Alexandrian revels; Antony
> Shall be brought drunken forth, and I shall see
> Some squeaking Cleopatra boy my greatness
> I' th'posture of a whore. (V.ii. 216–21)

'Again for Cydnus/To meet Mark Antony', she dresses royally, admits the clown with the asps, and keeps her assignation with death as if meeting a lover. When Iras falls dead, Cleopatra suffers a last pang of jealousy lest her maid 'first meet the curled Antony' and usurp his kiss. Even as she applies the asp her thoughts of cheating Octavius out of his triumph balance her thoughts of Antony. Charmian's eulogy,

> Now boast thee, death, in thy possession lies
> A lass unparallel'd, (V.ii. 318–19)

sweetens her memory. The queen whom age cannot wither nor custom stale dies nobly. High-minded Octavius honours the lovers' grave:

> High events as these
> Strike those that make them; and their story is
> No less in pity than his glory which
> Brought them to be lamented. (V.ii. 363–6)

The 'Imperial Magnificence' of *Antony and Cleopatra*, to borrow Knight's phrase, remains one of the most astonishing acts of creation in Shakespearean drama. There is nothing niggardly about the world that Shakespeare has built for his peerless amorists to win and lose. There is nothing overtly ascetic, nor do we find any of that moral snobbishness that mars the Senecan plays about the lovers. Yet this golden world is tarnished. Shakespeare is always shifting his viewpoint so that each magnificent wayward gesture is countered either by a glimpse of its futility or by a sober estimate of its cost both to the lovers and to the universe. We are left feeling as the earlier dramatists wanted us to feel but did not succeed in making us feel, that the most magnificent love affair the world had ever known blazed like a fire in the night and left sad ashes in the morning. The sensuality and luxury of the play, its scale and size, shock us by paradox. The *contemptus mundi* which other playwrights preach in vain follows upon our awe at the sight of the most glittering world conceivable lying in ruins.

SOURCE: Author's revision of passages in *Not Wisely But Too Well* (San Marino, Calif., 1957).

NOTES

1. The attitude is neo-Hegelian. A. C. Bradley, the noblest Hegelian of them all, admires Antony for the violence and single-mindedness of his love. The 'passion that ruins Antony also exalts him, he touches the infinite in it'. *Shakespearean Tragedy* (1905) p. 83.

2. This stirring declaration comes from Donald Stauffer's illuminating *Shakespeare's World of Images* (New York, 1949) p. 234.

3. *The Poems of Horace ... Rendred in English Verse by Several Persons ... Printed for Henry Brome* ... M.DC.LXVI, p.48. Cf. LCL, ll. 6–12; also Brome, p. 168, in LCL, ll. 11–16.

4. *The Historie of the World. Commonly called, The Naturall Historie*, trans. Philemon Holland (1601) 1, sig Z 3; Oo 4 verso. Cf. Macrobius, *Saturnalia*, II,xiii.

5. *An Auncient Historie and Exquisite Chronicle of the Romanes Warres* (1578), sigs. Rr verso and Rr 3 verso; Shakespeare used details for *Julius Caesar* as well as for *Antony and Cleopatra*.

6. Favorable mentions of her are slight and few. In the anonymous *Grete Rayson Cleopatra is by kyndnesse*, falsely attributed to Chaucer, she is a heroine. Turberville's 'Disprayse of Women' (1567) mentions her as an example of a woman faithful to death. Cf. Utley, *The Crooked Rib*, no. 356.

7. Sig. B 4 verso; sigs. D 3 verso–D 4.

8. Cf. Lodowick Lloyd, *The Pilgrimage of Princes* [1573], sig. D verso; sig. Nn 3 verso; sig. Tt verso; sig. Bbb 5; sig. Eee 2 verso; sig. Fff 2: Thomas

Rogers, *The Anatomie of the Minde* (1576) fo. 61 verso, fo. 134; La Primaudaye's *French Academie* (1586) ed. of 1618, sig. G 4 verso; sig. H 3 verso; sig. I 2 verso: Florio's *The Essays of Montaigne* (1603), in *Tudor Translations*, ed. Saintsbury (1892–3) II 474: Thomas Beard's *The Theatre of Gods Judgements* (1597) sigs. Z 3 verso–Z 4: *Politeuphuia: Wits Commonwealth* (1597) fo. 272; Sir Richard Barckley, *A Discourse of the Felicitie of Man* (1598) sig. D 6: Robert Allott, *Wits Theater of the Little World* (1599) fo. 240 verso, fo. 260 verso, fo. 263: Bodenham's *Belvedere or The Garden of the Muses* (1600) p. 164: Barnabe Rich, *Faultes Faultes* (1606) sig. G 3 verso: Richard Reynoldes's *A Chronicle of all the noble Emperours of the Romaines* (1571) folios 17–18: Others might be cited, including Bacon.

9. See Willard Farnham, *The Medieval Heritage of Elizabethan Tragedy* (Berkeley, 1936), and Lily B. Campbell, *Shakespeare's Tragic Heroes* (Cambridge, 1930).

10. Ed. Alice Luce (Weimar, 1897).

11. Cf. *Medieval Heritage*, 170 ff.

12. Cf. Leo Kirschbaum, 'Shakespeare's Cleopatra', in *Shakespeare Association Bulletin*, XIX (1944) 161–71.

Maurice Charney The Imagery of *Antony and Cleopatra* (1961)

Shakespeare's Antony resembles Hamlet in at least this one respect: both have an acute awareness of their moral situation, but they are seemingly without the power to change it. Their tragedies do not come from a blindness or error of judgment, but from a deep-seated defect of will. Hamlet, however, is catapulted into a tragedy to which he remains alien and unreconciled, whereas Antony seems to choose his fate deliberately and knowingly. He goes through the motions of suicide, for example, only to learn that Cleopatra is 'playing' dead in her monument. But this ruse seems to make no difference to him, and his dying wish to be carried to her is an acknowledgment and acceptance of his fate. In this way the death scene in IV.xv passes from tragedy to rhapsodic affirmation, and 'the visions of comedy and tragedy merge'.[1]

These movements in the fate of Antony grow out of the tragic conflict between the values of Egypt and Rome and may be illustrated in three image themes: sword and armor, vertical dimension, and dissolution. The sword and armor Antony wears are the visible signs of his soldiership and empire; but as the play progresses, the power of Antony's sword is undercut by his association with Cleopatra, and his unarming is a formal dumbshow for his renunciation of Rome. This pattern of Antony's tragedy is also reflected in images of lowness and height and in a very characteristic imagery of dissolution. Out of many possible themes, these three express the fate of Antony with most significance and originality.

Antony is visibly present in sword and armor for a good part of the play. This is a presentational image of his role as soldier and triumvir, his 'royal occupation' (IV.iv. 17), and the verbal imagery helps to support this impression. We see him in military dress throughout the scenes of war (from III.vii to IV.xiv. 35, when he begins to disarm), and probably also in the conferences with Caesar (II.ii; III.ii) and with Pompey (II.vi, vii) – the formal dress of sword and armor would be in keeping with the gravity of public affairs in these scenes. As a matter of fact, Lepidus very specifically indicates 'soldier's dress' (II.iv. 4) for the scene with Pompey. Antony is also probably in sword and armor when he first appears in the play. This would give Philo's allusions to 'plated Mars' (I.i. 4) and 'The buckles on his breast' (I.i. 8) an immediate reference to the Antony we see enter a few lines further. Philo wishes to indicate that the sword and armor are only a false appearance for Antony's present 'dotage'.

The basic application of sword and armor imagery is to the Roman concerns of war and soldiership. These are part of that public world of hard material objects and practical business that stands in sharp contrast to the luxuriousness and indolence of Egypt. Originally, it is the 'civil swords' (I.iii. 45), or civil war, in Italy that calls Antony back to Rome. But after his shameful flight from battle at Actium, his sword becomes only an image of his former glory. He recollects that the now triumphant Octavius

> at Philippi kept
> His sword e'en like a dancer, while I struck
> The lean and wrinkled Cassius; and 'twas I
> That the mad Brutus ended. He alone
> Dealt on lieutenantry and no practise had
> In the brave squares of war. Yet now – No matter.
> (III.xi. 35–40)

Now Caesar, whose sword served no more function than a dancer's ornament, has defeated Antony, and the extent of Antony's present shame is indicated by the prolonged and emphatic 'now'. Antony tries to restore the power of his sword by challenging Caesar to single combat:

> I dare him therefore
> To lay his gay comparisons apart
> And answer me declin'd, sword against sword,
> Ourselves alone. (III.xiii. 25–8)

It is an unreal, histrionic effort, for Caesar is not interested in this public display of bravery; he has, indeed, already refused Antony (III.i. 31–5). The aside of Enobarbus serves as chorus here:

> Yes, like enough high-battled Caesar will
> Unstate his happiness and be stag'd to th' show
> Against a sworder! (III.xiii. 29–31)

'Sworder' is a contemptuous word, and it signifies that Antony now wears his sword 'e'en like a dancer'; the power of war has gone out of it. Enobarbus, tragically divided between the qualities of Antony and Caesar, decides at this point to desert his master. His ominous and incisive comment closes the scene:

> When valour preys on reason,
> It eats the sword it fights with. I will seek
> Some way to leave him. (III.xiii. 199–201)

The Roman virtue of 'reason' is valor's true sword, and Caesar's conquest of the 'three nook'd world' (IV.vi. 6) shows how well he has learned this lesson.

There is an ironic comment on the ineffectiveness of Antony's sword in his suicide scene. He entreats Eros to draw 'thy honest sword' (IV.xiv. 79) and kill him, but Eros takes his own life instead. This gives Antony the courage to fall on his sword, but he is only able to inflict a mortal wound. He prays the Guard, then Diomedes, to make an end of his blundering work: 'Draw thy sword and give me / Sufficing strokes for death' (IV.xiv. 116–17). Antony's sword is powerless even for death – a graphic image of his tragedy. The inadequacy of his sword reflects the abandonment of his Roman role of soldier and world conqueror.

Our final image of Antony's sword balances the fall of Antony against the rise of Caesar. Once again the sword enters significantly into the stage action. As Antony lies dying, Decretas[2] steals his sword, which 'but shown to Caesar, with this tidings, / Shall enter me with him' (IV.xiv. 112–13). We see Decretas again at the beginning of Act V, where his portentous entrance with the bloody sword of Antony in his hand gives Caesar a sudden fright – it is a final reflection of the power of Antony. This sword, once the symbol of his Roman virtue and dominion, is handed over to Caesar, who is now indeed 'Sole sir o' th' wòrld' (V.ii. 120). Compare the symbolic stage business in *Julius Caesar*, where both Cassius (V.iii. 45–6) and presumably Brutus (V.v. 50–1) stab themselves with the same swords they used to kill Caesar. This ironic reciprocity presents the poetic justice of the play in strong theatrical terms. In *Antony and Cleopatra* the presentation of Antony's sword to Octavius acts out the tragic transfer of power that is a central issue in the play, and the ritual stage business serves as a brusque investiture for Caesar.

In a sense 'sword' has one set of connotations in Egypt and another in Rome. This difference reflects Antony's tragedy, for his sword in its Roman role is rendered powerless in Egypt, and his association with Cleopatra develops the sexual overtones of the image. Although the theme is directly stated only two or three times in the play, it underlies a good part of the action in Egypt. As Agrippa tells us, Cleopatra has the ability to charm swords to inaction: 'She made great Caesar lay his sword to bed. / He plough'd her, and she cropp'd' (II.ii. 232–3). This utterly unShavian Julius Caesar is the model for Antony, and the strong connotations of 'sword' here indicate its transformation from a military to a procreative term. The passage suggests Cleopatra's recollection of the time she drank Antony to his bed, 'Then put my tires and mantles on him, whilst / I wore his sword Philippan' (II.v. 22–3). In both passages Cleopatra's dominance involves control of her lover's sword, the symbol of his manliness and soldiership. There is perhaps an allusion to Hercules' enslavement by Omphale here, for Omphale forced Hercules to wear her clothes, while she dressed in his lion-skin and carried his club.[3] The identification is very specifically indicated in the 'Comparison' that follows the life of Antony in North's Plutarch:

> We see in painted tables, where Omphale secretlie stealeth away Hercules clubbe, and tooke his Lyons skinne from him. Even so Cleopatra oftentimes

unarmed Antonius, and intised him to her, making him lose matters of great importaunce, and verie needeful jorneys, to come and be dandled with her, about the rivers of Canobus, and Taphosiris.[4]

This is the sort of effemination that Cleopatra has inflicted on Antony, and it is no wonder that when Cleopatra enters in I.ii Enobarbus says sardonically: 'Hush! Here comes Antony' (I.ii. 83).[5]

The reversal of roles between Antony and Cleopatra is illustrated by the battle of Actium: it is to please her and against all reason that Antony accepts Caesar's dare to fight at sea. A Soldier warns him against it, but the Soldier's 'sword' and 'wounds' (III.vii. 64) cannot persuade Antony against the whims of Cleopatra, who insists on appearing at Actium 'for a man' (III. vii. 19). Antony blames her for his defeat at the same time as he acknowledges his own 'dotage' in Egypt:

> You did know
> How much you were my conqueror, and that
> My sword, made weak by my affection, would
> Obey it on all cause. (II.xi. 65–8)

'My sword made weak by my affection' is a key statement for the tragedy of Antony. His power to act, represented by the Roman sense of 'sword', has been overwhelmed by his power to feel ('affection'). Enobarbus, too, blames 'affection' for the defeat at Actium. When Antony followed Cleopatra from battle, 'The itch of his affection should not then / Have nick'd his captainship . . .' (III.xiii. 7–8). The word 'nick'd' implies that Antony's 'captainship' is conceived as the blade of a sword, which Cleopatra has damaged and made useless. He is thus being made aware of the price of Egypt, and this gives a tragic dimension to what began as frivolity and indulgence of the senses.

There is a final reflection of the theme in the scene of Antony's suicide. The entrance of Cleopatra's Eunuch, Mardian, sends Antony into a rage: 'O, thy vile lady! / She has robb'd me of my sword' (IV.xiv. 22–3). This is another way of stating the tragedy of Antony. Cleopatra has deprived him of the power to act and conquer that made him 'triple pillar of the world'. 'Sword' is being used in its obvious Roman sense, but there is also a play on the sexual connotations of the word. From a Roman point of view, Antony has become as impotent as the Eunuch Mardian: his sword is only an instrument of 'affection', the symbol of his dominance by

Cleopatra. But in the values of Egypt this is sufficient and in itself can offer a transcendence. When Antony learns that Cleopatra has not betrayed him to Caesar but has committed suicide in her monument, there is a marvellous change in his attitude. His sword is no longer his concern, nor is any temporal thing, as he prepares to follow his lady. It is a final, tragic acceptance of the values of Egypt, and it marks a strong poetic heightening for Antony.

The 'turn' in the dramatic action begins with his request to Eros: 'Unarm, Eros. The long day's task is done, / And we must sleep' (IV.xiv. 35–6). Antony by disarming now visibly abandons his Roman role of soldier just as Cleopatra assumes the role of queen by putting on robe and crown; both are the final symbolic acts of the protagonists, and in both costume has strong thematic significance. Antony's arming on the morning of the second battle prepares us for the symbolic tone of the later passage. Cleopatra insists on helping in spite of his protest: 'Ah, let be, let be! Thou art/The armourer of my heart. False, false! This, this!' (IV.iv. 6–7). Cleopatra, the 'armourer' of Antony's 'heart', is improperly assuming a Roman role in trying to arm his body, and the 'False, false!' and 'This, this!' refer to her ineptness at this sort of arming. It is another way of indicating that Antony's sword has been made weak by 'affection', and the ill omen of 'False, false!' echoes in his final defeat: 'O this false soul of Egypt!' (IV.xii. 25).

Antony's public position of Roman soldier and triumvir has been expressed by sword and armor throughout the play, so that his unarming in IV xiv marks a new, and final, movement in the action. The bitterness and misgivings of tragic conflict are gone; there is only a desire for haste (compare Cleopatra and Iras, V.ii. 283 ff):

> Off, pluck off!
> The sevenfold shield of Ajax cannot keep
> The battery from my heart. O, cleave, my sides!
> Heart, once be stronger than thy continent,
> Crack thy frail case! Apace, Eros, apace. –
> No more a soldier. Bruised pieces, go;
> You have been nobly borne. (IV.xiv. 37–43)

'No more a soldier' indicates the end of the unarming, and Antony feels that he is now suddenly entering a new spiritual state. It is as if he had put off some external Roman self with this 'sevenfold shield of Ajax' and these 'Bruised pieces'. His mortal body ('continent', with a play on the etymological and geographical senses) is now in itself too much armor to bear against death, and he prays that the 'battery' from his 'heart' be strong enough to 'Crack' his 'frail case' and 'cleave' his 'sides'. And he eagerly anticipates the fate of his unarmed self, the lover of Cleopatra. Her death set him an example of nobility, which evokes memories of his former glory as he prepares to follow her:

> I, that with my sword
> Quarter'd the world and o'er green Neptune's back
> With ships made cities.... (IV.xiv. 57–9)

But he is now 'No more a soldier', and his world-quartering sword is only a recollection of the past.

The fall of Antony is also marked by a persistent imagery of vertical dimension, which is a simpler and more literal theme than sword and armor, but keeps us vividly aware of the movement of the action. The basic pattern here is the contrast in vertical dimension between high and low, up and down, in a manner quite similar to that used in *Richard II*.[6] This is best seen in two presentational images. Antony's despair and remorse after Actium are summed up in a significant stage direction: '*Sits down*' (III.xi. 24). The action here is an absolute contrast to the movement of the battle scenes, and its tone suggests the homely opening of *Coriolanus* I.iii: 'Enter *Volumnia* and *Virgilia*, mother and wife to *Marcius*. They set them down on two low stools and sew.' It is not part of the 'decorum' of majesty for Antony to be sitting down, and the action becomes a literal stage image for his lowness at this point: 'He is unqualitied with very shame' (III.xi. 44). Similarly, one of the symbolic suggestions of Pompey's lowness in the political world is his reluctance to obey Menas' pregnant aside, 'Rise from thy stool' (II.vii. 62). One may easily overlook these presentational images in reading the play, but in the theatre they are an effective and eloquent expression, perhaps just because of their extreme simplicity. The image of Antony sitting down is supported by verbal references that do not allow us to forget his position. Cleopatra wishes to join him: 'Let me sit down. O Juno!' (III.xi. 28), but Antony protests bitterly: 'No, no, no, no, no!' (III.xi. 29) – the comment in its intensity recalls the 'never's' of King Lear (V.iii. 308). And Antony is still seated at III.xi. 46, when Eros says: 'Most noble sir, arise. The Queen approaches.' It is not presumably until a few lines further (III.xi. 50) that Eros, after four unsuccessful attempts (III.xi. 30, 34, 42, 46–8), is finally able to draw Antony's attention to Cleopatra and to compel him to stand. Antony deliberately turns his back to the queen (III.xi. 52), but the action of standing brings with it a recovery of equilibrium.

Antony reaches a different kind of height from Caesar's in IV.xv, when he is lifted, dying, to Cleopatra's monument. The action, '*They heave Antony aloft to Cleopatra*' (IV.xv. 37 s.d.), presents a literal image of height in the use of the upper stage. We see Antony being raised by his Guard, and they are assisted by Cleopatra and her girls from 'aloft'. The theatre thus provides us with a metaphor of elevation for Antony's death, which is accompanied by a corresponding heightening of style. Cleopatra's speech is full of ironic puns about the stage business:

> Here's sport indeed! How heavy weighs my lord!
> Our strength is all gone into heaviness:
> That makes the weight. Had I great Juno's power,
> The strong-wing'd Mercury should fetch thee up
> And set thee by Jove's side. (IV.xx. 32–6)

Antony's heaviness as he is raised to the monument is made the symbol of heavy grief; we can see that Cleopatra very obviously does not have 'great Juno's power'. She uses 'sport' ironically to fit in with the action, as if all the Egyptian pleasures should end in this final sport, the awkward manual labor of lifting a dying captain to his place of death. There are also obvious sexual overtones in 'sport' and 'heavy'. But Antony's place is an elevated one (both literally and figuratively) and in its own way defies the temporal height of Caesar. The note of fulfillment and reconciliation in this image places the fate of Antony outside the toils of tragedy. . . .

Antony's fallen state is represented most brilliantly by the imagery of dissolution. The pattern in the play is one of melting, fading, dissolving, discandying, disponging, dislimning, and losing of form that marks his downward course after Actium, 'for indeed I have lost command' (III.xi. 23). As Antony says, 'Authority melts from me' (III.xiii. 90), and this is clearly acted out when he orders Caesar's servant, Thidias, to approach (I supply in brackets what the stage action appears to be):

> Approach there! – [*Thidias stands insolently still*] Ah, you kite! – [*Spoken to Cleopatra:* You are responsible for this.] Now, gods and devils!

> Authority melts from me. Of late, when I cried 'Ho!'
> Like boys unto a muss, kings would start forth
> And cry 'Your will?' Have you no ears? [*Thidias is still insolently ignoring Antony*] I am
> Antony yet. (III.xiii. 89–93)

It was Antony who once declared with so much disregard: 'Let Rome in Tiber melt and the wide arch / Of the rang'd empire fall!' (I.i. 33–4). Now Antony's Rome has indeed melted and his own 'rang'd empire' fallen, for his authority is gone. Thidias refuses ceremony to what is no longer a reality, so that the use of politeness or its denial becomes an important dramatic means for indicating an attitude. To the dismay of Enobarbus, Antony's power in this scene expresses itself only in the empty form of violence: 'Take hence this Jack and whip him' (III.xiii. 93). Incidentally, we are already prepared for Thidias' insolence by Cleopatra's comment just before his entrance:

> What, no more ceremony? See, my women!
> Against the blown rose may they stop their nose
> That kneel'd unto the buds. (III.xiii. 38–40)

The declaration at the end of Antony's speech, 'I am / Antony yet', forces a contrast between the name and the reality. The real commanding presence of 'Antony' – 'That magical word of war' (III.i. 31) as Ventidius called it – has melted away, has suffered dissolution, while the name itself remains as hollow reminder of the past. In the same mood Antony in his next speech questions the reality of 'Cleopatra': 'what's her name / Since she was Cleopatra?' (III.xiii. 98–9). The resolution of this play on names comes at the end of the scene in a reaffirmation of reality: 'since my lord / Is Antony again, I will be Cleopatra' (III.xiii. 186–7).

The dissolution theme is acted out on a mythological plane in IV.iii, where the god Hercules, Antony's supposed ancestor and tutelary deity, abandons him. Shakespeare develops this scene from a marginal note in Plutarch: '*Strange noyses heard, and nothing seene*.'[7] One company of soldiers is relieving another on the night before the second day of battle, and '*They place themselves in every corner of the stage*' (IV.iii. 7 s.d.). The sense of isolation and dispersal over a large area would be intensified on the rectangular Elizabethan stage, which projected into the middle of the audience. Suddenly, after the third Soldier has said, ''Tis a brave army, / And full of purpose' (IV.iii.10–11), '*Music of the hautboys is under the stage*'

(IV.iii. 11 s.d.). This muffled, distant-sounding oboe music belies the false optimism of the soldiers.[8] It is a striking, portentous effect, and they listen with attentive fear:

2nd Soldier. Peace! What noise?
1st Soldier. List, list!
2nd Soldier. Hark!
1st Soldier. Music i' th' air.
3rd soldier. Under the earth.
4th Soldier. It signs well, does it not?
3rd Soldier. No.
1st Soldier. Peace, I say!
What should this mean?
2nd Soldier. 'Tis the god Hercules, whom Antony lov'd
Now leaves him. (IV.iii. 11–16)

This scene is in the symbolic tradition of the medieval pageant wagon, where the stage itself represented the world, with heaven above and hell below. As a matter of structure, the departure of Hercules occurs at almost the same time as the desertion of Enobarbus; in some sense Enobarbus has been Antony's Hercules, and IV. iii gives his desertion a mythological compulsion. By the strange voice of oboes from the underworld we are being prepared for Antony's defeat and tragic end. The image is harbinger of the 'discandying' and 'dislimning' that are to follow.

After his final defeat Antony speaks again in the imagery of dissolution:

All come to this? The hearts
That spaniel'd me at heels, to whom I gave
Their wishes, do discandy, melt their sweets
On blossoming Caesar. . . . (IV.xii. 20–3)

Antony's fawning and fickle allies now 'discandy' and 'melt' and make Caesar flourish while Antony languishes. Compare Cleopatra's melting imagery in III.xiii; if she be cold-hearted to Antony,

From my cold heart let heaven engender hail,
And poison it in the source, and the first stone
Drop in my neck; as it determines, so
Dissolve my life! The next Caesarion smite!
Till by degrees the memory of my womb,
Together with my brave Egyptians all,
By the discandying[9] of this pelleted storm,
Lie graveless, till the flies and gnats of Nile
Have buried them for prey! (III.xiii. 159–67)

Cleopatra imagines death in Antony's terms as a dissolving and a 'discandying'. The latter word is a vivid indication that the sweetness and strength are going out of life. 'Disponge' is used similarly for Enobarbus' death, when he prays that

> The poisonous damp of night disponge upon me,
> That life, a very rebel to my will,
> May hang no longer on me! (IV.ix. 13–15)

This is the earliest example of 'disponge' (spelt 'dispunge') in the *Oxford English Dictionary*, and its status as an unfamiliar word strengthens its poetic effect; 'discandy' also appears to be a coinage of Shakespeare's.

The most extended imagery of dissolution is in the pageant of cloud shapes Antony sees in IV.xiv, which melt and dissolve into each other and cannot hold their form:

> That which is now a horse, even with a thought
> The rack dislimns, and makes it indistinct
> As water is in water. (IV.xiv.9–11)

'Dislimns' is another of those arresting words of dissolution which give a characteristic quality to this play. Shakespeare seems to be creating his own vocabulary to establish the feeling of disintegration in the Roman world. The firm substance of life is being undone, things are losing their form, changing and fading with the indistinctness of water in water – this image is the essence of the dissolution theme. There is no bitterness here but only resignation and a certain aesthetic pleasure. The play of thought follows the same progress of forms, mingling as water in water. The complexity of the image lies in the fact that 'water' and 'water' are the same substance, yet in their being together, or in one's being in the other, subtle differences appear. Perhaps it is the idea of difference approaching similarity, as cloud shapes ('The rack') soon merge into simple clouds. The whole process of indiscernible change is expressed by 'dislimning'. Antony sees his own inner state reflected in this insubstantial show:

> My good knave Eros, now thy captain is
> Even such a body. Here I am Antony;
> Yet cannot hold this visible shape, my knave.
> (IV.xiv. 12–14)

It is ironic that the name remains – 'Here I am Antony' – while the physical reality, 'this visible shape', cannot be retained.

Finally, Cleopatra marks the moment of Antony's death with these words: 'O see, my women, / The crown o' th' earth doth melt. My lord!' (IV.xv. 62–3). Antony is not only her 'lord' but the 'crown o' th' earth'; the image attempts to objectify, to hyperbolize the personal dimension of the play. There is a peace and effortlessness in 'melt', as if there were no barrier between life and death, and one could flow easily into the other. It is a fitting close for Antony. His end is not a 'tragic' one as King Lear's is, or Othello's, or Macbeth's. Rather than being resolved, the conflict between Egypt and Rome ceases to exist, and the hard 'visible shapes' of Rome are dissolved into an ecstatic, poetic reality. In this sense *Antony and Cleopatra* looks ahead to the mood of Shakespeare's last plays.

SOURCE: Extract from *Shakespeare's Roman Plays: the Function of Imagery in the Drama* (Cambridge, Mass., 1961), pp. 125–41

NOTES

1. Geoffrey Bush, *Shakespeare and the Natural Condition* (Cambridge, Mass., 1956) p. 130.

2. As M. R. Ridley points out in his New Arden edition, the Folio has 'Decretas' six times and 'Dercetus' only once (pp. 203–4). The latter is a variant of Plutarch's 'Dercetaeus'. G. L. Kittredge (*Antony and Cleopatra*, 1941) gives the name as 'Dercetas'.

3. See *The Tragedie of Anthonie and Cleopatra*, ed. H. H. Furness (Philadelphia, 1907) p. 131. For the similarity with book V of the *Faerie Queene*, see F. M. Dickey, *Not Wisely But Too Well* (San Marino, Calif., 1957) p. 157; see also Sidney's *Defense of Poesy*, ed. Albert S. Cook (Boston, 1898) p. 51. Compare Strindberg's powerful use of Omphale in *The Father*. The identification between Antony and Hercules is developed in some detail in Plutarch.

4. *North's Plutarch*, the Tudor Translations, ed. W. E. Henley (1896) VI 91.

5. According to the Folio, Cleopatra enters (I ii 82), and then Enobarbus makes his deliberately ironic comment. Kittredge shifts Cleopatra's entrance to the end of this line (I ii 83), making Enobarbus' remark a casual oversight. See Elkin Calhoun Wilson, 'Shakespeare's Enobarbus', in *Joseph Quincy Adams Memorial Studies*, ed. James G. McManaway *et al.* (Washington, 1948) p. 392, no. 3.

6. See Paul A. Jorgensen, 'Vertical Patterns in *Richard II*', in *Shakespeare Association Bulletin*, XXIII (1948) 119–34, and Arthur Suzman, 'Imagery and Symbolism in *Richard II*', in *Shakespeare Quarterly*, VII (1956) 355–70.

7. *Four Chapters of North's Plutarch*, ed. F. A. Leo (1878) p. 1004.

8. Compare the awesome effect of the Ghost of Hamlet's Father, who '*cries under the stage*' (I. v. 148 s.d.). *Hamlet* begins with the abrupt anxious talk of the changing of the guard that resembles the conversation of the soldiers in *Antony and Cleopatra*, IV iii (see Cumberland Clark, *Shakespeare and the Supernatural* (1931) p. 150). *Macbeth*, too, makes portentous use of 'hautboys', which play as the Witches' cauldron sinks (IV.i. 106 s.d.).

9. This is an emendation suggested by Thirlby for the Folio 'discandering'.

L. C. Knights The Realism of *Antony and Cleopatra* (1959)

In *Macbeth* we are never in any doubt of our moral bearings. *Antony and Cleopatra*, on the other hand, embodies different and apparently irreconcilable evaluations of the central experience. There is the view, with which the play opens, of those who stand outside the charmed circle of 'Egypt':

> Take but good note, and you shall see in him
> The triple pillar of the world transform'd
> Into a strumpet's fool. (I.i. 11–13)

This attitude is strongly represented in the play; there are repeated references to 'lascivious wassails', 'the amorous surfeiter', 'salt Cleopatra', 'the adulterous Antony' who 'gives his potent regiment to a trull', and so on. The 'Roman' world of war and government – the realm of political 'necessity' (III.vi. 83) rather than of spontaneous human feelings – is of course itself presented critically; but although the way we take the Roman comments is partly determined by our sense of the persons making them, they do correspond to something of which we are directly aware in the Egyptian scenes. We do not need any Roman prompting to be aware of something cloying in the sexual insistence (in the opening of I.ii, for example), and of something practised in (to borrow a phrase from North) the 'flickering enticements of Cleopatra unto Antonius'.

On the other hand, what Shakespeare infused into the love story as he found it in Plutarch was an immense energy, a sense of life so heightened that it can claim to represent an absolute value:

Eternity was in our lips, and eyes,
Bliss in our brows' bent; none our parts so poor,
But was a race of heaven. (I.iii. 35–7)

This energy communicates itself to all that comes within the field of force that radiates from the lovers, and within which their relationship is defined. In Enobarbus' description of the first meeting of Antony and Cleopatra (II.ii. 190 ff) the energy counteracts the suggestion of a deliberate sensuousness; the inanimate is felt as animate; and the passage, although a set-piece, modulates easily into a racy buoyancy:

The city cast
Her people out upon her; and Antony,
Enthron'd i' the market-place, did sit alone,
Whistling to the air; which, but for vacancy,
Had gone to gaze on Cleopatra too,
And make a gap in nature.

Wilson Knight rightly insists on 'the impregnating atmosphere of wealth, power, military strength and material magnificence', the cosmic imagery, and 'the continual suggestion of earth's fruitfulness', in terms of which Antony and Cleopatra are presented to us,[1] and the suggestions of scope and grandeur are blended with continual reminders of what is common to humanity. It is the richness and energy of the poetry in which all this is conveyed that, more than any explicit comment, defines for us the vitality of the theme.

Shakespeare, in short, evokes the passion of the lovers with the greatest possible intensity, and invests it with the maximum of positive significance. But, more realist than some of his critics, he makes it impossible for us not to question the nature and conditions of that very energy that the lovers release in each other. The sequence of scenes between Actium and the final defeat of Antony opens, as Granville-Barker noticed,[2] with a suggestion of dry and brittle comedy. In an apparent abeyance of feeling the lovers are more or less pushed into each other's arms by their respective followers; and there is an inert resignation in the reconciliation that follows. Here indeed the most memorable verse is not love poetry at all; it is Antony's bare and emphatic statement,

Egypt, thou knew'st too well,
My heart was to thy rudder tied by the strings,

And thou shouldst tow me after. O'er my spirit
The full supremacy thou knew'st, and that
Thy beck might from the bidding of the gods
Command me. (III.xi. 56–61)

Feeling does not well up in Antony until he discovers Caesar's messenger kissing Cleopatra's hand. It is a perverse violence of cruelty – 'Whip him, fellows, Till like a boy you see him cringe his face' – that goads him into a semblance of energy; and it is in the backwash of this emotion that Cleopatra can humour him until she is, as it were, again present to him. Shakespeare, however, leaves us in no doubt about the overwrought nature of Antony's feelings: the very look of him is given us by Enobarbus – 'Now he'll outstare the lightning' (III.xiii. 195).

Antony, in short, is galvanised into feeling; there is no true access of life and energy. And the significance of this is that we know that what we have to do with is an emphatic variation of a familiar pattern. Looking back, we can recall how often this love has seemed to thrive on emotional stimulants. They were necessary for much the same reason as the feasts and wine. For the continued references to feasting – and it is not only Caesar and his dry Romans who emphasise the Alexandrian consumption of food and drink – are not simply a means of intensifying the imagery of tasting and savouring that is a constant accompaniment of the love theme; they serve to bring out the element of repetition and monotony in a passion which, centring on itself, is self-consuming, leading ultimately to what Antony himself, in a most pregnant phrase, names as 'the heart of loss'. Indeed, the speech in which this phrase occurs (IV.xii. 9–30) is one of the pivotal things in the play. In its evocation of an appalled sense of insubstantiality it ranks with Macbeth's, 'My thought, whose murder yet is but fantastical . . .'. With this difference: that whereas Macbeth is, as it were, reaching forward to a region 'where nothing is, but what is not', Antony is driven to recognise the element of unreality and enchantment in what he had thought was solid and enduring. The speech has a superb sensuous reality that is simultaneously felt as discandying or melting, until the curious flicker of the double vision – both intensified and explained by the recurrent theme of 'Egyptian' magic and gipsy-like double-dealing – is resolved in the naked vision:

O sun, thy uprise shall I see no more,
Fortune and Antony part here, even here

Do we shake hands. All come to this? The hearts
That spaniel'd me at heels, to whom I gave
Their wishes, do discandy, melt their sweets
On blossoming Caesar: and this pine is bark'd
That overtopp'd them all. Betray'd I am.
O this false soul of Egypt! this grave charm,
Whose eye beck'd forth my wars, and call'd them home;
Whose bosom was my crownet, my chief end,
Like a right gipsy, hath at fast and loose
Beguil'd me, to the very heart of loss. (IV.xii. 18–29)[3]

Cleopatra's lament over the dying Antony, her evocation of his greatness and bounty, have perhaps weighed too heavily in the impression that many people have taken from the play as a whole. That these things are great poetry goes without saying. But the almost unbearable pathos of the last scenes is for what has not in fact been realised.[4]

Cleopatra. For his bounty,
There was no winter in't: an autumn 'twas
That grew the more by reaping: his delights
Were dolphin-like, they show'd his back above
The element they lived in: in his livery
Walk'd crowns and crownets: realms and islands were
As plates dropp'd from his pocket.
Dolabella. Cleopatra!
Cleopatra. Think you there was, or might be such a man
As this I dreamt of?
Dolabella. Gentle madam, no.
Cleopatra. You lie up to the hearing of the gods.
But if there be, nor ever were one such,
It's past the size of dreaming: nature wants stuff
To vie strange forms with fancy, yet to imagine
An Antony were nature's piece 'gainst fancy,
Condemning shadows quite. (V.ii. 86–100)

The figure that Cleopatra evokes may not be fancy – the poetry invests it with a substantial reality; but it is not the Antony that the play has given us; it is something disengaged from, or glimpsed through, that Antony. Nor should the power and beauty of Cleopatra's last great speech obscure the continued presence of something self-deceiving and unreal. She may speak of the baby at her breast that sucks the nurse asleep; but it is not, after all, a baby – new life; it is simply death.

It is, of course, one of the signs of a great writer that he can afford to evoke sympathy or even admiration for what, in his final judgment, is discarded or condemned. In *Antony and Cleopatra* the sense of potentiality in life's untutored energies is pushed to its limit, and Shakespeare gives the maximum weight to an experience that is finally 'placed'. It is perhaps this that makes the tragedy so sombre in its realism, so little comforting to the romantic imagination. For Shakespeare has chosen as his tragic theme the impulse that man perhaps most readily associates with a heightened sense of life and fulfilment. It has not seemed necessary here to explore the range and depth of the poetry in which the theme of vitality twinned with frustration, of force that entangles itself with strength, is expressed; but it is, of course, the range and depth of the poetry that make Antony and Cleopatra into universal figures. At the superb close, Cleopatra – both 'empress' and 'lass unparallel'd' – is an incarnation of sexual passion, of those primeval energies that insistently demand fulfilment in their own terms, and, by insisting on their own terms ('Thy beck might from the bidding of the gods Command me'), thwart the fulfilment that they seek. 'There is no evil impulse', says Martin Buber, 'till the impulse has been separated from the being.'[5] It is precisely this that *The Tragedy of Antony and Cleopatra* reveals.

SOURCE: Extract from *Some Shakespearean Themes* (London and Toronto, 1959), pp. 144–50.

NOTES

1. See 'The Transcendental Humanism of *Antony and Cleopatra*', in *The Imperial Theme* (1931).

2. *Prefaces to Shakespeare, Second Series* (1930) p. 146.

3. Shakespeare, Granville-Barker rightly says, 'is never the vindictive moralist, scourging a man with his sins, blind to all else about him' (op. cit. p. 196), and the play certainly emphasises Antony's admirable qualities, especially his ability to make friends with the men he commands and his generosity. But it is in this very respect also that Shakespeare shows himself so far from 'blind'. When Antony reproaches 'the hearts . . . to whom I gave their wishes', we are compelled to ask, What had he given? The answer of course is, gifts ranging from kingdoms to mule-loads of treasure – visible and tangible symbols of worldly power. He has 'play'd' as he pleased 'with half the bulk o' the world . . . making and marring fortunes' (III.xi. 64–5); 'realms and islands were As plates dropp'd from his pocket' (V.ii. 91–2); and

at his call 'kings would start forth', 'like boys unto a muss' (III.xiii. 91). If all this – which forms the background of his bounty – is felt as discandying it is, surely, not just because Antony is defeated, but because it is of the very nature of the wealth that he deals in to betray an exclusive trust. It is certainly vain and arrogant pomp that is insisted on in the account of the distribution of the kingdoms in Act III, scene vi:

> I' the market place, on a tribunal silver'd,
> Cleopatra and himself in chairs of gold
> Were publicly enthroned . . .
> . . . she
> In the habiliments of the goddess Isis
> That day appear'd . . .

The resounding catalogue of proper names (lines 14–16, 68–76) is to the same effect. I do not think it matters that the description is made by the unsympathetic Caesar; Shakespeare need not have dwelt on it at such length, and the fact that he does so suggests that he was deliberately following Plutarch's lead: 'it was too arrogant and insolent a part, and done . . . in derision and contempt of the Romans' – *Shakespeare's Plutarch*, ed. C. F. Tucker Brooke (1909) II. 86.

4. A view of the play in some ways similar to this is expressed by Professor John F. Danby in *Poets on Fortune's Hill: Studies in Sidney, Shakespeare, Beaumont and Fletcher* (1952) ch. 5: 'Antony and Cleopatra: a Shakespearean Adjustment'. An excellent description of the imaginative effect of the passage from the play next quoted in my text is given by Mr L. G. Salingar in his essay on 'The Elizabethan Literary Renaissance', in the Pelican *Guide to English Literature*, 2: *The Age of Shakespeare*, pp. 106–9.

5. Martin Buber, *I and Thou*, trans. Ronald Gregor Smith (1937) p. 48.

H. A. Mason *Antony and Cleopatra*: Telling *versus* Showing (1966)

The central issue, however, concerns what Bradley calls Antony's 'inward recovery'. Since my account of the fall owes so much to Bradley's, it is awkward not to be able to subscribe to the sequel:

Then Shakespeare begins to raise him again. First, his own overwhelming sense of shame redeems him. Next, we watch the rage of the dying lion.

Then the mere sally before the final defeat – a sally dismissed by Plutarch in three lines – is magnified into a battle in which Antony displays to us, and himself feels for the last time, the glory of his soldiership. And, throughout, the magnanimity and gentleness which shine through his desperation endear him to us. How beautiful is his affection for his followers and even for his servants, and the devotion they return! How noble his reception of the news that Enobarbus has deserted him! How touchingly significant the refusal of Eros either to kill him or survive him! How pathetic and even sublime the completeness of his love for Cleopatra! His anger is born and dies in an hour. One tear, one kiss, outweighs his ruin. He believes she has sold him to his enemy, yet he kills himself because he hears that she is dead. When, dying, he learns that she has deceived him once more, no thought of reproach crosses his mind: he simply asks to be carried to her. He knows well that she is not capable of dying because he dies, but that does not sting him; when, in his last agony, he calls for wine that he may gain a moment's strength to speak, it is to advise her for the days to come. Shakespeare borrowed from Plutarch the final speech of Antony. It is fine, but it is not miraculous. The miraculous speeches belong only to his own hero:

> I am dying, Egypt, dying; only
> I here importune death awhile, until
> Of many thousand kisses the poor last
> I lay upon thy lips;

or the first words he utters when he hears of Cleopatra's death:

> Unarm, Eros: the long day's task is done,
> And we must sleep.

If he meant the task of statesman and warrior, that is not what his words mean to us. They remind us of words more familiar and less great – 'No rest but the grave for the pilgrim of love'. And he is more than love's pilgrim; he is love's martyr.

The tone, manner and rhythms of this prose have led me in the past to dismiss this passage as 'tosh', yet it is only with people capable of siding so extremely with Antony that I would care to advance the opposing thesis, that in his closing scenes Antony both talks himself out and is talked by others out of reality.

A mild beginning towards this conclusion might be made by noticing a deliberate device employed by Shakespeare to throw a classical aura round Antony. Every classical reference takes Antony off the earth we know and delivers him over to hyperbole and bombast. Taken one by one, we may not find these allusions out of place: for instance, when the soldier tells Enobarbus

> Your Emperor
> Continues still a Ioue

we may murmur, 'generous, yes, but not quite so superlative as to require the introduction of the divine', yet as they accumulate we both become aware of the author's intention and build up our resistance to the 'try-on'. When Antony tells his men 'you haue shewne all *Hectors*' we note that Antony is characteristically inflating a petty skirmish into a major campaign. The whole mode of this scene smacks of Marlowe:

> Ile giue thee Friend
> An Armour all of Gold: it was a Kings.
> He has deseru'd it, were it Carbunkled
> Like holy Phoebus Carre.

and ends on a crude boyish note:

> Trumpetters
> With brazen dinne blast you the Citties eare,
> Make mingle with our ratling Tabourines,
> That heauen and earth may strike their sounds together
> Applauding our approach.

The effect on me of Antony's self-comparison with Herakles, so far from casting over him a heroic or mythical tragic grandeur, is to make him a mere stage figure:

> The shirt of *Nessus* is vpon me, teach me
> *Alcides*, thou mine Ancestor, thy rage.
> Let me lodge *Licas* on the hornes o' th' Moone,
> And with those hands that graspt the heauiest Club,
> Subdue my worthiest selfe.

Cleopatra reinforces the impression:

> Oh hee's more mad
> Then *Telamon* for his Shield, the Boare of Thessaly
> Was neuer so imbost.

This is stock Elizabethan rhetoric: it mars Antony's efforts to meet death squarely. He is ranting in the same vein here:

> The seuen-fold shield of *Aiax* cannot keepe
> The battery from my heart. Oh cleaue my sides.
> Heart, once be stronger then thy Continent,
> Cracke thy fraile Case.

Weighing more heavily against Antony is this speech:

> Stay for me,
> Where Soules do couch on Flowers, wee'l hand in hand,
> And with our sprightly Port make the Ghostes gaze:
> *Dido*, and her *Aeneas* shall want Troopes,
> And all the haunt be ours.

This was a never-never land, even for a Roman. It makes a terrible draught on the previous scenes of the play and forces us to weigh once again the relative significance of what we have seen for ourselves and what has been merely said about the lovers. This speech itself has power, but cannot remove the impression of weak evasion: instead of living in the present and ending as a full person, Antony projects himself into an unreal future.

What turns the scale for me is the emphasis on the admiration Antony thinks they will get from the Elysian spectators. Shakespeare seems anxious to support this conceit by praising Antony up well beyond any deserts shown in the play. First, we have the repeated assertion that suicide is noble as well as prudent, and then the various forms of commentary. The most ludicrous to my mind, is that of the two soldiers who find that Antony was unable to make a clean job of his own death:

> The Starre is falne
> And time is at his Period.

Qui est-ce qu'on trompe ici? Is Shakespeare inviting our irony or an implicit acceptance? For Cleopatra merely says the same in more moving words:

> Oh Sunne,
> Burne the great Sphere thou mou'st in, darkling stand
> The varrying shore o' th' world.

It is the same Shakespeare who makes Cleopatra joke at the ludicrousness of the scene where sixteen stone of dying Antony are lugged into the monument, and immediately after makes her say:

> Had I great *Iuno's* power
> The strong wing'd Mercury should fetch thee vp,
> And set thee by Ioues side.

Here, quite inconsistently, I find in the context this allusion helps. For Antony goes off by contrast with pleasing sobriety: he merely says what North said.

But what can we do with the wonderful epitaph Cleopatra speaks before she faints?

> Oh see my women:
> The Crowne o' th' earth doth melt. My Lord?
> Oh wither'd is the Garland of the Warre,
> The Souldiers pole is falne: young Boyes and Gyrles
> Are leuell now with men: The oddes is gone,
> And there is nothing left remarkeable
> Beneath the visiting Moone.

I am unable either to feel it as generated out of her own mind or to relate it to the Antony of the play. The lines are written in by Shakespeare, and it is a pity that he did not organise a play around them. When I compare these lines with their repetition in Cleopatra's next speech this impression is reinforced. The former seem to come all the more from a mind such as we may imagine was Shakespeare's – they are his commentary on a situation he has imagined but not embodied: the latter strike me as theatrical in the best sense. They are what make Cleopatra a 'fat part', good to declaim . . . at the lips' ends, but not going deep. (Who, for instance, could believe she is fully 'there', *all* behind

> Then is it sinne,
> To rush into the secret house of death?)

A possible sign of a general loss of grip is that Antony is not the only leading personage to become the slave or dupe of words. The consequence of Cleopatra's lending herself to the self-deception of the pacification after the quarrel over the messenger may have been the frigidity of:

> Ah (Deere) if I be so
> From my cold heart let Heauen ingender haile,
> And poyson it in the sourse, and the first stone
> Drop in my necke: as it determines so
> Dissolue my life, the next Caesarion smite,
> Till by degrees the memory of my wombe,
> Together with my braue Egyptians all,
> By the discandering of this pelleted storme,
> Lye grauelesse, till the flies and Gnats of Nyle
> Haue buried them for prey.

And even before Antony's death Cleopatra has played up to his illusion about the grandeur of his petty operations:

> Lord of Lords,
> Oh infinite Vertue, comm'st thou smiling from
> The worlds great snare vncaught?

Yet though Cleopatra speaks like this to his face, she may still have a shrewd idea of the real proportions, for behind his back, we must not forget, she had said:

> He goes forth gallantly: That he and *Caesar* might
> Determine this great Warre in single fight;
> Then *Antony*; but now. Well on.

What puzzles me more, and makes me wonder what Shakespeare thought he was doing, is the deliberate insertion of a favourable Roman epitaph for Antony. We have had the Roman verdict before our eyes throughout the play. Although there have been many small suggestions that it was not to be taken as the last word on Antony, since it was based on an external view of his behaviour, yet it has often enough been sustained by internal evidence. Nothing, for instance, coming from within, has mitigated the verdict on Antony's flight at Actium. Yet now we find the Romans uniting to lament Antony as a fallen *hero*. We cannot mistake the author's intention here. Shakespeare lets himself go in his self-indulgent delight in hyperbole and gives incongruously to Caesar the following words:

> The breaking of so great a thing, should make
> A greater cracke. The round World
> Should have shooke Lyons into ciuill streets,
> And Cittizens to their dennes. The death of *Antony*
> Is not a single doome, in the name lay
> A moity of the world.

This is reinforced by 'choric' commentary:

> His taints and Honours, wag'd equal with him.
> A Rarer spirit neuer
> Did steere humanity.

But what brings out the contrast between the Antony who walked the earth and the fiction that might have been but never was, is

Cleopatra's scene with Dolabella. This is the true counterpiece to the description of Cleopatra at Cydnus:

> I dreampt there was an Emperor *Antony*.
> Oh such another sleepe, that I might see
> But such another man.

(which might remind us of Caliban:

> and sometime voices
> That if I then had wak'd after long sleepe,
> Will make me sleepe againe, and then in dreaming
> The clouds methought would open, and shew riches
> Ready to drop vpon me, that when I wak'd
> I cri'de to dreame againe.)

This at any rate is what Cleopatra says she saw in her dream:

> His face was as the Heaun'ns, and therein stucke
> A Sunne and Moone, which kept their course, & lighted
> The little o' th' earth . . .
> His legges bestrid the Ocean, his rear'd arme
> Crested the world: His voyce was propertied
> As all the tuned Spheres, and that to Friends:
> But when he meant to quaile, and shake the Orbe,
> He was as ratling Thunder. For his Bounty,
> There was no winter in't. An Automne it was,
> That grew the more by reaping: His delights
> Were Dolphin-like, they shew'd his backe aboue
> The Element they liu'd in: In his Liuery
> Walk'd Crownes and Crownets: Realms & Islands were
> As plates dropt from his pocket.

But then comes the significant exchange where, as in the piece on Cleopatra, Fancy is played off against Nature:

> Thinke you there was, or might be such a man
> As this I dreampt of?
> Gentle Madam, no.
> You Lye vp to the hearing of the Gods:
> But if there be, nor euer were one such
> It's past the size of dreaming: Nature wants stuffe
> To vie strange formes with fancie, yet t'imagine
> An *Antony* were Natures peece, 'gainst Fancie,
> Condemning shadowes quite.

What a remarkable play, we might reflect, *Antony and Cleopatra* would have been if Cleopatra had shown in her behaviour that she had often had such dreams in Antony's lifetime! Yet this is the only mode in which Antony can now be presented. It is equally significant that when Cleopatra prepares to meet Antony in the other world she recalls the part they played at Cydnus.

Do these observations taken together and shorn of what is merely personal in them call for a judgment on the play? Will it now be generally agreed that the promise of the first scene was never realised? The Antony we were to see was never shown. We are *told* I don't know how many times that he was a supreme specimen of humanity, so lofty indeed that to indicate the scale it was necessary to suppose that his nature partook of the divine. The Antony who is presented dramatically never makes us believe in these reports. Shakespeare's Antony, in fact, is not markedly more heroic and god-like than what we divine to have been Plutarch's conception. The critics who have defended Shakespeare against the charge of selling his soul to Plutarch (North) could easily point to many departures in the plot, they could also tell of departures in the drawing of Antony's character, but they say nothing of the relative stature of the two figures in the narrative and in the play. I cannot believe that Shakespeare tried very hard to make us feel, feel intimately, what he so often talks about. He has not made us know what it is for a man to be like Mars, nor has he brought us near knowing what it would be for a man to be like Bacchus. We do not get near enough to the root and springs of action that could make a life of love-making and drinking and general jollity seem the expression of a force of nature. And for those who do not require the values of Love and War to seem god-like before they can be deeply roused by them, I would say that on the human level we do not get the effective answer to the common-sense moral judgment on Antony's behaviour. I am quite sure that Shakespeare could have challenged the Elizabethan norms and given us the inside picture of a valuable love with all its attendant stresses as it conflicted with the normal judgment of decent men. I can't feel that Shakespeare could not have endowed his hero with the necessary articulateness or made us feel what was going on inside a man who could not tell us directly. So I am bound to conclude that Shakespeare was seduced by his 'angelic strength' into organic weakness. Nobody can deny that Shakespeare was playing with the heroic suggestions he failed to make dramatic. Professor G. W. Knight was not making his Antony out of nothing: but he certainly strikes me as too often having taken the will for the deed. But the will is plainly in the text: which makes the failure very painful to contemplate. Humanly, of course, we can understand that a poet might not want to repeat the agony of pushing matters painfully home. We are so greedy for the supreme pleasure of tragedy that we overlook what it costs the poet to provide it. When I call this play a failure, I do not mean that Shakespeare tried for tragedy and failed: it seems to me he just did not try. . . .

The difficulties facing all critics of this act are inherent in the play. Comment can only challenge when it refers to the palpable. So much of the play is now a matter of suggestion, of response to an almost magical play with words, to activities of what I must be content to style the imagination without providing a working definition of the word, that one man's say-so becomes unusually impertinent. I shall therefore confine my comment to a few marginal notes on Bradley, which query some of the terms but do not point to a radical difference of judgment.

First, then, as to the love that has been before us for most of the play and now comes up for a last scrutiny. Cleopatra, says Bradley, ruins a great man but shows no sense of the tragedy of his ruin. This seems true: it is fatal to the continuity of the play, if Antony's ruin has mattered to us, for it simply disposes of the question of honour. The difficulty of this is that it takes the grandeur out of her contempt for the world Antony and she have lost. Since her pronouncements on that world have not the merit of 'weighed and found wanting', we must look to what she puts in place of all that she fails to understand and respond to. A great difficulty is that it severely qualifies the meaning we can give to her 'love'. We do not require Cleopatra to be herself a great warrior – though we think the less of her as a *queen* when having claimed the right to lead her contingent at Actium she funks the issue and turns tail: but we do expect a woman in love to be able to imagine what it must mean for a man, a great general and leader of men, to imitate her. So, as our first point, we might say that after Actium Cleopatra sinks back and is no longer a sustaining partner in the love relation, somewhat as Lady Macbeth ceases to be a help to her husband after the banquet scene. She seems dazed and puzzled by the catastrophe and has to question Enobarbus – and then makes no comment when she hears his verdict. Bradley thinks she seriously meditated giving up the fallen Antony: Enobarbus clearly thought so too:

> Sir, sir, thou art so leakie
> That we must leaue thee to thy sinking, for
> Thy deerest quit thee.

The meaning of 'love' is narrowly circumscribed by what follows the reconciliation:

> Come,
> Let's haue one other gawdy night: Call to me
> All my sad Captaines, fill our Bowles once more:
> Let's mocke the midnight Bell.

Cleopatra does not suggest that their love requires a different celebration; she yields to the invitation. Although I have not been able to find the texts to support Professor L. C. Knights when, starting from the point, he comments:

> Antony ... is galvanized into feeling; there is no true access of life and energy ... Looking back, we can recall how often this love has seemed to thrive on emotional stimulants. They were necessary for much the same reason as the feasts and wine. For the continued references to feasting ... serve to bring out the element of repetition and monotony in a passion which, centring on itself, is self-consuming ...

nevertheless it reminds us how restricted are the lights Shakespeare throws on the love relation: an awful lot has to be taken for granted. Nevertheless we must not press everything equally hard in making out the case against Cleopatra. Some critics, for instance, have included Cleopatra's failure to understand what was happening to Antony in the second scene of the fourth act. I would suggest that the presence of Cleopatra and Enobarbus in that scene is merely as *ficelles* to help the author 'dramatise' the following passage from North:

> So being at supper (as it is reported), he commaunded his officers and household servauntes that waited on him at his bord, that they should fill his cuppes full, and make as muche of him as they could: for said he, you know not whether you shall doe so much for me tomorrow, or whether you

shall serve an other maister: and it may be you shall see me no more, but a dead bodie. This notwithstanding, perceiuing that his frends and men fell a weeping to heare him say so: to salue that he had spoken, he added this more vnto it, that he would not leade them to battell, where he thought not rather safely to returne with victorie, then valliantly to dye with honor.

But though this detail may not be telling, we cannot avoid a general impression. Suppose a man entered the theatre during Act IV, would he have supposed that love between Antony and Cleopatra was the central theme? More than this, would he have understood that Cleopatra was the dominant partner who had caught Antony in her toil? Although one can't measure these things, I should say we are more engaged with Cleopatra in the early part of the play when Antony is in Rome than we are in the fourth act when she is always popping in and out.

Again, if we were not already convinced that the couple were tied by love, if we merely followed the text, what would we say was uppermost in Antony's mind when he hears the false news of Cleopatra's death? Antony's mind is not easy to know: at one moment in a rage, at the next unmanned. At least he knows he ought to be dead but that he must kill Cleopatra first. When the eunuch says:

> My Mistris lou'd thee, and her Fortunes mingled
> With thine intirely.

Antony replies:

> Hence sawcy Eunuch peace, she hath betraid me,
> And shall dye the death.

And when he takes in the news, it never crosses his mind that it might have been the result of his rage. He immediately thinks, she has done the noble thing I ought to have done, she recovers stature in his eyes and becomes a queen. We see this again when Eros kills himself:

> Thrice-Nobler then my selfe,
> Thou teachest me: Oh valiant *Eros*, what
> I should, and thou could'st not, my Queene and *Eros*
> Haue by their braue instruction got vpon me
> A Noblenesse in Record.

Now although we must allow for the conventions of the theatre – Antony is going to have another dying speech – dramatically Antony thought those were his last words on earth. He returns to them when he is brought to Cleopatra:

> Not *Caesars* Valour hath o'rethrowne *Antony*,
> But *Anthonie's* hath Triumpht on it selfe.

and his actual last words are:

> A Roman, by a Roman
> Valiantly vanquish'd.

And the more I ponder this death scene the harder it becomes to think of the lovers as united. The lines that stand out are:

> Hast thou no care of me

and

> Come, away,
> This case of that huge Spirit now is cold.

Secondly, some notes and a judgment on the final scene of the play. In a sense the play picks up from Act IV, scene ii. The remainder of the play makes a continuous whole, but closes on a less ambitious note, it draws to a fine single point. There is, however, a certain amount of vain repetition. The interview with Proculeius goes over the same ground as the earlier interview with Thidias, and Cleopatra's rage against Seleucus is pale after her previous outburst and Antony's. One repetition, however, Act V, scene ii, lines 51–62, is an improvement on Act III, scene xiii, lines 158–67 (quoted above). Cleopatra is still play-acting, but she is truer here to her theatrical self. We feel she is rapidly trying out all her repertoire, and the contrast between her poses and her real calculating self is thrilling. Especially after the dream fantasy about Antony this line is very moving: 'Know you what *Caesar* meanes to do with me?' This contrast is even more poignant after the play-acting with Caesar:

> He words me Gyrles, he words me,
> That I should not be Noble to my selfe.

Yet Iras' reply, though in itself impressive, seems without relation to its context:

> Finish good Lady, the bright day is done,
> And we are for the darke.

But when Cleopatra comes to grips with her probable fate she surpasses anything previously said about suicide. Here we touch reality, for if Cleopatra in no sense can diminish the greatness of Rome, as an imperial power, she can deny Caesar the most piquant element in his triumph. What Cleopatra does is in fact to stage a *rival show*, a final show as like as possible to that which began her career with Antony, a show which requires dressing up – only this time there will be words.

These words are the natural focus for a debate on the play. The extreme at one end may well be Professor G. W. Knight's remark, 'We find an imaginative parallel in the Crucifixion.' We may wonder whether 'parallel' is the right word for

> Now no more
> The iuyce of Egypts Grape shall moyst this lip

and

> I will not drink the fruit of the vine, until the kingdom of God shall come

when we think of the manner of the two deaths. For Cleopatra's is to be a painless triumph:

> As sweet as Balme, as soft as Ayre, as gentle.

I should not dare to assert that Shakespeare had no interest at this point in possible forms of after-life and immortality, but I would advance confidently that full participation in the text requires us to note the paradox of the apparent claim to be leaving the body and the recurrent stress on 'lip' and all the other allusions to the body. If we say that Cleopatra now refines her essence, it is still an exquisite sensuality that goes out with her dying words. Her power is to be able to keep it up to the last and to show her sensual nature dominant, to end with velvety jokes drawn from memories of love passages involving the complexities of bodily touch. Unlike Bradley, I find myself now recapturing the mystery of Cleopatra, the sense that she somehow brings the qualities we associate with the spirit to bear centrally on matters we normally classify as of the flesh. Not that I find myself tempted to create a 'mystique' or 'philosophy' of the extremes of love. I come naturally to the literary query: how to characterise what I have just called her jokes? They have something of the conceit in them and extend from the merely fanciful to the 'metaphysical' or Donne-like play of the mind. I have elsewhere spoken of the finest intelligence as that which is one with what it works on. Sometimes her mind seems distinct from what she is attending to, but in the lines that move us we have to ask what faculty is at work, and what she turns death into in such flights?

The more I am willing to grant that there is no limit to the reverberations in the imagination of lines such as

> Now boast thee Death, in thy possession lyes
> A Lasse vnparalell'd

the more I would contend that what we have is a flight of imagination rather than an embodied dramatic creation. And difficult as it would be to contrast the supreme imagination and the real when we are thinking of a play, yet if we agree with Bradley that this death does not trouble us, if we feel that its import is seriously diminished by the sense that Cleopatra could have died saying 'All's had, nought's spent', then we can say that the interest aroused by Cleopatra at the end is too ideal and that she has ceased to be part and parcel of the real. In claiming that the play draws to a fine point, I am expressing a feeling that the end does not bring the whole of our minds into play and as it were set a new pattern on our being.

SOURCE: Extract from '*Anthony* [sic] *and Cleopatra*: Telling *versus* Shewing', *Cambridge Quarterly*, i (1966), 340–54.

Michael Long *Antony and Cleopatra* and the Song of Dionysos (1976)

... *Antony and Cleopatra*, opens with space, leisure and laughter ... No sooner has [Philo] been the play's first spokesman for the official

Roman view than the words and action of the play move on out of his range of vision to suggest orders of lyric intensity quite beyond Roman knowledge. If we follow his advice to 'take but good note' we shall not find our responses being much in line with his. His Roman words 'measure' and 'temper' seem comically minute as the spacious range of Antony's words is set against them. The impeding hardness of 'plated Mars' and 'the buckles on his breast' is mocked by the sinewy and voluptuous ease of movement which informs Antony and Cleopatra's speeches. The 'scuffles' of Roman imperialism seem like petty brawls in this atmosphere of leisured extravagance. And the Roman, racial jeering contained in 'a tawny front' and 'a gipsy's lust' is belied as a ludicrous insolence by the laughing and delighted civility which, coquetry notwithstanding, lives in Cleopatra's words. It is nothing like 'dotage' that we are seeing and hearing but the modes of a life incomparably richer than the precious Roman rhetoric of solemnizing grandiosity – 'office and devotion' – can ever reach. The Roman version of Egypt is at once set against the realities of Egyptian life; and at once that version is seen not only to be far from the truth but – a vital point – *comically* far from the truth. A few lines down and Cleopatra will invite the continuance of that comic comparison, mocking 'the scarce-bearded Caesar' and caricaturing the strutting rhetoric of imperial command:

> 'Do this or this;
> Take in that kingdom and enfranchise that;
> Perform't, or else we damn thee'. (I.i. 22–4)

These are the first notes of Dionysos' song, simultaneously lyrical and ribald, which will dominate the first half of the play and colour our view of Rome and Egypt throughout.

Of all the things commonly missing from criticism of *Antony and Cleopatra* a sense of this comedy is the most important. The creator of Rome in this play is the creator of Rome in *Coriolanus*; but he is also, and pre-eminently, the creator of the imperial grandiosities of the Greeks in *Troilus and Cressida*; or the creator of Hotspur, that 'mad fellow of the north' who talks in his sleep about parapets and culverins and who would have agreed with Caesar that a capacity for drinking horse-piss and stagnant water was a sufficient proof of manhood; or the creator of Falstaff with his ribald opinions about 'honour' and 'the rusty curb of old father antic the law'. The ribald, anti-imperial comedy of *Troilus and Cressida* and *Henry IV* has contributed a great deal to the portrait of Rome in *Antony and Cleopatra*; while on the other hand the comedy of lyric delight and love-play has given to the Egyptian part of the play a Bacchanalian romanticism which makes Egypt so impervious to the moralistic objections of Romans and critics alike.

In *Coriolanus* Rome was the society of anti-nature and, horribly, of anti-Eros. Its predatory attitude to Eros fuelled its cruelty and fanaticism. In *Antony and Cleopatra* Rome is similarly passionless, but the tone in which this is seen is now very different. This Rome has none of the frightening predatory language and blood-soaked violence of Cominius' praise of the warrior-hero. Neither Caesar nor Pompey, as the strong-men of the Roman world, has the terror of Coriolanus in him. Octavia, as the apogee of Roman womanhood, is a lightweight in comparison with the horrendous Volumnia; and, though formal and cold, she is almost garrulously fulsome in comparison with the scarcely audible Virgilia. Rome here, and particularly Rome in the first part of the play, has something Chaplinesque about it; or something of Rome as we might have been brought to see it by the Good Soldier Švejk; or something of the Rome of imperial inflatedness which Ezra Pound presents for the purposes of scurrilous comedy (and also for the critique of its 'anti-Eros' quality) in his *Homage to Sextus Propertius.*[1]

The Rome of the first half of *Antony and Cleopatra* is seen with airy and scurril comedy as absurd. Its great Titans, Caesar and Pompey, are petty and rather ludicrous men, peevish when they are defied, tetchy about rank and status, 'queasy' (as Agrippa happily puts it) at the 'insolence' of one who falls out of line – in Cleopatra's final opinion 'paltry' and 'absurd'. In the Rome of this part of the play we see little ('scarce-bearded') men living solemnly amid antic visions of themselves wherein they pace the world from edge to edge, frown at levity in the name of 'our graver business' and chase such farcical ambitions as that of Pompey who wants to own the sea. Its characteristic language is of a kind for which Pound's *Homage* will provide description – the language of the 'large-mouthed product' designed to 'expound the distentions of empire'. Pound has his Rome see its great imperial destiny in terms of laughable pettiness: 'Tibet shall be full of Roman policemen'. In Shakespeare's play imperial Caesar, in triumph, is no more than 'the universal landlord'.

We must be clear as to this tone, and have ears attuned to it, for though it seems to me extremely pervasive it has also been subtle enough to elude many critics and producers altogether. But subtlety is of its essence, for Shakespeare uses it not to provide the open torrent of spoof and parody of Pound's poem (or indeed to repeat the scurrilous acerbity of his own *Troilus and Cressida*) but, more gently, to ripple with disbelieving laughter and a quiet sense of knowingness beneath the orotundities and gaucheries of Roman rhetoric, politicking, propriety and self-opinion.

In I.i, as we have seen, the tone announces itself – its humour brought into play when Egypt is first made to sound so delightfully different from Philo's Roman severity on the subject, and then pointed to and enjoyed by the Cleopatra who mimics the order-giving Caesar. I.ii and I.iii then give much of their time to creating a mood of playfulness and levity, lived in Egypt in the bawdy-talk of the soothsayer and Cleopatra's women, inhabiting Enobarbus' 'light answers' of a bawdy kind on Cleopatra's 'celerity in dying' etc., and inhabiting the coquetry and love-play which is interlaced with incandescent lyricism in Cleopatra's farewell to Antony. We note, in I.ii, that the 'Roman thought' which has struck Antony is said by Cleopatra not to have destroyed his 'passion' or his 'love' but his 'mirth'; and we note too that while we have been asked to begin to create the figure of Antony as the 'Herculean Roman' in our minds as part of our conception of him, we have also been asked to see

> How this Herculean Roman does become
> The carriage of his chafe (I.iii. 84–5)

– a picture of a hero in a pique, whereby delighted levity comes to the rescue of what might have been overly grandiose.

Thus attuned we come to I.iv to find the dead weight of a solemn slab of Caesarism interposing its ludicrous presence in this lightened world. In Caesar's opening declaration we catch the authentic tone of weighty self-opinion which Cleopatra has already mimicked out of court:

> You may see, Lepidus, and henceforth know,
> It is not Caesar's natural vice to hate
> Our great competitor. (I.iv. 1–3)

And in the ensuing moralistics, which clearly carry the hatred he has just disavowed, the ripples of our amusement are set going at the expense of an ignorant, scarce-bearded man pouting with a sense of moral outrage:

(Antony) is not more manlike
Than Cleopatra, nor the queen of Ptolemy
More womanly than he (I.iv. 5–7)

He is a slight man talking largely; and talking primly too (on the immaturity of which pleasure-seeking is a sign), and snobbishly (his distaste for Antony's keeping company with 'knaves that smell of sweat'), and parsonically (sermonizing to Lepidus on the man who is 'the abstract of all faults', from the observation of whom moral lessons can be learnt provided the observer is not 'too indulgent'). Throughout the scene Shakespeare's delicate humour, summoned to our minds already by the delighted levity which Egypt has presented, stalks Caesar subtly, making us quietly aware of every trace of stiffness, self-importance and inflatedness with which the universal landlord, chaste spokesman for old father antic the law, is replete.

The opening Act is so structured as to give Caesar little chance against the ripples of mirthful disbelief inspired by the airy lightness of tone in which life in Egypt is conducted. His appearance in this scene, to talk with a pout and a stamp of the imperial foot against Antony's 'lascivious wassails', has much mischief done to it by having to come after we have seen Antony, Cleopatra, Enobarbus, Charmian, Iras and the Soothsayer living a life which in no way prompts our enthusiasm for his judgments of it; and by having to come before the closing scene of the Act wherein Egyptian blood flows again not only in the language of passion

Be'st thou sad or merry,
The violence of either thee becomes,
So does it no man else (I.v. 59–61)

but also in the language of mirth or gamesomeness, as in Cleopatra's inability to take pleasure in aught an eunuch has or Charmian's baiting her with the memory of her 'salad days'. If we know how to hear the Act's subtly mirthful tone we shall know that we have seen the antics of Caesarism subjected to the *vif* of an easeful but probing scepticism which is given life and licence by the counter-comedy of Egypt where moments of incandescent lyricism rise repeatedly from a fertile chaos of humour, bawdy and animal vitality, all tangled together in a 'gamesome' vision of Dionysos' powers.

Built upon this basis, Act Two and the first six scenes of Act Three take the comedy of delicate derision and the comedy of festivity and play to exuberant heights. On the Roman side Pompey appears, full of self-importance, with:

> If the great gods be just, they shall assist
> The deeds of justest men (II.i. 1–2)

and then spends his time in II.i gloating over his watery dominions ('the sea is mine') and rearing the higher his opinion of himself. In II.ii the fop Lepidus, beginning already to look like a figure from Donne's satires, is pushed about by Enobarbus' sharp tongue just as hopelessly as he was by Caesar's moral lessons; and, in the negotiations that follow, Antony (now struck by Roman thoughts) and Caesar (trying to pretend he never spoke 'derogately' about the lascivious wassailer) experience a rough passage at the hands of Shakespeare's wanton laughter, aided as it is by some fine stage-business:

> *Caes.* Sit
> *Ant.* Sit, sir.
> *Caes.* Nay then. (*They sit.*) (II.ii. 30–2)

and by Enobarbus' capacity for an irreverent assessment of the politicking of the 'noble partners' who are in the act of becoming 'brothers':

> Or, if you borrow one another's love for the instant, you may, when you hear no more words of Pompey, return it again. You shall have time to wrangle in when you have nothing else to do. (II.ii. 107–10)

Enobarbus, though told to be quiet and mend his manners, clearly wins his playful skirmish, and celebrates his victory with the famous description of Cleopatra in her barge, which has the Roman Maecenas boggle-eyed with amazement yet still Roman enough to miss the point entirely. 'Now Antony must leave her utterly', he ventures. 'Never!', says Enorbarbus, with probability enough. Then Maecenas:

> If beauty, wisdom, modesty, can settle
> The heart of Antony, Octavia is
> A blessed lottery to him. (II.ii. 245–7)

to the extraordinary unlikeliness of which there can be no reply, so the scene ends without Enobarbus bothering to give one.

In II.iii the blessed lottery makes its sad contribution to the proceedings as we first see the frigid formality of the Antony/Octavia marriage; and then, after Egypt has interposed with another sumptuously playful extravagance of unbridled emotionalism and mirth:

> *Cleo.* Give me some music – music, moody food
> Of us that trade in love.
> *All.* The music, ho!
>
> *Enter* MARDIAN *the Eunuch*
>
> *Cleo.* Let it alone! Let's to billiards, (II.v. 1–3)

the Act concludes with the delicious hilarity of the scene on Pompey's galley.

The scene stirs one's memories of Gadshill, or of the great set-pieces on the Greek and Trojan camps in *Troilus and Cressida*. Lepidus is now clearly a character from Donne – the semi-travelled fop who is quick to believe and pass on reports of the marvels of foreign parts:

> Nay, certainly, I have heard the Ptolemies' pyramises are very goodly things. Without contradiction I have heard that.
> (II.vii. 33–5)

And Enobarbus duly makes haste to derive as much amusement as possible from the spectacle of a member of the great triumvirate in his cups:

> *Eno.* There's a strong fellow, Menas.
> (*Pointing to the servant who carries off Lepidus.*)
> *Men.* Why?
> *Eno.* 'A bears the third part of the world, man; see'st not?
> (II.vii. 87–9)

But Caesar and Pompey scarcely fare better. The great Pompey responds like a shoddy little gangster (but burdened with a sense of propriety) to the proposal that his guests should have their throats slit:

> In me 'tis villainy:
> In thee't had been good service. (II.vii. 73–4)

Caesar, feeling himself befouled by food and drink, 'antick'd' by merriment, and opining solemnly that 'our graver business/Frowns at this levity', is no more prepossessing. And when the Egyptian Bacchanals scatter the 'great fellows' and the revelry goes below stairs with Enobarbus and 'Hoo' and 'Hoo' we have watched a scene in which the spirit of the Lord of Misrule has done his traditional comic damage to the stiffnesses, repressions and formalisms of the law.

Egypt in this Act has been represented by the scene which began with Cleopatra calling for 'music, moody food' and went on with her wild rampage of haling the messenger up and down – both of which performances are too gustily alive with emotional turmoil, the creative chaos of Dionysos, for moral point-making to constitute an adequate response to them. And it has also been represented by the description of the barge. Here Dionysos is brought alive as a breeding chaos of self-replenishing energies creating kinds of luxury and magnificence which have nothing to do with mere 'ornament' or 'ostentation'. All is swarming with life; and once again it is all laughter-filled, gamesome.

Shakespeare found for this passage in Plutarch a description of luxury as lavish exhibition and show for which the moderate-minded historian had a tempered disdain. It was a part of the headily flamboyant spirit of over-played laxity which caught Antony in its trammels and made him fritter away his manhood in 'childish sports ... and idle pastimes'. All the emphasis of Plutarch's description, as translated by North, is on the lavish expense of 'gold and silver and of riches and other sumptuous ornaments' used by a calculating woman, mature in the ways of the world, to create a pageant of idle splendour:

(her barge) ... the poop whereof was of gold, the sails of purple, and the oars of silver, which kept stroke in rowing after the sound of the music of flutes, howboys, citherns, viols, and such other instruments as they played upon in the barge. And now for the person of herself: she was laid under a pavilion of cloth of gold of tissue, apparelled and attired like the goddess Venus commonly drawn in picture; and hard by her, on either hand of her, pretty fair boys apparelled as painters do set forth god Cupid, with little fans in their hands, with the which they fanned wind upon her. Her ladies and gentlewomen also, the fairest of them were apparelled like the nymphs Nereides (which are the mermaids of the waters) and like the Graces, some steering the helm, others tending the tackle and ropes of the barge, out of which there came a wonderful passing sweet savour of perfumes, that perfumed the wharf's side, pestered with innumerable multitudes of people.[2]

Shakespeare's lyrical imagination transformed this pageant of artifice into a picture of richness which seems like the florescence of nature itself. Inanimate things become animated in this general florescence of the world – the winds 'love-sick', the water 'amorous', the ropes of the barge swelling in (sexual) response to animate touch, the banks of the river having 'sense'. And the whole spectacle, in Shakespeare's version of it, is filled with a self-fuelling and self-replenishing fire wherein 'fancy' and 'nature' dance a playful dialectic of their respective powers. As part of this every-burning energy the fans carried by Cleopatra's boys

> did seem
> To glow the delicate cheeks which they did cool,
> And what they undid did. (II.ii.207–9)

As another manifestation of it Cleopatra, hopping through the public street until she is breathless,

> spoke, and panted,
> That she did make defect perfection,
> And, breathless, pow'r breathe forth. (II.ii. 234–6)

And again:

> she makes hungry
> Where most she satisfies; for vilest things
> Become themselves in her, that the holy priests
> Bless her when she is riggish. (II.ii. 241–4)

This is the poetry of Shakespeare's lyric-romantic mind at its finest. The innermost power of it is in that phrase 'become themselves', or on the rhythm of 'undid did', 'defect perfection' and 'breathless, pow'r breathe forth'. It is the poetry of the metamorphoses and transformations of Queen Mab, building an extravagant lyric power out of a rapid and close apprehension of the processes of the organic. It is a poetry incomparably kinetic – or comparable only with the poetry of the world of light and space which Macbeth lost. Egypt's ability to generate such powers, with their attendant human qualities of sexual vitality and laughter, not only mocks the absurd pretension and juvenile insolence of Roman imperialism. It mocks all moralistics too, having in itself as it does the very essence of the Dionysiac which is seen by Shakespeare, here as in festive comedy, as a *sine qua non* of full psychic life.

So in the first Act the interposition of Rome in a predominantly Egyptian world makes Rome look petty and ludicrous. In the second Act, which has an opposite structure, the interposition of Egypt in a predominantly Roman world annihilates Romanness by its fire and colour and demands an absolute of recognition from the audience. In the Third Act the slow and swaying comedy of Dionysos' song continues, revelling through the contrast between the frigidity of Octavia/Antony and the gusty exaggerations of Cleopatra's enthusiasms: through Enobarbus and Agrippa's merriment at the sham courtesies of the politicians (to which language Lepidus then makes a characteristically ludicrous contribution); and through Enobarbus' later comments on the fall from the triumvirate of the 'poor third':

> Then, world, thou hast a pair of chaps – no more;
> And throw between them all the food thou hast,
> They'll grind the one the other. (III.v. 13–15)

It all leads excellently to III.vi (before the change in the play's tone) where Rome's deflation by laughter is at its best again.

In this scene the ribaldry of Dionysos does its worst with Caesar before the catastrophe of the play becomes imminent in III.vii. It begins with another stamp of the imperial foot – 'Contemning Rome, he has done all this' – and another petulant exhibition of his snobbery – 'I' th' common show-place'. It sees Agrippa hitting that exact and unfortunate word 'queasy' to describe Rome's feelings about Antony's 'insolence'. It sees Caesar hoarding up bits of the world for himself (like Lepidus' 'Revenue'), and wanting to hoard up more (like 'Armenia'), while sending off messengers with cheap lies to excuse himself. Then, suddenly, it sees the arrival of Octavia: too suddenly for Caesar, who is thereby prevented from laying on 'an augmented greeting' to show 'the ostentation of our love' – though after forty lines or so he has gathered himself and is launched:

> Welcome to Rome;
> Nothing more dear to me. You are abus'd
> Beyond the mark of thought, and the high gods,
> To do you justice, make their ministers
> Of us and those that love you. (III.vi. 85–9)

On that claim, made by the universal landlord, to some kind of ministerial status in a platonic, celestial empire, the scene's chicane at the expense of Caesarism has reached its climax. It is quickly finished off by Maecenas with his mouth very full of outrage:

> Only th' adulterous Antony, most large
> In his abominations, turns you off,
> And gives his potent regiment to a trull
> That noises it against us. (III.vi. 93–6)

Rome has been dealt with by comedy. The catastrophic product of its imperial power will now begin to come forth.

We have reached what is almost exactly the mid-point in this tragedy and yet still the comedy of Dionysos dominates the play with its interlinked tones of scurrility and playful lyricism. Rather as in *Romeo and Juliet*, a 'tragedy of love' spends the bulk of its earlier energies in the creation of a dramatic life both festal and ribald. I labour the point about the play's comic vitality because if we do not feel both the festal laughter of Egyptian lyricism and the ribald laughter directed at Rome we shall read the play more solemnly than it requires and miss the very essence of the vision of the Dionysiac which it has to impart.

It is in one way similar to the case of *Macbeth*, which, without that quality of festal delight in its basic vision of the Apollonian, would have been a solemn, religious-pastoral pageant of Order. Without the delighted levity of the Dionysiac, *Antony and Cleopatra* would be a far lesser play than it is – serving either to advance a beglamoured myth of romantic love or (by undermining such a myth with moral detraction) to advance a cautionary tale. But (again as with *Macbeth*) the play's vision is less 'organized' or 'fixed' into a system of opinion than either myth-making or myth-deflating. It captures alive its vision of the Dionysiac – as much a *sine qua non* of human vitality as was the Apollonian a *sine qua non* of humane ordonnance.

Humour is of the essence of this. The ribald comedy of disbelief in Rome is as much a part of Dionysiac life as is the lyricism of Egyptian passion. It carries the playful intelligence of the Dionysiac, its quick-witted vitality and humane freedom from code and law; and in the case of Egyptian passional life itself, interlaced with festive notes of topsy-turvy and misrule, the playfulness of the Dionysiac is again of supreme importance. It distinguishes the lyric of Egypt from the 'heroic' or 'transcendental' lyricism of many high romanticisms of love. This is not the love of Wagner's *Tristan and Isolde* or of Rubek and Irena in *When We Dead Awaken*. It has no other-wordly attachments and involves no flesh-despising or flesh-transcending. It lacks the fierce and self-isolating egotism of heroic passion and it lacks that hankering after darkness and dissolution which brings the language of mystery-religions into the romance of love. It does not thrive upon the sublimation of Eros into religious or aesthetic terms, bent as it is neither upon purity nor upon divinization.[3]

In comparison with the passion of *Tristan and Isolde*, the passional life of Egypt is full of the richness of the commonplace and the mundane. With the fibrous tangle of its roots deep in the slime of the Nile it is bent upon flowering in the light of the sun, not plunging into the darkness of religious mystery to find therein redemption from the false appearances of the daylight world. Being thus commonplace, rooted in the organic and content with the real, it is in essence laughter-filled. The uninhibitedness of laughter is essential to it, as is laughter's commonplace, social gaiety. The exuberance of laughter is, as in many great eroticisms, including those of Blake and Pound whom I have already brought forward for assistance, seen as an intrinsic part of the exuberance of sexuality. It is therefore as characteristic of Egyptian passion to be both *playful* and *erotic* as it is for Wagner's image of passion to be *heroic, sublimated* and *unsmiling*. In that difference the greater humanity and greater *vif* of Shakespearean romanticism seem to me to lie.

So we come to the play's imminent catastrophe with such a vision fully realized before us, and the fulness of romantic life which the vision carries determines our response to the catastrophe. It determines our response to Rome's menace, which now takes over in our minds from our earlier sense of its derisoriness; and it also determines our response to the havoc and panic created by the Dionysiac quality of Egypt itself in response to threat. Both factors are important – Rome's destructive power and thrust and Egypt's own propensity for calamity.

Rome's destructive intrusion into the Egyptian world is terribly swift and quite decisive. In four scenes of scarcely 100 lines between them the organized power of Rome will 'cut the Ionian sea' and rout the forces of Antony and Egypt. Canidius says:

> This speed of Caesar's
> Carries beyond belief (III.vii. 74–5)

and with that we get a chilling sense of the irresistible. For the rest of the play Caesar in Egypt is a colonialist ravager, bearing the armoured and calculating weight of an empire to the destruction of a flamboyantly alive culture. By III.xii he is installed and trading in the ugly 'realities'. Thyreus talks of his protective influence as 'his shroud', aptly thereby catching the tone of his regimen. At the beginning of Act Four more Realpolitik sees him pleased to use Antony's own soldiers to 'fetch him in' like a hunted animal. In IV.vi he is talking of 'universal peace' – an idea which is made hollow and unlovely by its placement in the midst of Enobarbus' desolation and his revelations as to Caesar's way with men who desert to him.

The low realism of Caesar's powers feels deadly and irresistible again in IV.xi:

> To the vales,
> And hold our best advantage. (IV.xi. 3–4)

The public humiliation envisaged as their fate in Rome first by Antony and then by Cleopatra is a characteristic part of his procedures; and while some of his grief for Antony's death is clearly very genuine he goes on from expressing it, unruffled and undeflected, to plan the capture and use of Cleopatra. His vaunted gentleness and promised civility are lies: the reality of his political presence, again swift and efficient, is caught in the scene where Proculeius follows his talk of a 'princely hand' which is 'full of grace' by rushing the monument with easy success. Caesar is not savage, as Coriolanus is; but there can be no doubting the bleakness and lowness of his presence, the humanly impoverished nature of his authority, the mere efficiency of his marshalling of things.

It is important to note that record of a low power and its deadly weight which the latter part of the play gives us. The hysterical note in Antony's response to it and the wild panic of Cleopatra's gyrations cannot fairly be seen for what they are unless we see that they take place in the path of an oncoming and irresistible machine of conquest. It is perhaps a little like the panic-stricken flight of the princes and then of Macduff in *Macbeth*, or the controversial scene IV.iii in that play where Malcolm and Macduff reveal some apparently absurd squirmings of the spirit – until we realize that this is a picture of men who are more delicately alive and therefore more vulnerable than the machine of power with which they are living. That does not fully 'explain' the crazedness of Cleopatra's and Antony's behaviour in the latter part of the play, nor is it intended to. But it gives us some necessary context whereby a part of the truth can be seen.

But the other part of the matter, and the major part, concerns the nature of the Dionysiac itself, and it sends us, as we consider it, back through the long history of Shakespeare's dealings in tragedy and comedy alike with the hazards and dangers which live in the volatile and creative chaos of kinesis. Even in comedy the experience of the dream-wood of Puck and the fairies was fraught with hazard and it confronted the adventurer with the fear of the unknowable. The journey through Dionysiac tumult turns out to be liberating, joy-giving; but while the journey lasts that outcome is far from clear and inevitable. It is easy to suppose a bush a bear. And indeed it may well have *been* a bear – for we always come from these comedies of the kinetic with a sense that those who have traversed the wild and come out of it replenished have done so with a fair amount of luck. Particularly in the later comedies, preceding the plays of the tragic period and carrying as they do certain premonitions of tragedy, this sense of people who are simply *lucky* is strong. Olivia and Orsino are, as luck would have it, steered through currents too turbulent for Malvolio; and Beatrice and Benedick are felt to be 'lucky to get away with it' when they harvest all the quickness of passional life contained in their wit while the chaff of its isolating aggression is blown carelessly away.

The comedies always record this sense of fortunate chance in the way that the kinetic is endured. It is their witness to Shakespeare's 'high-force' world of a romanticism which is tough and realistic rather than complacent. To live in the tumult of Dionysos is to live creatively, but also to live exposed – without the stabilizing certainties of social evaluation and selection which support dwellers in an unmagical, workaday world. And in tragedy a realistic record of what that tumult feels like to one upon whom its forces are unleashed is given in the life of Lear, the 'poor perdu' on the heath. From contact with the wild flows energy, and the greatest imaginative forces of the psyche. But such contact can only be got from being perilously close to destruction and perilously exposed to torment.

In some sense it will therefore always involve the 'shirt of Nessus' which Antony wears when he is convinced that Cleopatra has betrayed him again. But it will also involve (with characteristic Shakespearean ambiguity) something far less 'elevated' than that – a kind of ludicrousness, exhibited by a mind subject to the mischief of Puck, the idiot bamboozlement of a mind tossed hither and thither without dignity, composure or ordonnance by the currents of racing mischief which are an intrinsic part of the high-force world finding their living emblems in Puck and Queen Mab. In comedy that mischief is hurly-burly, though it can occasionally hurt people as it hurts Malvolio. In tragedy it is the awful mischief that the world does to Lear, introducing that element of the grotesque into his tragic experience which was recorded when the thunder *laughed* at the folly of an old man venting his rage on the non-existent daughters of Poor Tom.

It is a sense of all this, generated by the laughing vision of a creative Dionysos, which we need for the latter part of *Antony and Cleopatra*. For there, under pressure from the dead hand of Rome, but also under the intrinsic pressure of the Dionysiac itself, Antony and Cleopatra go through a double process which is humiliating and exalting at the same time, grotesque and magnificent, an ebbing and decrescence of the spirit which is at the same time a spiritual triumph. There is no point in trying to sort out the pros and cons of it all to award moral points for and against. There is a certain moralizing tardiness of the imagination in the mind which wishes to conceive of one part existing without the other – the same moralizing tardiness which wants to feel that Lear is 'learning' and 'being redeemed' but which also wants to reserve the right to make a moral point or two about some of the things he says while the terrible process is going on. In *Antony and Cleopatra* the whole tangle of Dionysiac elements can only be taken as being of a piece, the whole chaos of it all taken as it is in the certain knowledge, imparted by this great romanticism, that without these grotesqueries there will be no creative life, without these indignities (painfully there when Antony botches his suicide, for example) there will be no possibility of Egyptian 'fire and air'. Again it is the case that if you banish Plump Jack you will banish all the world: banish the triple-turned whore and the strumpet's fool and you will simply make over the world to the bleak conveniences of Caesarism.

If we have heard the full power and range of Dionysos' song in the first half of the play, and understood both its high lyricism and its low humour, we should have no difficulty with the double progress of its major creators in the second half. Instead it will come with beautiful inevitability – the absurd bravado of Antony which Caesar summarily snubs, the hysterical and self-indulgent notes that now run through the vitality of his mind, the desperation of his efforts to recreate with his 'sad captains' the old life of supper, carousing and 'rattling tabourines', his humiliating failure to bring off the noble death he proposes; and the hideous whimsicality of Cleopatra's feigned death, the vacillating distractedness that runs through all her dealings with Caesar, the hysterical notes that she too sounds at moments in her grief and confusion: all of it will come through as the inevitable, essential, inalienable concomitant of that spirit which produces the contrary movement of the play's great lyric and triumphant end. Even Caesar catches a glimpse of the duality in the end – the 'strong toil of grace' catches exactly the unavoidably paradoxical nature of the forces involved. If it is for a moment within the mental compass even of the universal landlord, I find it hard to think that it should be beyond the powers of critics and producers.

That 'lyric and triumphant end' is, of course, what we get in the play's incomparable exhibition of the poetry of wanton, romantic exuberance and charmed flight which I have traced through from the plays of the mid-1590s. It reaches its apex in Cleopatra's speech of 'immortal longings' and 'fire and air', but it has been growing steadily to that peak ever since the 'sad captains' and the eclipse of the 'terrene moon' in III.xiii, where the decrescence of Egypt first began to produce the poignantly continuing autumnal fire which comes from a bounty with 'no winter in't'. Shrunk and dispersed almost to extinction, Egypt simply cannot help bringing forth from the strong toil of its grace the succession of wonderful images of exultation which share the last two Acts with the grotesque twists and turns of panic and humiliation. Out of the continually reiterated opposites of light and dark, sprightliness and collapse and (again) the dancing dialectic of nature and fancy whereby Cleopatra expresses what in Antony was 'past the size of dreaming' – out of these reiterated contraries comes the progression of this living and branching lyric.

I can find no more spirit of hesitation or qualification accompanying this song of Dionysos than I could find such a spirit accompanying the song of Apollo in *Macbeth*. Here as there the lyric is created in the full, wakeful knowledge of the power of the actual. But that does not mean that it is the function of the actual to make us receive the lyric in a qualified way; rather it makes our acclaim of it, again, a *tragic* acclaim. In *Macbeth* the humane fulness of the Apollonian involved a price, which served to remind us that the Apollonian dream was part of a tragic vision. The price was to be seen in that precariousness or vulnerability with which (as in Banquo) an unarmoured, humane ordonnance sustained itself in open and hence dangerous contact with a wild world containing witches. So too in *Antony and Cleopatra* the fulness of Dionysos involves a price, which again has to do with precariousness and vulnerability, and again makes it a part of an essentially tragic vision. The life of Egypt gets its exuberant and wanton energy from constant proximity to the tumult of the kinetic. It is thence that it draws into itself the tremendous resources of energy that place the quality of its life so far beyond the reach of Rome. But by virtue of that very proximity its life is lived in constant peril. It is constantly on a brink of self-destruction or self-dissolution; and it is people living on that brink whom we see create the song of Dionysos but also the panic and hysteria of their later life.

In *Macbeth*, as I said, Shakespeare's sense of this precariousness prompts him to no shuddering back from it into the securities of the Doric. So too in *Antony and Cleopatra* there is no shuddering back into the arms of Caesar. The critics who have had their 'reservations', let alone those who have followed T. S. Eliot in feeling that this play was a study in infatuation, seem to me to have been involved in just such a retreat from the furious but generous energies of Shakespeare's tragic metaphysic. That retreat might have been avoided had the connexions between tragedy and festive comedy been better understood; or had more people known as surely as Nietzsche did that 'one must still have chaos in oneself to be able to give birth to a dancing star'.

SOURCE: Extract from *The Unnatural Scene: a study in Shakespearean tragedy* (London, 1976), pp. 241–59.

NOTES

(Renumbered by the editors.)

1. Ezra Pound, *Collected Shorter Poems* (London 1952), 225–47. I quote below from this edition.

2. *Shakespeare's Plutarch*, ed. T. J. B. Spencer (Harmondsworth, 1964), p. 201.

3. This is much indebted to Denis de Rougemont's excellent study of the idea of divinizing love as carried by the Tristan myth (*Passion and Society*, tr. Montgomery Belgion, London 1956, revised edn).

Leonard Tennenhouse *Antony and Cleopatra* and the Theater of Punishment (1986)

We might consider *Antony and Cleopatra* as both the easiest and the most difficult of Shakespeare's tragedies for us to read. The language of the play translates so well into modern cultural terms that more than one critic has read the play as if it were a Renaissance version of a modern romance on the order of *Wuthering Heights*. For this very reason, it proves most difficult to understand this play in relation to other Jacobean tragedies and the poetics of display which gave them their form. The sexual relationship between Antony and Cleopatra displaces the political struggles within the Roman empire to the point where sexuality – at least from a modern perspective – appears to transcend politics in the play. Even the most dedicated historical critic feels hard pressed to think otherwise and therefore to maintain his or her concern for the vicissitudes of state power in this play. But, I will argue, this temptation to say the play is about love rather than politics is a form of seduction which Shakespeare himself has built into *Antony and Cleopatra*. He sees to it that his audience feels the seduction of a world independent of patriarchal power all the while knowing such a world is impossible. Where the modern reader feels the utopian attraction of a private world free of ideology, however, the early seventeenth-century theater-goer would have rejected it because of the undesirable political features inherent in such a utopia.

Contrary to novelistic strategies, Shakespeare's drama sets up the possibility of detaching sexuality from politics only to demonstrate the preposterousness of thinking of the body this way. *Antony and Cleopatra* resembles *King Lear* in the respect that kinship and kingship constitute a single strategy for distributing political power and thus for understanding the operations of such power in the world. But if *Antony and Cleopatra* seems somehow more mythic in its presentation of this theme, it is because the play self-consciously interweaves the various themes of Jacobean culture and works through the same problematic terms of its most important categories – sexuality and politics. Like other assaults on the political body – the senate's willingness to overrule Desdemona's father, Lear's attempt to divide his kingdom among his daughters, or Lady Macbeth's usurpation of patriarchal prerogatives – Antony's profession of love flies in the face of political reality to threaten the most basic law of Renaissance culture:

> Let Rome in Tiber melt, and the wide arch
> Of the rang'd empire fall! Here is my space,
> Kingdoms are clay; our dungy earth alike
> Feeds beast as man; the nobleness of life
> Is to do thus [*embracing*] – when such a mutual pair
> And such a twain can do't, in which I bind,
> [On] pain of punishment, the world to weet
> We stand up peerless. (I.i. 33–40)

In making this statement, Antony obviously calls for a complete separation of love from nationalism, but his claim for the legitimacy of this relationship ultimately requires much more in the way of a cultural transformation than this. In his affection for, or his dotage on the Egyptian queen – depending on whose view one adopts – nobleness springs neither from aristocratic birth nor from the metaphysics of blood. It is engendered by the queen's embrace. Their relationship, in short, requires nothing less than a semiotic apocalypse. The basis of meaning itself – and with it the mating and mismating of terms – will henceforth be decided according to nature rather than the distinctions culture makes between nations or even between east and west. Any Jacobean audience would, I think, have recognized instantly the nature of the delusion. Antony can not actually separate politics from sexuality in this speech or for that matter anywhere else in the play. The very desire to have sovereignty over one's sexual relations and therefore to construct a private world within the public domain is an inherently political act. The play clearly demonstrates that by desiring a Cleopatra rather than a Fulvia or an Octavia, Antony does not remove himself from political history. Rather, the consequences of his desire change the course of history itself.

In the Elizabethan plays, union with the aristocratic female was always a political act. In fact, desire for the female and desire for political power could not be distinguished one from the other. But in Jacobean drama, we have noted, the iconic bond between the aristocratic female and the body politic is broken. No longer conceived as a legitimate means for access to membership in the corporate body, the aristocratic female has the potential to pollute. Nowhere is this clearer than with Cleopatra. Using her, Shakespeare undertakes his most thorough revision of that figure of the autochthonous female which had uses so central to Elizabethan representations of power. Cleopatra is Egypt. As such, however, she embodies everything that is not English according to the nationalism which developed under Elizabeth as well as to the British nationalism later fostered by James. It is perhaps difficult for us to see Cleopatra as such a threat to the political body. She contrasts Egyptian fecundity, luxury and hedonism to Rome's penury, harshness and self denial. The fact is, however, that no matter how well we romanticize her, Shakespeare has represented her in much the same terms Bakhtin uses to identify the grotesque – or popular – body in Renaissance culture. Shakespeare clearly endows her with all the features of carnival. These define her as the ultimate subject and object of illicit desire as Enobarbus's well known description suggests.

> Age cannot wither her, nor custom stale
> Her infinite variety. Other women cloy
> The appetites they feed, but she makes hungry
> Where most she satisfies; for vilest things
> Become themselves in her, that the holy priests
> Bless her when she is riggish. (II.ii. 234–9)

A body that incorporates the basest things represents the very antithesis of aristocratic power. It is that which threatens to pollute the aristocratic community. Egypt's queen thus resembles other Jacobean females who in desiring or being desired become a source of pollution. That such a sexual threat poses a threat to the political body is repeated in several different variations. His sexual bond to Cleopatra strips Antony of his military judgement, deprives him of prowess in battle, and deceives him into committing suicide.

Unlike this Jacobean rendering, Elizabethan versions of the Antony and Cleopatra story, like the sources for *King Lear*, represent the threat to the body politic in terms of division and inversion. *The Tragedie of Antonie* (1595), the Countess of Pembroke's translation of Garnier's play, begins with the following, "After the overthrowe of Brutus and Cassius, the libertie of Rome being now utterly oppressed, and the Empire settled in the hands of Octavius Caesar and Marcus Antonius. . . ."[1] In Daniel's *The Tragedie of Cleopatra* (1599), the action begins after Antony has committed suicide. Tragic consequences develop, then, from competition for political supremacy. In his version of this story, however, Shakespeare makes certain that the threat to Rome comes from an external rather than internal source. This is the first condition for the staging of pollution and its resolution, the scene of punishment. First Labienus with Parthian troops attacks Roman garrisons on the Asian border, and then Pompey attacks Rome's "borders maritime" in the Mediterranean. In both cases, the play makes it quite clear that Rome is thus besieged because Antony has been, in Caesar's words, "rioting in Alexandria." For one thing, Pompey readily agrees to a truce when he hears that Antony has returned to Rome. For another, we see that the Roman world can tolerate division; even competition between Antony and Caesar is not in itself a bad thing. As long as they can exchange women as Caesar and Antony do, these powerful men remain part of a common political body. Even when Caesar seizes Lepidus or breaks the treaty with Pompey, he does not really endanger the nation. In a word, all serious threats to Rome stem from Antony's alliance with Cleopatra.

To so locate the source of political disorder is to represent such disorder as pollution. Why else would Shakespeare dwell on the danger of the offspring of Antony and Cleopatra. As Caesar explains to his friends Maecenas and Agrippa, Antony's mismating with Egypt has engendered another illegitimate aristocracy whose blood will contend for legitimate authority over Rome:

I' th' market-place, on a tribunal silver'd,
Cleopatra and himself in chairs of gold
Were publicly enthron'd. At the feet sat
Caesarion, whom they call my father's son,
And all the unlawful issue that their lust
Since then hath made between them. Unto her
He gave the stablishment of Egypt, made her
Of lower Syria, Cyprus, Lydia,
Absolute queen.
Maec. This in the public eye?
Caes. I' th' common show-place, where they exercise.
His sons [he there] proclaim'd the [kings] of kings . . .
(III.vi. 3–13)

To his sister, Caesar more bluntly describes the danger Antony's alliance with Cleopatra poses: "He hath given his empire / Up to a whore" (III.vi. 66–7).

In destroying Antony and Cleopatra, Shakespeare accomplishes two things. First he relocates the sources of legitimate authority in Rome. Secondly, he establishes the figure of uncompromising male power over that of the autochthonous female. Shakespeare not only illegitimizes this figure of power by linking it to that of the grotesque body, he also subjects the body of the other to ritual purification. Shakespeare gives Cleopatra the entire last act to gather up the features associated with illegitimate authority. Having denied her the privilege of committing suicide in the Roman manner, he dresses her as Queen of Egypt, surrounds her with her eunuch and ladies in waiting, and then kills her off with an Egyptian viper. This elaborate scene of punishment purges the world of all that is not Roman. In this manner of delivering the world over to patriarchy, however, Shakespeare makes it very clear that a whole way of figuring out power has been rendered obsolete. One might call his play Shakespeare's elegy for the signs and symbols which legitimized Elizabethan power. Of these, the single most important figure was that of the desiring and desired woman, her body valued for its ornamental surface, her feet rooted deep in a kingdom.

SOURCE: Extract from *Power on Display: the politics of Shakespeare's genres* (London and New York, 1986), pp. 142–6.

NOTE

1. *Narrative and Dramatic Sources of Shakespeare*, ed. Geoffrey Bullough (New York, Columbia Univ. Press, 1966), V. 358.

Kay Stockholder The Sweetened Imagination of *Antony and Cleopatra* (1987)

Antony, like Hamlet and Macbeth, is distinguished by his self-awareness. Like Hamlet he inspects his inner state and consciously crafts the figure he cuts among those who populate his world, and like Macbeth he intuits the inner consequences of his actions as he performs them. In one respect he has more awareness than the earlier figures, for there is less of a gap than there is for Hamlet or for Macbeth between the elements that compose his figure and those he confronts. The views of him expressed by other figures and the images in which they render his conflicting drives more often than not resonate in Antony's own consciousness, and there are no figures who, by representing a repudiated set of values, function as *alter egos* to him. The protagonist of *Antony and Cleopatra* has at least partial awareness of the major conflicts that structure its action. Therefore in tracing Antony's relations to the various figures who compose his world we will be concerned with changing levels of emotional immediacy and degrees of awareness rather than with the sharp breaks that characterized the dreamscapes of previous protagonists. It is rather in the play's framework and structure of action that Antony confronts the unconscious dimensions of the ideas and fears that polarize the Roman martial honour and the Egyptian gratification by both of which he defines himself.

Antony's self-awareness is an aspect of the autonomy that initially defines his figure. Unlike Hamlet or Macbeth, he inhabits a world free of parents or parentally symbolized power relations. This freedom from overt parental forms frees him as well from moral ones. Unlike his predecessors, Antony asserts both mature authority and desire and does not surround his lover with an aura of either the demonic or angelic. The axis of conflict for Antony is not between good and evil but, as for Lear in his final state, it is between conflicting desires for self-assertion and for loss of selfhood. Consequently, in contrast to Hamlet or Macbeth, Antony is not in pursuit of furtive pleasures while dodging parental spying eyes or hiding beneath a blanket of the dark. Rather, openly coupling himself with Cleopatra, he confronts the equally unabashed gaze of an audience whom he challenges to witness his peerless love. However, his grasp on his freedom from the miasma that surrounds heterosexual love for other protagonists is tenuous, for, as in Othello's psychic economy, the martial valour that allows him to define himself as a lover is undermined by his doing so. . . .

Antony's defiance of Roman values . . . reveals his complicity in them. The same dual impulse structures the sequence of action in which Antony and Cleopatra have their first exchange in the context of Antony's refusal to see the messenger from Rome. With the conditions for his withdrawal already provided by the presence of the Roman messenger in the wings, Antony dares to 'let Rome in Tiber melt.' In the juxtaposed images he makes his union with Cleopatra dependent upon the dissolution of the Roman self that makes them a peerless couple, so that he can commit himself to her only with the conditions for his betrayal of her already in place. As Cleopatra taunts him to see the messenger, he expresses in her figure the network of associations that produce the self-defeating polarity in which he is caught.

The associations that comprise that polarity become apparent in their exchange. She implies that his apparent pre-eminence in age and stature conceals a childlike relation to 'the scarce bearded Caesar' and the 'shrill-tongued' Fulvia. Her words reveal that he, to his shame, has empowered these Roman figures and Rome itself with parental force. His grandiloquent counter-assertion that he will force the world 'on pain of punishment' to acknowledge him with Cleopatra only confirms Cleopatra's implied accusation that Antony on her account feels diminished in Roman eyes, and thereby gives parental force to Caesar and the militaristic honour he represents. A further dimension appears when Cleopatra in disbelief contrasts herself to the legitimate Fulvia and asks, 'Why did he marry Fulvia, and not love her?' His loveless but legal relation to Fulvia will be replaced by one with the 'holy, cold Octavia,' the 'married woman' who, unlike Cleopatra, can generate the 'lawful race' that alone insures his place and lineage in the Roman paternal arena.

With Rome, therefore, Antony associates full maturity, and parental powers that he can inherit only by forgoing love and sexuality, and to which he otherwise remains in childlike subjection. His associations with love and sexuality that oppose them to Roman honour appear in his definition of Cleopatra. On the periphery of consciousness he first attributes to her the kind of knowledge of his secret duplicity that Lady Macbeth has of Macbeth or Goneril and Regan do of Lear. Having empowered her to undermine the stance he needs to keep her at a distance, he also associates her with resentful distrust and anger at the illegitimacy and consequent social barrenness within which he defines her figure. The shame that is correlative with this complex of associations prevents him from knowing himself as making a free choice in loving her. Instead he attributes to her charms a quasi-magical power, and feels his will compelled by them, thus simultaneously enhancing and evading his shame by defining his love as compulsive rather than as freely chosen. In this way he avoids knowing that her power derives from, rather than despite, her challenge to the Roman values by which he defines himself.

Feeling himself compelled by her charms further erodes Antony's confidence in his Roman autonomy and makes him feel that his 'soft hours' with her signify his dotage. Therefore when he silences Cleopatra's demands that he give audience to the messenger by saying, 'Fie, wrangling queen! / Whom every thing becomes, to chide, to laugh, / To weep: how every passion fully strives / To make itself, in thee, fair and admired!' (I.i. 48–51), he also distantly expresses his sense of self-abasement in Demetrius's comment on their retreating figures, 'I am ful sorry / That he approves the common liar, who / Thus speaks of him at Rome' (I.i. 59–61). Antony has generated the Roman world to protect him against a sexuality that he associates with a network of threatening emotions, but finding it loveless and cold, he seeks to regain love with Cleopatra. He can do so only in conjunction with a sense of illegitimacy, which in turn shames him before the Roman eyes that were designed to repress sexuality and that therefore threaten the image of himself as heroic lover that initially bound the two together.

In this first scene between himself and Cleopatra, Antony sketches the countervailing forces that will determine the ebb and flow of action between Rome and Egypt. The remainder of the first swing of action, which culminates in his departure for Rome, shows him internalizing the previously externalized image of himself as debased by his relation to Cleopatra, at the same time as he interprets his love and desire as the consequence of her preternatural powers.

Antony intensifies his shame by directing the messenger to 'name Cleopatra as she is called in Rome,' and identifies with the Roman view of himself when he says, 'These strong Egyptian fetters I must break, / Or lose myself in dotage' (I.ii. 113–14). The news that Fulvia has died expresses both aspects of his desire. On the surface level it expresses his need to shore up the Roman aspect of his self-definition, for it is her death that calls him away from Egypt. But on a deeper level the same news represents a deep stirring of his desire to be with Cleopatra and constitutes the counter-current, for he has eliminated with Fulvia's death the barrier to his union with Cleopatra.

As a consequence he feels vague and nameless fear, regrets Fulvia's death, and concludes, 'I must from this enchanting queen break off, / Ten thousand harms, more than the ills I know, / My idleness doth hatch' (I.ii. 125–7). His mind turns not to known, but to unknown dangers; moved not by the specific needs of Rome but by the vague fear associated with the enchanting queen, he announces to Enobarbus that 'I must with haste from hence.' Antony emphasizes not the Roman need of him, but his need to flee Egypt. While Enobarbus mockingly anticipates the love-death consummation with his comments on Cleopatra's 'celerity in dying,' Antony reacts not to the jest, but to that image of death with which he associates her now ominous power: 'She is cunning past man's thought.' He concludes, 'Would I had never seen her!' but shows an imagination already infected when he describes the Roman situation in images that throughout characterize Egypt: 'Much is breeding, / Which like the courser's hair, hath yet but life / And not a serpent's poison' (I.ii. 190–2). . . .

As a consequence of externalizing the passions that he previously acknowledged, on his return to Egypt Antony falls into a dreamlike world in which he is pursued by incomprehensible powers. The sense of a magical component in the action is rendered in the scenic structure, which, unlike that in Plutarch's narrative, leaps from Caesar's decision in Rome to attack Antony, to Antony's opening lines in Egypt in which he marvels that Caesar 'from Tarentum and Brundusium / . . . . could so quickly cut the Ionian sea, / And take in Toryne?' (III.vii. 21–3). A little later, when told that Caesar has taken Toryne, Antony muses, 'Can he be there in person? 'tis impossible; / Strange, that his power should be' (III.vii. 56–7). Antony's sense of Caesar's magic outweighs Cleopatra's skeptical 'Celerity is never more admir'd / Than by the negligent' (III.vii. 24–5), when it is confirmed by the more impartial Canidius, who comments that 'This speed of Caesar's / Carries beyond belief' (III.vii. 74–5). In this preternatural speed Antony attributes to Caesar the martial superiority that he himself once claimed. Together with the Soothsayer episode and the strange music that signifies Hercules' departure, this scene shows Antony divesting himself of his martial powers and translating them into a supernaturally punitive paternal force to which he, like Lear to the storm, becomes victim. In doing so he manages to defy a paternal witness while he claims a maternal Cleopatra, and simultaneously punishes himself for this Oedipal crime.

Just as in *Macbeth* both naturalistic and supernatural components bring Birnam wood to Dunsinane, so Antony's self-victimizing impulses manifest themselves as well on a more naturalistic level when he courts defeat by irrationally insisting on fighting by sea. His flight from that battle is the decisive moment in which his previously interior world explodes and reshapes itself as external circumstance. Following Cleopatra out of battle 'like a doting mallard,' Antony becomes the child who seeks his mother's protection from the wrath of his father to whom she has betrayed him, and by blaming her for his defeat he renders her an image of the mother who seduces the son and then betrays him to an avenging father. That configuration remains below the surface, for having externalized his emotional forms, Antony can only observe and wonder at himself for violating 'experience, manhood, honour' and becoming a 'noble ruin of her magic.' He must now 'to the young man send humble treaties, dodge / And palter in the shifts of lowness' (III.ix. 63–4) in a way that represents the collapse of his attempt to assume a maturity that is free of Oedipal mystification. Anticipating Coriolanus, Antony becomes a boy in relation to reinstated parental figures. Only amid this shame and humiliation can he allow himself an unqualified love. For a moment he rises, dolphinlike, above the cataclysm to assert his heroic love: 'Fall not a tear, I say, one of them rates / All that is won and lost: Give me a kiss. / Even this repays me' (III.xi. 69–71), giving substance to what previously was hypocritical hyperbole: 'Let Rome in Tiber melt.' . . .

Once having ceased to struggle Antony rescues a moment of the equal love he envisioned. Earlier his sensuality and Cleopatra's have been expressed indirectly by others in images of food and feasting, but when the lovers have been together they have sparred or have been estranged from each other. Only within the aura of death do they display sensuous affection and intimacy, as Cleopatra first fumblingly and then deftly buckles Antony's armour, and he feels rejuvenated – 'This morning, like the spirit of a youth / That means to be of note, begins betimes' (IV.iv. 26–7). He gives her a 'soldier's kiss,' and boyishly wants her to witness his prowess in 'the royal occupation.' Like Othello and later protagonists in the romances, Antony can afford to indulge erotic love only when he feels his identity protected by martial honour. The armour he dons as he prepares to challenge Caesar both permits and restrains intimacy. Coming triumphant from the battlefield in a short-lived victory, he declares a fully sexualized love for Cleopatra when he exclaims, 'O thou day o' the world, / Chain mine arm'd neck, leap thou, attire and all, / Through proof of harness to my heart, and there / Ride on the pants triumphing!' (IV.viii. 12–16). She responds, 'Lord of lords, / O infinite virtue, com'st thou smiling from / The world's great snare uncaught?' (IV.viii. 16–18). Though a battlefield might not be thought of as a snare, the image is apt for the emotional snare that has been pulling tighter around him, the strands consisting on the one hand of his weakness in relation to Caesar because of his love of Cleopatra, and on the other his incapacity to love Cleopatra fully because of his shame before Caesar. But for this moment he has escaped the snare, and openly declares his love. He does not return to her as to a mother, but as a loving partner when he says,

> My nightingale,
> We have beat them to their beds. What, girl, though gray
> Do something mingle with our younger brown, yet ha' we
> A brain that nourishes our nerves, and can
> Get goal for goal of youth. (IV.viii. 18–22)

Momentarily free from guilt and shame, he invokes an admiring audience to blast the city's ear with trumpets and 'brazen din . . . That heaven and earth may strike their sounds together, / Applauding our approach' (IV.viii. 36–8). But he quickly succumbs to the psychic snare that made the achievement so difficult as Cleopatra becomes the 'triple-turn'd whore' who 'beguil'd [him] to the very heart of loss' (IV.xii. 19, 29). As her image darkens he, like Lear before him, generates polarized images of the 'good' but sexless woman punishing the evil and sexual one:

> Let him take thee,
> And hoist thee up to the shouting plebeians,
> Follow his chariot, like the greatest spot
> Of all thy sex. Most monster-like be shown
> For poor'st diminutives, for dolts, and let
> Patient Octavia plough thy visage up
> With her prepared nails. (IV.xii. 33–9)

In an accelerating vacillation between giving Cleopatra to Caesar and taking her back he, like Hamlet, sees himself as Hercules in the 'snare of Nessus.' Antony escapes that intolerable and intractable polarity only by fully experiencing the dissolution that he had sought and feared from the beginning. He feels himself melting like the clouds, like 'black vesper's pageants' in which,

> That which is now a horse, even with a thought
> The rack dislimns, and makes it indistinct
> As water is in water....
> My good knave Eros, now thy captain is
> Even such a body: here I am Antony,
> Yet cannot hold this visible shape, my knave.
>
> (IV.xiv. 9–14)

Out of his desire Antony has generated the image of the archetypal mother; out of his fear and guilt he has turned that image to a whore, and struggled to escape its power by an unsuccessful effort to align himself with the paternal Caesar. Having returned to Cleopatra, for a brief moment he has mastered his fear of sexuality and transformed her into a sexual and loving companion in enterprise, only to fall prey more fully to his image of her as poisonously destructive. Finally he escapes the snare only by losing his 'visible shape.'[1]

Earlier Antony has said that the 'poisoned hours' he spent with Cleopatra 'bound him up from [his] own knowledge'; as though to fulfil a prediction, as he asserts his love he loses his sense of identity. When he thinks Cleopatra dead, the opposition between Roman virtues and Egyptian sexuality disappears, for he attributes to her those virtues that, living, she undermined. He can fully embrace both her and death, since in losing his 'visible shape' he has foregone his body's lusts that had poisoned his imagination. When he is about to give himself his death wound, he finally imagines legitimizing his union with Cleopatra in marriage: 'but I will be / A bridegroom in my death, and run into't / As to a lover's bed' (IV.xiv. 99–101). But the marriage bed remains associated with the twin fears of violence and dissolution of the self.

Antony interprets his death as a punishment, one that substitutes for, as well as evades, punishment by Caesar. He says, 'Not Caesar's valour hath o'erthrown Antony, but Antony's hath triumph'd on itself' (IV.xv. 14–15), and 'Bid that welcome / Which comes to punish us, and we punish it / Seeming to bear it lightly' (IV.xiv. 136–8). In the act of suicidal self-punishment Antony defeats Caesar by becoming his own father, and claims a disembodied Cleopatra: 'Where souls do couch on flowers, we'll hand in hand, / And with our sprightly port make the ghosts gaze: / Dido and her Aeneas, shall want troops, / And all the haunt be ours' (IX.xiv. 51–4). If Lear penetrates the infantile Oedipal dream implied by but not realized in Hamlet's story, Antony and Cleopatra partially fulfil what is potential in the relation between Hamlet and Ophelia. Like Hamlet in his charisma and self-reflection, though without his thoughtfulness, Antony falls back into the filial self-definition from which he has tried to free himself. But more explicitly than Hamlet at the moment of his suicide he defies the paternal ghost and accepts the slime of sexuality as the price of the visionary fulfilment of his love for Cleopatra in death. He embraces the loss of self that his predecessors avoided, and disappears into Cleopatra's language. He dissolves out of his own dream, and passes on to Cleopatra the task of rescuing romance from images of betrayal and corporeal decay.[2]

In order to summarize the configurations Antony has generated in Cleopatra, I will take her as protagonist-dreamer, and discuss the significance of the last act for her, before considering it as Antony's dream.[3] The uncertainty with which Antony surrounds her figure becomes her uncertainty about herself. Within the vagueness, she emerges as an older and wiser Ophelia, or as one who plays the nurse to her own Juliet or Emilia to her own Desdemona. She is as deeply divided as Antony when her love for him conflicts with keeping her eye on the main chance. In that confusion, she rests her sense of herself on her capacity to charm and captivate men, which she in subliminal ways identifies with an archetypal image of herself as the eternal mother, giving birth and destroying, necessarily unfaithful, and always surviving. The infidelity of the earth mother defines her as a whore, which in turn makes her fear men's betrayal. Her serpentine charm becomes her means of reprisal. Associating her generative capacity with death, she fears the destructiveness of her own loving. Therefore she generates in Antony a lover whose Roman discipline will put distance between him and her inner sense of her corrupting sexuality. She wants Antony when she sees him as a Roman father whom she can seduce from the corresponding Roman mother figure, Fulvia or Octavia. But if she succeeds, then he becomes a weak father, and a betrayer of the legitimate mother figure whom she despises, but with whom she identifies. Therefore, she is outraged by Antony's callousness when Fulvia dies, at the same time as she blames him for not making her, Cleopatra, the 'married woman.' She seduces Antony into sensuous pleasures, but cannot fully succeed because his image would then be besmirched by her own inner life. She needs him at a heroic distance to keep him worthy of her love, safe from its dangers, and to lift her self-image from the mire that threatens it. But that distance increases the danger by intensifying her image of herself as whore. In that dilemma she, like Antony, vacillates between rejecting him and drawing him back. But the more she wins him, the more she must betray him in punishment for the crime of loving her. Her decision, like Antony's, appears when she sees his heart tied to her rudder, and she almost immediately generates Thidias with whom to dally. She now sees herself through Antony's eyes no longer a morsel for a monarch, but as garbage, 'A morsel, cold upon / Dead Caesar's trencher,' and in her quasi-denial of having betrayed Antony reveals that she associates her sexuality with death and decay. She keeps Antony apart from those images by envisioning their loving moment in conjunction with Antony's warlike and Roman self, as he arms for battle and comes victorious from it, but that distance threatens her hold on him. Therefore, to draw him closer she betrays him, and finally evades her fear of her own deadly sexuality by having him die into her language.

With that Cleopatra has accomplished her revenge, has taken Antony from the Roman realm, has allowed him to escape her snare long enough to envision herself elevated by his heroic love, before his proximity to her threatens to transform him into one of the rotting products of her womb. His death frees her from the terrors of her own destructiveness. Having dismissed from her horizon the possibility of corporeally fulfilled love, she realizes and distances herself from the 'baser elements,' earth and water that together make mud, slime, and rotting things. In the 'air and fire' of an imagination that has dismissed living bodies, she achieves a vision of herself merging into her own archetype and joining a bodiless Antony as both wife and mother.

She transforms the images of dissolution into the means of Antony's exaltation when she says, 'The crown o'the earth doth melt. My Lord? / O, wither'd is the garland of the war, / The soldier's pole is fall'n' (IV.xv. 63–5), and becomes a fair warrior, one with her Roman lover in resolving to die 'after the high Roman fashion.'

However, she can generate sufficient hatred of her betraying body to overcome the will to live only through the vicissitudes of the last act. Like Hamlet pressing his nose to Yorick's skull, or like Lear envisioning himself born from foul-smelling genitals before his reunion with Cordelia, or like Antony in asking to hear himself named in Rome, in slow stages Cleopatra disgusts herself with the vilest images of her living self in order to generate the vision of them united in death. Only after Dolabella has finally assured her that Caesar will not only lead her in triumph, but will do so 'within three days,' does she assert her determination to die rather than be chastised by Octavia's 'sober eye,' or mocked by censuring Rome's 'shouting varletry.' In these images she gives parental power to both Octavia and the generalized image of the Roman crowd, but first she avoids the imagination of their censure by repeating the image of her womb and dead Egyptians being buried by the 'flies and gnats' of the Nile when she says, 'Rather on Nilus' mud / Lay me stark-nak'd, and let the water-flies / Blow me into abhorring;' before giving herself more visibility in changing the image to one in which she will hang in chains on her 'country's high pyramides' (V.ii. 58–62). Her next speech brings her imagination a stage closer to seeing herself through Roman eyes when she tells Iras that puppets will represent them in Rome where 'mechanic slaves / With greasy aprons, rules, and hammers shall / Uplift us to the view.' The general humiliation focuses on the word 'greasy,' which brings in its wake images of food when she adds that 'In their thick breaths, / Rank of gross diet, shall we be enclouded, / And forc'd to drink their vapour' (V.ii. 206–12). Though still thinking of the puppets, she incorporates the images of rotten food that at a remove previously defined her, like Cressida, as a whore, before finally seeing herself as a whore when she says that saucy lictors

> Will catch at us like strumpets, and scald rhymers
> Ballad us out o' tune. The quick comedians
> Extemporally will stage us, and present
> Our Alexandrian revels: Antony
> Shall be brought drunken forth, and I shall see
> Some squeaking Cleopatra boy my greatness
> I' the posture of a whore. (V.ii. 214–19)

She makes immediate to her imagination, though not to her body, the mocking audience that Antony feared, defied, and evaded, and in that process finally gives her voice to the names 'whore' and 'strumpet' that have throughout hovered around her.

Having fully associated her body with the most corrupt version of sexuality and generation, she becomes 'absolute for death,' but wants a death cleansed of the odours of corruption. As Hamlet expressed his divided imagination of death by opposing the charnel-house images of the body's corruption to his own glorification through the bird imagery in the words of both Horatio and Fortinbras, so Cleopatra opposes the Clown's description of the asp to the use she will make of it. The Clown imagistically emerges from and embodies the slime of the Nile, while his jokes, of two kinds, express ironic distrust of the transcendence she later imagines.

First, he plays on the polarity between immortality and the finality of death; 'for his biting is immortal: those that die of it, do seldom or never recover' (V.ii. 245–6). Like those of Hamlet's grave-digger, his jests about death merge with jests about women when he tells of the very honest woman who 'died of the biting of it,' and gave a 'very good report o' the worm.' He refocuses the imagistic link between women and food when he warns that the deadly worm 'is not worth the feeding.' Cleopatra asks, 'Will it eat me?' and he responds, 'I know that the devil himself will not eat a woman: I know that a woman is a dish for the gods, if the devil dress her not' (V.ii. 269–73). In his jests, which give some of Lear's cannibalistic grotesqueness to this play's otherwise softer oral images, Cleopatra remains food for monarchs, but only after passing through the guts of a beggar.

The Clown embodies in the asp the images of Nilus' slime from which Cleopatra escapes into visions of air and fire. He also calls attention to the missing middle term, the ordinary fertility she forgoes in death. After the Clown exits, Cleopatra says, 'Give me my robe, put on my crown; I have / Immortal longings in me. Now no more / The juice of Egypt's grape shall moist this lip' (V.ii. 279–81). Her lines stand in ironic juxtaposition to the Clown's story of the 'very honest woman' who told of her own death, and his warning that the worm's 'biting is immortal; those that die of it seldom or never recover.' As he repeatedly wishes Cleopatra the 'joy o' the worm,' these ironic plays on death's finality call into question and cast doubt on the status of the love-death fantasy that so deliciously permits erotic fulfilment without taint from the world, the flesh, or sexuality.

That actualization in the clown scene of what previously was vague pushes Cleopatra's mind over the hurdle posed by the fear of death and its associated images of decay. Now envisioning death as a realm of purity and reunion with Antony, she dons her robe and crown and takes leave of the Nile's shifting tides to become, like Othello's heavens, 'marble constant.' She identifies now with the beneficent aspect of the archetypal Isis, and finally claims Antony as her 'husband.' Like Antony earlier, she associates her imagined marriage with death, both in Iras' spontaneous death, which parallels Enobarbus', and when she says 'the stroke of death is as a lover's pinch, / Which hurts, and is desired' (V.ii. 294–5). The image reduces to erotic play the violence Antony associated with his death, and adds a familial dimension absent from Antony's language. In a detail not to be found in Plutarch's account, she puts the asp to her breast. As she says, 'Peace, peace! / Dost thou not see my baby at my breast, / That sucks the nurse asleep' (V.ii. 307–9), she restores to their innocent source the images of monstrous devouring, and substitutes for an image of archetypal maternity one of ordinary maternal tenderness unique in Shakespeare's plays.[4] When she murmurs, 'As sweet as balm, soft as air, as gentle. / O Antony!' (V.ii. 310–11), she transforms Nilus' slime into an image of Antony that she embraces within that tenderness. She becomes, indeed, 'a morsel for a monarch,' even though doing so simultaneously kills her.[5]

The episode suggests that Shakespeare's imagination of mothering grew more benign between the time he imagined the infant at Lady Macbeth's breast and writing this play. Though outraged by the sexual smells of the world, King Lear manages to imagine himself as an infant, and Antony, after dying into Cleopatra and being born through her words to more than his former glory, allows himself at a distance, like a dreamer absent from his dream, and at the price of becoming a slime-born asp, the last luxury of these gentle maternal words.

This excursion into Cleopatra's psychic structure necessarily duplicates Antony's own, but emphasizes the ways in which he has embodied in her figure both his association of sexual desire with shame, and has endowed her with maternal power to draw him into corruption and death that will fulfil his desire in its punishment. Once he ceases to struggle against that tide and merges himself into Cleopatra he gains everything and nothing. In her vacillation he, on the one hand, joins the offended paternal Caesar to satisfy his desire that she be humiliated and punished for her betrayal. On the other hand, by submitting totally to her he has bought a vision of himself resurrected as heroic lover, lifted dolphinlike by a disembodied eternal Isis out of the watery element. In Cleopatra's image of him, 'past the size of dreaming,' with legs bestriding the ocean that divides Rome from Egypt, he achieves an imagined resolution to his conflict even while he defines it as irresolvable.[6] He can claim her as lover, as wife, and more secretly retain a diminished corporality in the slimy asp in order to suck his nurse asleep.[7] In a strategy worthy of Hamlet, Antony can enjoy Caesar's tribute to and blessing on their union, while his escape into the grave acknowledges and defeats Caesar's paternal power.

But in the Clown's words Antony has also expressed the limitations of the disembodied imagination – those who have the joy of the worm 'do seldom or never recover.' Antony's fullest achievement, and in my view Shakespeare's, lies in his victorious invocation to Cleopatra to ride on the triumphant pants of his heart, even though that victory remains subject to the ebb and flow of life and time.

In *Romeo and Juliet* the hatred and betrayal that characterize later protagonists are externalized into the surrounding figures who, along with fortuitous time and circumstance, bear responsibility for the young lovers' death. All negative components are present, but in a form that obscures their relevance to the lovers. Juliet, as an early Cleopatra, gives her self-preservative impulses and capacity for betrayal to the Nurse, and insofar as Romeo stands behind Antony, his struggle away from love and sexuality are expressed through Mercutio, the fortuitous plague, and accidental mistiming. More deeply than *Othello, Antony and Cleopatra* invites us into the psychological morass that underlies the seduction of love-death romance, but in the process more fully engages, and momentarily overcomes the conflicted sexuality that underlies the form. In the protagonists' capacity to love each other despite their betrayals, the play's generous embrace of the imperfect makes it the tragic counterpart to *As You Like It*.

SOURCE: Extracts from *Dream Works: Lovers and Families in Shakespeare's Plays* (Toronto, 1987), pp. 148–68.

NOTES

(Renumbered by the editor)

1. In *The Common Liar: An Essay on* Antony and Cleopatra (New Haven: Yale University Press, 1973) Janet Adelman thinks that Antony's transfor-

mation of his fear of dissolution into a desire for it resolves the tension that we all experience in loving (160).

2. Roger Stilling in *Love and Death in Renaissance Tragedy* (Baton Rouge: University of Louisiana Press, 1976) sees Antony as vacillating between a romantic and an anti-romantic conception of love (278), and finally embracing a romantic conception that courts death rather than being subverted by it. Richard Wheeler in *Shakespeare's Development and the Problem Comedies* (Urbana: University of Illinois Press, 1981) sees Antony 'reborn through the fertile womb of [Cleopatra's] imagination' (202). Views closer to mine are those of Norman Rabkin in *Shakespeare and the Common Understanding* (New York: Free Press, 1967) and Matthew N. Proser in *The Heroic Image in Five Shakespearean Tragedies* (Princeton: Princeton University Press, 1965). Rabkin sees these protagonists, like Romeo and Juliet, linking love to the death-wish. Proser argues that 'the grave's worm and the worm as phallus' fuse symbolically in a kind of sexual act (238), and that in the final scene Cleopatra does not transcend but rather asserts the amoral passion that defined her all along.

3. In 'Egyptian Queens and Male Reviewers: Sexist Attitudes in *Antony and Cleopatra* Criticism,' *Shakespeare Quarterly* 28 (1977) 297–316, Linda Fitz in a refreshing approach sees Cleopatra as similar to male protagonists in her struggle against her theatricality rather than as essentially enigmatic (314).

4. Leslie Fiedler in *The Stranger in Shakespeare* (New York: Stein and Day, 1972) finds a contradiction in Cleopatra's both renouncing the feminine principle by associating herself with 'air and fire' and defining herself as wife, and then as mother (76).

5. These images of eating monstrously or of being eaten are similar to those in *King Lear*, but taken in conjunction with Cleopatra's 'baby,' and with all the images of food previously discussed, they are softened and reduced to jesting. David Willbern in 'Rape and Revenge in *Titus Andronicus,' English Literary Renaissance* 8 (Spring 1978) 159–82, sees in the horrible dinner in *Titus* the first expression of the deepest fear in Shakespeare's plays – not of castration, but of the pre-Oedipal devouring mother (171). He is right that fears from the oral level pervade the plays, but characteristically Shakespeare's protagonists bring these fears to Oedipal situations. The fusion of the two vastly magnifies the horror of both.

6. In 'Shakespeare through Contemporary Psychoanalysis,' *Representing Shakespeare* (Baltimore: Johns Hopkins University Press, 1980), 21–32, Murray M. Schwartz ignores the slime into which the lovers disintegrate, arguing that this play 'transcend[s] the dilemma of the other tragedies' because opposites interpenetrate (30). Charles R. Lyons in *Shakespeare and the Ambiguity of Love's Triumph* (The Hague: Mouton, 1971) sees this play, like the problem plays, as displaying a 'surfeited disgust at sexuality' despite the creative aspects of sexuality shown in the lovers' feeling that their commitment is infinite (162).

7. In 'New Heaven, New Earth: The Escape from Mutability in *Antony and Cleopatra,' Shakespeare Quarterly* 33 (Autumn 1982) 328–35, William D. Wolf sees the worm replacing the sword as the symbol of sexual pleasure (335).

SELECT BIBLIOGRAPHY

The most useful and economical texts for study are the New Penguin, edited by Emrys Jones (Penguin, 1977) and the Signet Classic edition by Barbara Everett (New English Library, 1964). The latter has the advantage of including extensive extracts from Plutarch and an anthology of criticism about the play.

A careful and detailed commentary, scene by scene, conscious of verbal texture and dramatic construction, is provided by D. A. Traversi's *Shakespeare: The Roman Plays* (Bodley Head, 1963). In Michael Scott's *Antony and Cleopatra: Text and Performance* (Macmillan, 1983), a discussion of the play's themes and a commentary on Act V, scene ii are followed by an account of five contrasted productions. Jonathan Miller's 1980 production for BBC Television, which is one of those discussed by Professor Scott, is available as a video cassette.

The complexity and unity of Cleopatra as a stage character were vindicated in a lively chapter of J. I. M. Stewart's *Character and Motive in Shakespeare* (Longmans, 1949). Here the play is also defended as a 'poetic drama', and this is the principal concern of the chapters on *Antony and Cleopatra* in G. Wilson Knight's *Imperial Theme* (rev. edn, Methuen, 1951); Knight argued that the 'spatial symbolism' of the play celebrates the power of 'transcendental humanism'. Many of the critics during the next several decades took much the same view, but then, gradually, a less romantic, more political and more ambivalent judgement on the play's effect began to predominate. Its ambiguities were carefully displayed by Ernest Schanzer in *The Problem Plays of Shakespeare* (Routledge, 1963) while Arnold Stein's article 'The Image of Antony: Lyric and Tragic Imagination', *Kenyon Review*, xxi (1959), 586–606, showed the double view which it offered of one of its leading characters. With this line of criticism most studies after the early 1960s belong: for example, Janet Abelman's *The Common Liar: an Essay on 'Antony and Cleopatra'* (Yale University Press, 1973), Howard Felperin, *Shakespearean Representation: Mimesis and Modernity in Elizabethan Tragedy* (Princeton University Press, 1977) and Robert Grudin, *Mighty Opposites: Shakespeare and Renaissance Contrariety* (University of California Press, 1979). J. Leeds Barroll's *Shakespearean Tragedy: Genre, Tradition and Change in 'Antony and Cleopatra'* (Associated Universities Presses, 1984) brings together a great deal of current thinking and research; it places *Antony and Cleopatra* at the centre of Shakespeare's work in tragedy, an extension and, in some ways, a summation of his exploratory *King Lear*.

The dramatic origins of the play were traced by Willard Farnham in *Shakespeare's Tragic Frontier* (Cambridge University Press, 1950) and important elements of its intellectual background by Michael Lloyd in two articles, 'Cleopatra as Isis', in *Shakespeare Survey*, xii (1959), 88–94, and 'Antony and the Game of Chance', in *Journal of English and Germanic Philology*, lxi (1962), 548–54, and by Eugene Waith in *The Herculean Hero in Marlowe, Chapman, Shakespeare and Dryden* (Chatto & Windus, 1962). J. L. Simmons's *Shakespeare's Pagan World* (University of Virginia Press, 1973) and Robert S. Miola's *Shakespeare's Rome* (Cambridge University Press, 1983) are both useful on the background for the dramatic action.

The verbal style of the play came under scrutiny in W. H. Clemen's influential *Development of Shakespeare's Imagery* (Methuen, 1951), by Granville-Barker in his *Preface*, a section from which is printed elsewhere in this anthology, by Wilson Knight in *The Imperial Theme*, and by B. T. Spencer in an article '*Antony and Cleopatra* and the Paradoxical Metaphor', in *Shakespeare Quarterly*, ix (1958), 373–8. The play is the subject of a lengthy chapter in T. McAlindon's *Shakespeare and Decorum* (Macmillan, 1973), a study which begins with an account of the Renaissance philosophy of language as an image of mind and soul, and as the basis of social order.

A full account of both analogues and sources is found in *Narrative and Dramatic Sources of Shakespeare*, volume v (Routledge, 1964), ed. Geoffrey Bullough. The most useful edition of the play's main source is T. J. B. Spencer's edition of *Shakespeare's Plutarch* (Penguin, 1964).

NOTES ON CONTRIBUTORS

ANDREW C. BRADLEY (1851–1935). Professor of Literature at Liverpool and Glasgow and, then, of Poetry at Oxford; his *Shakespearean Tragedy* (1904) analysed character in *Hamlet, Othello, Lear* and *Macbeth* and has become the most lasting book of its kind.

MAURICE CHARNEY. Professor of English at Rutgers University; specialises in American literature and civilisation as well as Shakespeare and Elizabethan drama.

FRANKLIN M. DICKEY (1923–76). A pupil of Lily B. Campbell, who became Chairman of the Department of English, the University of New Mexico; he published numerous poems and was active as a Renaissance scholar.

HARLEY GRANVILLE-BARKER (1877–1946). Playwright, actor, theatre director and critic: his productions of plays by Shaw, Euripides and others during the Barker–Vedrenne management at the Court Theatre (1904–7) were followed by Shakespearian productions at the Savoy; his *Prefaces to Shakespeare* were published in several volumes (1927–47).

L. C. KNIGHTS. Professor Emeritus of English Literature, University of Cambridge; his books include *Drama and Society in the Age of Jonson, Explorations: Essays in Literary Criticism* and *An Approach to 'Hamlet'*.

MICHAEL LONG. Fellow of Churchill College, University of Cambridge, and University Lecturer in English.

H. A. MASON. Author of *Humanism and Poetry in the Early Tudor Period* (1959) and an editor of the *Cambridge Quarterly*.

JOHN MIDDLETON MURRY (1889–1957). Professional writer of reviews, novels, criticism, philosophy and autobiography; last editor of the *Athenaeum* and founder editor of the *Adelphi*; he wrote studies of Keats, Blake, D. H. Lawrence and Shakespeare.

KAY STOCKHOLDER. Professor of English at the University of British Columbia, Vancouver; she has published numerous articles on the psychological understanding implicit in Shakespeare's characterisations.

LEONARD TENNENHOUSE. A member of the Center for Humanities, Wesleyan University, Connecticut; he has published on political implications of both Elizabethan and Jacobean plays, notably in anthologies edited by Stephen Greenblatt and by Jonathan Dollimore and Alan Sinfield.

INDEX